The 71st Highlanders

Revised version

Other Books by Daniel McDonald Johnson

THIS CURSED WAR
Lachlan McIntosh in the American Revolution

FIGHTING THE BATTLES OF AMERICA
John McIntosh in the American Revolution,
East Florida Rebellions and War of 1812

SAVANNAH, AUGUSTA & BRIER CREEK
The Conquest of Georgia in the American Revolution

The 71st Highlanders
in the American Revolution

Revised version

Daniel McDonald Johnson

Independently published
Distributed by Ingram Content Group

Daniel McDonald Johnson
Post Office Box 747
Allendale, South Carolina 29810

ISBN: 979-8-218-05625-4

About the Cover

"One Gallant Stand" by Jeff Trexler shows the 71st Regiment at the Battle of Brier Creek. The image is used by arrangement with Trexler Historical Art.

About the revised version

I wrote the original version before I became aware of *71st Fraser Highland Regiment in the American War of Independence* by Ed Brumby (Anchorprint, 2012). I believe that my book and his book complement one another because I give narrative structure and he gives details derived from archives and other sources. For my revised version, I expanded the biographical sketches of Roderick Mackenzie and Aeneas Mackintosh using information from Brumby's research on the officers of the 71st Regiment.

This version also describes recent archaeological research at the Camden Battlefield that resulted in the reburial of a soldier in the 71st Regiment.

Author's Note

Spelling, punctuation, and place names have been modernized in many cases to make the story easier to understand.

Contents

(Continued on next page)

(Contents continued from previous page)

Part 2: Additional Information

Part 3: Biographical Sketches

The 71st Highlanders

Revised version

Part 1: A Narrative History

New York and New Jersey

SCOTTISH HIGHLANDERS ENLISTED by the thousands to subdue the rebellion in America. Their sea voyage from familiar territory to a strange land presented numerous hazards. "The difficulties in securing transports have been very great," a British secretary told the commander in America, but expected "the corps of Highlanders, consisting of the 42nd and 71st regiment making together 3466 men which are nearly if not entirely completed, will embark in the Clyde" by the middle of April, 1776.[1]

After the troops set sail from Glasgow, storms scattered the ships. Privateers took advantage of the situation by attacking single ships isolated from the fleet; two vessels carrying members of the 71st Regiment fell prey to the privateers.

Four other transports carrying companies of the 71st Regiment were captured as they neared their destination. Lieutenant Colonel Archibald Campbell—commander of the 2nd Battalion of the 71st Regiment—reported "the circumstances which have occasioned this disaster" to the British commander in America:

> On the 16th of June the *George* and *Annabella* transports, with two companies of the Seventy First Regiment of Highlanders, made the land off Cape Ann, after a passage of seven weeks from Scotland, during the course of which we had not the opportunity of speaking to a single vessel that could give us the smallest information of the British troops having evacuated Boston. On the 17th, at daylight, we found ourselves opposite to the harbor's mouth at Boston; but, from the contrary winds, it was necessary to make several

tacks to reach it. Four schooners (which we took to be pilots or armed vessels in the service of his majesty, but which were afterwards found to be American privateers, of eight carriage-guns, twelve swivels, and forty men each) were bearing down upon us at four o'clock in the morning. At half an hour thereafter two of them engaged us, and about eleven o'clock the other two were closing alongside. The *George* transport (on board of which were Major Menzies and myself, with one hundred and eight of the Second Battalion, the Adjutant, the Quartermaster, two Lieutenants, and five volunteers, were passengers) had only six pieces of cannon to oppose them; and the *Annabella* (on board of which were Captain Mckenzie, together with two subalterns, two volunteers, and eighty-two private men of the First Battalion) had only two swivels for her defense. Under such circumstances, I thought it expedient for the *Annabella* to keep ahead of the *George,* that our artillery might be used with more effect and less obstruction. Two of the privateers having stationed themselves upon our larboard quarter and two upon our starboard quarter, a tolerable cannonade ensued, which, with very few intermissions, lasted till four o'clock in the evening, when the enemy bore away, and anchored in Plymouth harbor. Our loss upon this occasion was only three men mortally wounded on board the *George*, one killed and one man slightly wounded on board the *Annabella.* As my orders were for the port of Boston, I thought it my duty, at this happy crisis, to push forward into the harbor, not doubting I should receive protection either from a fort or some ship of force stationed there for the security of our fleet.

Towards the close of the evening we perceived the four schooners that were engaged with us in the morning joined by the brig *Defence*, of sixteen carriage guns, twenty swivels, and one hundred and seventeen men, and a schooner of eight carriage guns, twelve swivels and forty men, got under way and made toward us. As we stood up for Nantasket Road, an American battery opened upon us, which was the first serious proof we had that there could scarcely be many friends of ours at Boston; and we were far too embayed to retreat, especially as the wind had died away, and the tide of flood not half expended. After each of the vessels had twice run aground, we anchored at George's Island, and prepared for action; but the *Annabella* by some misfortune got aground so far astern of the *George* that we could expect but a feeble support from her musketry. About eleven o'clock four of the schooners anchored right upon our bow, and one right astern of us. The armed brig took her station on our starboard side, at the distance of two hundred yards, and hailed us to strike the British flag. Although the mate of our ship and every sailor on board (the Captain only excepted) refused positively to fight any longer, I have the pleasure to inform you that there was not an officer, non-commissioned officer, or private man of the Seventy First but what stood to their quarters with a ready and cheerful obedience. On our refusing to strike the British flag, the action was renewed with a good deal of warmth on both sides, and it was our misfortune, after the sharp combat of an hour and a half, to have expended every shot that we had for our artillery. Under such circumstances, hemmed in as we were with six privateers, in the middle of an enemy's harbor, beset with a dead calm, without the power of escaping, or even the most distant hope of relief, I thought it became my duty not to sacrifice the lives of gallant men wantonly in the arduous attempt of an evident impossibility. In this unfortunate affair Major Menzies and seven private soldiers were killed, the Quartermaster and twelve private soldiers wounded. The Major was buried with the honours of war at Boston.[2]

The next day, a British transport carrying the grenadiers of the 2nd Battalion of the 71st Regiment blundered into Boston Harbor and was seized. Privateers patrolling offshore captured a transport carrying the light infantry of the 1st Battalion of the 71st Regiment and took it to Marblehead. Members of the 71st Regiment taken prisoner from the four transports included twenty-two officers, fifteen sergeants, sixteen corporals, eight drummers, and 362 privates.[3] "This unfortunate accident makes a considerable addition to their number of prisoners," the British commander in New York informed officials in London, "and increases my anxiety for their relief, for which end I shall use every means in my power to improve and avail myself of this agreement [with General George Washington of the Continental Army] for the exchange of prisoners."[4]

The soldiers of the 71st Regiment who landed safely in America went into battle with scant military training.[5] British Major General William Howe determined to wrest New York from American possession. Convoys of transports and warships brought twenty thousand troops from Canada and Britain to Staten Island. General Henry Clinton returned from an expedition against Charleston and placed another 2,500 troops at Howe's command. A fleet arrived on August 12, raising the total strength to 32,000 British and Hessian soldiers and ten thousand seamen. At the time, it was the largest expeditionary force ever sent from Britain.

On August 22, 1776, fifteen thousand British troops commanded by General Charles Cornwallis crossed from Staten Island to Long Island in flat-bottom boats and landed without resistance. The British seized Flatbush and challenged the American outposts at Long Island Heights. The 71st Regiment took post at Flatlands Church.[6] When Americans attacked a Hessian position the next day, Highlanders mounted two cannons on a breastwork on Flatbush Road and exchanged fire with American artillery throughout the afternoon.[7]

The British continued to shuttle soldiers and artillery to Long Island, increasing their troop strength to nearly twenty thousand, double the number of American defenders.[8] Under a full moon on the night of August 26, Howe led an army of ten thousand soldiers and twenty-eight pieces of artillery into action.[9]

SHORTLY AFTER MIDNIGHT on the unusually cool morning of August 27, 1776, ten thousand British soldiers advanced against the American defenses at Long Island near the city of New York. Americans at an outpost on the Gowanus Road opened fire, and British infantry attacked two American regiments.[10]

The attack on the right flank was a diversion. The main British army—including the 71st Regiment—marched through the night toward the left flank of the American defenses at Long Island Heights. By 9 a.m. they were in position to attack barricades at the Flatbush Pass. Most of the Americans at the pass ran away, pursued nearly to the American position at Brooklyn by British and Hessian troops wielding bayonets. The British took hundreds of prisoners.[11]

The diversionary force resumed its attack on the American position on the Gowanus Road near the marsh along Gowanus Creek. Fifteen hundred Americans staunchly held their position against seven thousand British troops. When the American commander heard sounds of battle at Long Island Heights, he realized the British had cut off his route of retreat to the American fortifications at Brooklyn. Meanwhile, Cornwallis's division—including the 71st Highlanders—advanced from the Flatbush Pass toward the Gowanus Road, blocking the Americans' route of retreat. A trail through the marsh offered the only possibility of escape. Three American regiments fell back and started to cross the trail through the marsh to safety. When Continental General George Washington saw the American troops retreating along the path through the marsh, he placed infantry and artillery on high ground overlooking the marsh to cover the retreat.

Howe reported that "the rebels, suspecting their retreat would be cut off, made a movement to their right in order to secure it across a swamp and creek that covers the right of their works; but being met in their way by a part of the 2nd grenadiers who were soon after supported by the 71st regiment, and General Grant's left coming up, they suffered considerably. Numbers of them, however, did get into the morass where many were suffocated or drowned."[12]

To cover their comrades' escape, five hundred Americans launched a charge against Cornwallis's troops. The British beat back the charge. The Americans charged again, and the British repulsed the charge. The Americans charged three more times and the British withstood the charge each time. When reinforcements joined Cornwallis's troops, the combined British forces surrounded the Americans and forced them to surrender. The Battle of Long Island ended at about noon.

American casualties were about two hundred killed or wounded, and eight hundred captured. Howe reported British casualties of sixty-one killed, 267 wounded, and thirty-one captured; casualties in the 71st Regiment were three killed and eleven wounded.[13]

AFTER THE BATTLE OF LONG ISLAND, the British constructed siege works in front of the American fortifications at Brooklyn Heights. The Americans evacuated the fortifications during a dark, rainy night. Boats carried men, supplies, and artillery across the East River to New York. A British patrol reached the East River just as the last boat pulled away from shore. The British fired muskets and a field piece but did not hit the boat as it crossed to safety.[14]

When the American army took up positions in New York, the British army and navy maneuvered into positions around the city, attempting to block escape routes. The Americans began moving supplies out of New York on September 12, three days before the British launched attacks on the American defenses. Cornwallis led four thousand British and Hessian troops in an advance division that soon received reinforcements as flatboats carried troops from Long Island. The Americans abandoned New York and took positions around Harlem Heights. Although casualties were light, the British captured ammunition, supplies, dozens of cannon and more than 350 American soldiers.

Shortly before dawn on September 16 an advance British unit encountered American defenders at Harlem Heights. Soon more than five thousand troops on each side engaged in battle. The Americans withdrew after a six-hour fight. British casualties were seventy killed and two hundred wounded; American casualties were thirty killed and ninety wounded. Fire broke out in New York on September 20 and the British struggled for two days to put out the flames.[15]

On October 12 the British moved ten thousand men toward the American positions on Manhattan Island. Cornwallis led an advance unit of four thousand English and Hessian light infantrymen onto a causeway through the marsh; about eighteen hundred Americans covering the causeway with rifle fire from behind piles of wood stopped the British unit.

On October 16 Washington decided to abandon Harlem Heights and withdraw to White Plains on the mainland. He left two thousand men at Fort Washington on Manhattan and sent three thousand men to Fort Lee on the Jersey shore.

Washington gave command of the troops at the two forts to General Nathanael Greene. The British, meanwhile, established a base at New Rochelle.[16]

Howe sent more than four thousand British and Hessian troops supported by artillery and cavalry against the American position at White Plains on October 28. American militiamen ran away, but Continental troops tried to hold their hilltop position. As the British and Hessians stretched their flanks around the hill, the Americans conducted an orderly withdrawal. The Americans moved northward and took up a position between the Bronx River and St. Marys Lake. American casualties at White Plains were about fifty killed and two hundred wounded. About fifty British and Hessian troops were killed and nearly two hundred were wounded.[17]

British reinforcements arrived over the next three days. In the dark of night, the Americans withdrew to higher ground on North Castle Heights. Four days later, the British relocated to the lower Hudson. Washington divided the American army, leaving seven thousand men at North Castle and leading about two thousand men to join another two thousand men who were protecting Fort Lee on the west bank of the Hudson River across from Fort Washington.

On November 16 eight thousand British and Hessian troops—including the 71st Regiment—moved against Fort Washington, which was perched atop steep, rocky terrain on a high bluff above the Hudson River. While other British generals moved against the fort from the other directions, Cornwallis led a column assigned to attack the fort from the east. The battle had been underway for three hours by the time Cornwallis's column managed to cross the Harlem River under heavy fire. As the four British columns closed in on the fort, the Americans surrendered. The British not only took 2,722 prisoners but also captured forty-three artillery pieces and a large amount of ammunition. American casualties were fifty-three killed and ninety-six wounded. British and Hessian casualties were seventy-seven killed, 374 wounded and seven missing.[18]

Three days later, Cornwallis led four thousand troops in a nighttime crossing of the Hudson River. Landing about five miles above Fort Lee, the British advanced on the fort at dawn. Greene organized a hasty evacuation, leaving behind thirty cannon and stores of ammunition and provisions. Shortly afterwards, the 71st Regiment reinforced the troops led by Cornwallis.

When the American army under Washington withdrew to Newark, Cornwallis waited a week at Hackensack and then advanced toward Washington's position. Washington withdrew to New Brunswick, and Cornwallis occupied Newark on November 28.[19]

Cornwallis continued to pursue Washington's army, which had dwindled to 3,400 men after the battles in New York, the surrender of Fort Washington, and the departure of two thousand men whose enlistments expired. British and American troops skirmished at New Brunswick on December 1 as Washington fell back toward Philadelphia, located across the Delaware River from New Jersey.

As Cornwallis approached Princeton on December 7, Washington led three thousand men from Princeton toward Trenton on the east bank of the Delaware. As the Americans withdrew, they destroyed bridges and blocked roads to delay the British pursuers. Washington's army crossed to the Pennsylvania side of the Delaware River on December 8. Although Cornwallis arrived at Trenton before all the Americans had reached the far side of the river, American artillery on the west bank protected the crossing. The British could not pursue the Americans across the river because Washington had arranged for all the boats in the region to be moved to the west side.

WITH WINTER SETTING IN, Howe called a halt to the campaign on December 14. The British had 23,000 troops in the region; about half of them remained in New York while the other half occupied posts in New Jersey. The 71st Regiment took up a position at Amboy, New Jersey—a former Scottish settlement also called Perth Amboy—across a tidal straight from Staten Island.[20]

Washington was desperate to salvage the revolution after being driven out of New York in a string of humiliating defeats. He decided to cross the Delaware and attack the British winter quarters. Washington's troops assembled on Christmas afternoon for their expedition across the Delaware. They reached McKonkey's Ferry as midwinter darkness descended. Chunks of ice careened down the swift current of the Delaware River and slammed into the fifty-foot-long boats that transported the troops. Snow fell steadily throughout the evening and, before midnight, sleet pelted the troops. The wind rose as the night went by, complicating not only the crossing but also the loading and unloading of men, horses and artillery. The expedition was hours behind schedule when the crossing was completed. The troops marched through the stormy night, and shortly after dawn reached the town of Trenton, where Hessian troops in the service of the British army had established winter quarters.

The American army of 2,400 men attacked the Hessian quarters in the early morning of December 26. After an American brigade blocked the route to Princeton, the Americans hemmed in the Hessians on three sides while a creek trapped the Hessians on the fourth side. The Hessian troops surrendered shortly after their commander died while leading a counterattack. In a battle lasting a little over an hour, the Hessian losses were twenty-two killed and 948 captured; about 430 Hessian and British troops escaped. Four Americans were wounded in the fighting, and two Americans froze to death shortly after crossing the Delaware. The Americans captured ammunition, arms and artillery.

After the battle, the Americans and their prisoners continued to suffer in wintry weather. Three Americans froze to death re-crossing the Delaware in daylight.[21]

On December 29 George Washington led the American army once again across the Delaware River into New Jersey and reoccupied Trenton. In response, General Cornwallis led a British army into the field. Cornwallis reached Trenton on the night of January 2 and decided to wait until morning to assault the American defenses. Washington executed a silent midnight evacuation and escaped around the left flank of the British forces.[22]

Meanwhile, another American force captured the British post at Princeton in a battle lasting less than half an hour. Washington led his force to a rendezvous at Princeton. The ragged American army confiscated British stockpiles of shoes, blankets and provisions. From his encampment at Trenton, Cornwallis heard gunfire at Princeton and sent reinforcements. The Americans left Princeton as the British reinforcements arrived. Both armies retired to winter quarters a few days later.[23]

Brandywine

TROOPS MANEUVERED across the territory between the British stronghold at New York and the American capital at Philadelphia throughout the summer of 1777. The 71st Regiment found "constant employment" in "skirmishing warfare" and marched out on expeditions to Willsbrough and Westfield. In June the 71st and three other regiments occupied a position at Bonhamtown, New Jersey, eight miles from a larger British encampment at Perth Amboy. At the end of June, the British evacuated New Jersey and crossed a tidal strait to Staten Island.[1]

Philadelphia's location on the Delaware River made it vulnerable to an approach by water. British General William Howe called on his brother Admiral Richard Howe to assemble an armada to transport 18,000 enlisted men and thousands of other personnel—including an authorized quota of women for each company averaging about one woman for every eight soldiers—along with provisions, artillery, ammunition, horses and fodder. The fleet contained 266 vessels organized into six divisions. The 71st Regiment boarded transports in the fleet's third division on July 8 and 9, but the fleet remained in place for more than a week. The soldiers pent up on the transports suffered in the summer heat and depleted supplies of fresh food. The fleet eventually got underway on July 20. Two days later, before the vessels reached open water, a storm struck. When the storm abated the next day, the fleet ventured into the Atlantic.[2]

With winds coming out of the south and southwest, the fleet moved only 150 miles in the first week. Foggy mornings faded into terribly hot days capped by thunderstorms. A particularly violent storm on July 27 scattered the fleet, requiring ships to fire guns every half hour to alert the other ships of their location; even with those precautions, some ships collided with one another. By the time the fleet entered Delaware Bay on July 30, it had lost at least thirty vessels.[3]

Instead of ascending the Delaware River toward Philadelphia, the fleet departed Delaware Bay on July 31 and sailed farther southward into even hotter, more humid conditions. "We are bound for the Chesapeake," a British sailor griped, "in which situation may God defend us from the fatality of the worst climate in America at the worst season of the year to experience it!"[4]

Sailing from Delaware Bay to the Chesapeake consumed two weeks, meaning the soldiers had been aboard ship for four weeks all together. They ate the last morsels of fresh food and survived on salt rations and putrid water while suffering from lice, motion sickness, and intense heat.[5] "I am forced to complain about the intolerable heat we have been having to bear so far," a sailor declared. "If I could own the whole of America, I would refuse it if I had to live in these hot regions." A soldier described "an intense suffocating heat, which we have experienced for several days and nights together. If possible, the nights were more disagreeable than the days."[6]

In a storm on the evening of August 3, "the lightning and thunder surpassed description and the heaviness of the rain," a sailor reported. He witnessed a sloop "laid on her beam ends—7 men and a woman took to their boat, but kept her towed, but the painter breaking got adrift and was lost. The sloop with four men on board righted an hour after."[7]

The fleet entered Chesapeake Bay on August 14. For ten days, the fleet maneuvered up the bay on the incoming tide and rested at anchor on the outgoing tide. After going without fresh food for weeks, the soldiers and sailor feasted on crabs. "It is remarkable in this bay the multitude of crabs that swim nearly to the surface of the water," noted a sailor. "The fleet caught thousands."[8]

Even in the shelter of the bay, summer storms continued to batter the fleet. "A thunderbolt killed 3 horses in the hold of a transport, and split her mainmast to shivers; but by God's infinite mercy there was not one man on board hurted," a British sergeant wrote in his diary for August 16. He added that a lightning strike blackened the muskets of three companies of soldiers. "A woman's shift being burnt upon her body, lying in a birth on a transport, and she asleep, by a flash of lightning, without the least damage to her skin or flesh," he continued. "Also, a man's coat and shirt was burnt likewise on his back, without his knowing of it till next morning."[9]

The fleet passed the mouth of the Potomac River on August 20, and passed Annapolis, Maryland, a couple of days later. As the fleet progressed inland along the bay, the passages became narrower and shallower; the larger ships could proceed no farther. On August 22 the fleet passed the inlet leading to Baltimore without threatening to attack the city. When the fleet reached its destination at the upper end of the bay, British commanders sought suitable places to land their troops. While the troops were still aboard, lightning struck the ship carrying General Charles Cornwallis, setting the main mast on fire and filling the general's cabin with a sulfurous smell.[10]

Transports moved up the Elk River at the head of the bay and soldiers began unloading at Elk Ferry without resistance from American military forces. The 71st Regiment was among the fifth wave of troops taken ashore in flat-bottomed craft. The men rejoiced at being ashore after seven weeks aboard ship, but their suffering did not end. Fresh provisions were not available at the landing site, and British officers punished plunderers severely, so the men continued to subsist on biscuits and salt pork. Rain began falling during the landing and continued falling for thirty-six hours, soaking soldiers and damaging their ammunition. Their tents were still aboard ship, so they constructed shelters of tree branches and whatever materials they could find.[11] A soldier described "living like beasts, no plates, no dishes, no table cloth."[12] The huts shed light rain but offered scant protection when a heavy thunderstorm struck. A British engineer said the men spent three days and nights "drenched to the skin by those torrents of rain common in the Southern climate."

To reach the objective of the campaign—capturing the seat of the Continental Congress at Philadelphia—the army would have to march sixty miles and cross two rivers. The army, however, could not move out from the landing site because the horrible voyage had killed or weakened not only the soldiers but also the horses need for pulling artillery and baggage wagons. An officer reported that twenty-seven men and 170 horses died aboard ship, and about 150 of the horses that survived were unfit for duty. Another official called the surviving horses "mere carrion," and noted that the soldiers were "not sufficiently refreshed." An initial plan to move out was canceled because "the rain continues, and the roads are bottomless," an officer reported, and "the horses are still sick and stiff."[13]

THE ARMY FINALLY MOVED OUT on August 28; the line of soldiers, wagons and artillery stretched for ten miles as the army traveled bad roads in intense heat. After traveling ten miles to Head of Elk at the upper tip of Chesapeake Bay, the British commander provided a rest period for the men and horses. Although plundering was forbidden, some soldiers—including some Highlanders—violated the regulations and encountered not only punishment by the British but also attacks by Americans. "Two men of the 71st found in the woods yesterday with their throats cut, and two grenadiers hanged by the

Rebels with their plunder on their backs," reported John Peebles, a grenadier with the 42nd Highland Regiment.[14]

After almost a week at Head of Elk, the soldiers moved into a new position where they remained five days, still without tents and other camp gear. Before daylight on September 8 the soldiers marched northward in three divisions, avoiding battle with American troops entrenched to the east. One battalion of the 71st Regiment marched in the second division under the command of General James Grant, a Scotsman who was a career soldier and a veteran of the Seven Years War in North America; the 1st and 2nd Battalions of the 71st marched in the third division led by General Wilhelm von Knyphausen, commander of the German troops serving with the British army. The march turned out to be "very disagreeable," an artilleryman in the third division said, "without anything to eat, and almost suffocated with dust, owing to the vast train of baggage wagons and cattle that were in front." The divisions passed through Newark, Delaware, and then maneuvered through steep, rocky hills and narrow gorges to cross White Clay Creek before encamping at Hockessin near the Pennsylvania border. The army then divided into two columns and marched on two separate roads to enter Pennsylvania on the night of September 9 and early morning of September 10.[15]

In response, the American army—with an estimated strength of seventeen thousand men—pulled out of its entrenched position and relocated to block the British army's route to Philadelphia. American commander General George Washington chose to make a stand at Chads's Ford, where the road between Baltimore and Philadelphia crossed the Brandywine River. The river was five to six feet deep in most places, but at the ford reached the height of a man's chest. Steep banks and thick woods enhanced the ford's suitability as a defensive position.[16]

General Howe conceived a plan for dislodging the Americans from their strong position. One division of the British army under Knyphausen would confront the Americans head-on at Chads's Ford while another division would conduct a flanking movement upstream of the American position. On September 11, the British army formed for action before sunrise in cool, foggy conditions. Knyphausen's column marched out of Kennett Square on a seven-mile trek to Chads's Ford along the Great Post Road. The 71st Regiment—containing 1,200 men organized in three battalions—brought up the rear, escorting a baggage train of 131 wagons and 524 horses as well as a herd of cattle. The travelers encountered rolling hills, valleys and ravines; heavy woods beside the road alternated with farms and clearings.[17]

The column's advanced detachment included Ferguson's Rifle Corps—led by Patrick Ferguson, who would later hold a commission in the 71st Regiment—and the Queen's Rangers, along with a dozen dragoons, for a total of four hundred men. The detachment soon encountered opposition from more than a hundred American infantrymen and a few horsemen. The Americans, Ferguson reported, "threw away their fire and ran off, with the loss of three or four men and a horse whom we shot flying."[18] The Americans retreated a short distance, joined forces with two hundred comrades, fired a volley at the oncoming advance detachment, and retreated again. Near Kennett Meetinghouse, the Americans fired yet another volley that inflicted several casualties among the advanced detachment; the Americans retreated once again and took cover behind a fence. Meanwhile, another American unit waited in ambush. When the British advanced detachment reached point-blank range, the Americans fired a volley that struck thirty members of the Queen's Rangers. The Americans continued to fall back and join forces with other units, reaching a combined strength of nearly a thousand men.[19]

The combined American forces, including light artillery, occupied breastworks made of logs at a position covering the intersection of roads leading to Chads's Ford and Chads's Ferry. By this point, the British advanced detachment had been fighting for three hours, taking casualties and becoming fatigued. Knyphausen, therefore, employed additional elements. He sent a battalion of the 71st Regiment into the woods with orders to maneuver behind the American breastworks. Another regiment moved to a hill overlooking Brinton's Ford. British artillery set up on a hill opposite the American defense works. British and American artillery exchanged fire while British and American infantrymen fought fiercely at Brinton's Ford. American reinforcements crossed the Brandywine River and joined the fight. A British regiment threatened the American left flank, causing the Americans to withdraw from the breastworks and retreat across a field. As the British continued to advance, the Americans continued to retreat until they reached another set of breastworks on a ridge near Chads's Ford.[20]

While the fighting continued near Chads's Ford, several British units advanced toward Chads's Ferry. The units included a battalion of the 71st Regiment in addition to Ferguson's Riflemen, the Queen's Rangers, and the 23rd Regiment. The Queen's Rangers launched a bayonet attack that drove Americans out of the woods and toward the Brandywine. Ferguson led thirty men in an attack on a nearby American breastwork; after taking a volley at short distance, Ferguson recalled, his men "scrambled into the breastwork and the dogs ran away." Coming under fire from another American position, Ferguson "threw my party immediately to the ground" to avoid casualties. "This fire continued for some minutes very heavy until we sickened of it,"

Ferguson said, “after which upon the signal to rise my lads like Bay’s dead men sprung up and not one hurt.”[21]

The British onslaught forced the Americans at Chads’s Ferry and Chads’s Ford to fall back across the Brandywine where the main American army under General George Washington occupied a strong defensive position. The British moved up to the banks of the Brandywine but did not attempt to cross. One battalion of the 71st Regiment remained among the British Forces near Chads’s Ferry while the other two battalions made up part of a reserve force and guarded the baggage. Knyphausen marched various units back and forth through the hilly terrain to deceive the Americans into thinking they faced the entire British army rather than only one division. The opponents continued to exchange artillery fire, and light infantry units occasionally skirmished; Ferguson received a debilitating bullet wound in his right elbow.[22]

Early in the afternoon, the Americans launched a counterattack. An American force crossed the Brandywine, pushed back the British pickets, and skirmished with the 4th Regiment, the Queen’s Rangers, and Ferguson’s Riflemen. Artillery fire intensified on both sides. Two British infantry regiments advanced on the Americans, who returned to the other side of the river.[23]

THE BRITISH DIVISION under General Cornwallis conducted a flanking maneuver while Knyphausen’s division confronted the Americans at Chads’s Ford. Two companies of the 71st Regiment served in a light infantry brigade in Cornwallis’s division, and another company of the 71st severed in a grenadier battalion. John Maitland—a major in the Royal Marines who would serve in the 71st Regiment later in the war—commanded the 2nd Light Infantry Battalion in Cornwallis’s division.[24]

The soldiers marched more than five hours and crossed the west fork of the Brandywine River at Trimble’s Ford without opposition. Then they marched two hours to Jeffries's Ford on the east fork where they waded through waist-deep water. Once across the river, Cornwallis's division presented a dire threat to the flank of the American army at Chads's Ford about seven miles away. The Americans became aware of the flanking maneuver early in the afternoon and dispatched units to face the new foe; about 5,300 Americans opposed about nine thousand British troops in Cornwallis's division. Taking advantage of the terrain, the Americans occupied a defensive position atop Birmingham Hill.[25]

The opponents exchanged artillery fire, resulting in gruesome casualties. At about 4 p.m., the British attacked while the Americans were still in the process of aligning for battle. Fierce fighting forced the Americans to withdraw from their defensive position. British losses included twenty-four killed and 141 wounded.[26]

Because so many Americans had been sent north to Birmingham Hill, the 6,700 British troops under Knyphausen faced fewer than six thousand Americans, and most of the Americans were militiamen instead of Continental troops. The 4th Regiment and 5th Regiment launched an assault across Chads's Ferry at about 5 p.m., followed by the 2nd Battalion of the 71st Regiment, Ferguson's Riflemen, the Queen's Rangers, the 23rd Regiment, and a light dragoon detachment; the Hessian brigade brought up the rear.[27]

The soldiers carried their muskets in one hand and their ammunition in the other as they waded fifty paces through chest-high water. Artillery fire killed and wounded soldiers crossing the river; their blood stained the water, and their bodies drifted downstream. The soldiers who survived the crossing remained exposed to artillery fire and musket fire as they advanced in column along a causeway stretching two hundred yards through a swamp. When they eventually reached dry ground, they spread into battle formation.[28]

While the British vanguard fought hand-to-hand to capture earthworks housing American artillery near the river, the 2nd Battalion of the 71st and the Queen's Rangers passed between the earthworks and the river to threaten other American artillery positions at Brinton's Ford. The American artillery crew attempted to flee but, as a British soldier noted, "being attacked by the Rangers and the 71st in a buckwheat field was totally scivered with the bayonets before they could clear the fence around it."[29]

The British assault overwhelmed the forces guarding the riverbanks; the Americans abandoned artillery and ammunition in a disorderly retreat. As the British advanced along the Great Post Road, an American force under General Anthony Wayne made a stand. "British troops came on with the greatest boldness and bravery," an American reported, "and began a most heavy fire on us." The battle raged on as the sun began to set and gun-smoke swirled in darkening haze. The Americans withdrew in good order along the Great Post Road. Nightfall prevented the British column under Knypausen from pursuing the Americans withdrawing from the vicinity of Chads's Ford, and also prevented the column under Cornwallis from pursuing the Americans withdrawing from the vicinity of Birmingham Hill.[30]

The Battle of Brandywine inflicted heavy casualties on both sides. About three hundred Americans were killed, six hundred wounded and four hundred captured. According to the official report, British losses were ninety-three killed, 488 wounded, and six missing; according to a memorandum, however, the column under Cornwallis had 1,032 casualties and the column under Knyphausen had 944 casualties, for a total of nearly two thousand British killed and wounded. Three men of the 71st

Regiment suffered wounds in the fighting around Chads's Ferry and Brinton's Ford.[31]

Because the fighting continued until nightfall, many of the soldiers waited in the darkness for medical treatment. General Howe gave orders for "A small party with a surgeon's mate and wagon from each corps to be sent off by day-break in the morning to pick up their wounded in the woods and bring them to the general hospital at Dilworth," referring to an inn at Dilworth that was being used as a temporary hospital. Captain John Andre reported that "Parties were sent from the different regiments to find their wounded in the woods and bury their dead."[32]

ON THE DAY AFTER THE BATTLE of Brandywine, the 71st Regiment and some light dragoons set out to capture Wilmington on the Delaware River, where the British army could establish a connection with the British fleet. As the Highlanders approached Wilmington's defensive perimeter, the American militia fled, abandoning seven artillery pieces. After entering Wilmington, the Highlanders arrested Delaware President John McKinley. Several British ships arrived at Wilmington within a few days.[33]

Soldiers wounded in the Battle of Brandywine were sent to Wilmington, a process consuming five days because of the ongoing scarcity of wagons and healthy horses. At first, the wounded were placed aboard ships, and soon a hospital was established in town.[34] In addition to the wounded British soldiers, several hundred wounded American prisoners of war arrived in Wilmington. A Hessian battalion escorted the prisoners and remained in Wilmington to reinforce the 71st Regiment.[35]

The British army, except for the units at Wilmington, resumed its mission to capture Philadelphia. The American army under George Washington withdrew to protect supplies stored in western Pennsylvania, allocating responsibility for protecting Philadelphia to local troops. Late in the night of September 15, British General Charles Cornwallis set out to confront Washington's troops. Darkness and muddy terrain slowed the march. A storm of wind and rain slowed the march even more, and the mud got even deeper as infantrymen, artillery carriages, horses, livestock and supply wagons churned the dirt.[36] "I wish I could give a description of the downpour which began during the engagement and continued until the next morning," a Hessian officer wrote. "It came down so hard that in a few moments we were drenched and sank in mud up to our calves."[37] With powder soaked, visibility cloaked, and roads choked with mud, the British army commanders decided to hunker down. The British had been traveling light, without tents, so they sought shelter in farm sheds or built huts with fence rails, tree limbs and brush.

Washington's troops, meanwhile, withdrew six miles away from the British because the rain had ruined their ammunition. Normally small creeks were so swollen that the men had to swim across. Moving artillery carriages up muddy hills required repeated changes of horse teams. Dripping-wet men shivered in the cold night.[38]

The storm continued to rage until the afternoon of September 17. The Schuylkill River rose eight feet, and when riders tried to ford creeks the water lapped against their horses' bellies. Washington moved out toward a supply of fresh powder to replace what the rain had ruined. The wagons and artillery lurched through the flooded countryside, and the men walked single file on logs laid across creeks. Although the lack of powder left the American army defenseless, pursuit by the British was frustrated by boggy ground and ravaged roads.[39]

The British and American armies maneuvered around the countryside for three weeks without finding an opportunity for a decisive battle. British forces under Cornwallis occupied

Philadelphia on September 26, fifteen days after the Battle of Brandywine.

In order to hold Philadelphia, the British had to bring supplies up the Delaware River. The Americans tried to thwart the British by placing obstacles in the river and establishing defensive posts along the banks. Several engagements resulted in opening the river to shipping from the coast to Philadelphia. In one of the engagements, the British 42nd Regiment and part of the 71st Regiment attacked a redoubt at Billingsport on October 2; the garrison of the redoubt fled.[40]

While the British held Philadelphia, the main British army encamped five miles away at Germantown. Washington launched a surprise attack against the encampment on the morning of October 4. British defenders, occupying stone houses in the middle of town and using garden walls as breastworks, held off the American attack. British General Cornwallis brought fresh troops from Philadelphia, creating a second line of battle. The Americans slowly retreated. Two weeks later, the British withdrew from Germantown into Philadelphia and constructed strong fortifications around the city.[41]

THE 71ST REGIMENT remained at Wilmington until November, when the Highlanders returned to New York. Two hundred recruits from Scotland reinforced the regiment.[42]

In the summer of 1778, the 71st Regiment under the command of Lieutenant Colonel Archibald Campbell remained encamped in McGowan's Pass on Manhattan Island in New York.[43] Later in the summer, the regiment relocated to King's Bridge near the marshes of the Harlem River. "About two hundred paces to the right of the spot on which the tents were pitched, was a tract of low and swampy ground," observed Robert Jackson, a surgeon's mate in the 1st Battalion of the 71st Regiment, "but the immediate situation was dry, and of considerable elevation."[44] Jackson—a doctor who had previously conducted observations of fever outbreaks in Jamaica—continued his observations as he treated the soldiers:

> The regiment in which I served was encamped during the months of June and July on a healthy part of York-island. Fevers were rare; and the time of invasion of such as did appear was chiefly confined to the second and last quarters of the moon.
>
> In the beginning of August, the encampment was removed to King's Bridge, where it occupied a very unhealthy situation. The intermitting fever soon made its appearance. It extended in some degree to the whole battalion, but raged with particular violence on the right, which bordered on low and swampy ground. The approach to new and full moon never failed, even in this climate, to increase the number of sick; yet it deserves to be remarked that this increase was always smaller in proportion in that part of the battalion which lay contiguous to the swamp, where the disease was highly epidemic than in the other extremity of the encampment where it prevailed in a less degree. But still, on the whole, when the regiment moved from their ground in the beginning of November, of a hundred cases of intermittent fever, which were marked on the almanac, eighty were found to have commenced in the usual period of invasion; that is, the second and last quarters of the moon. It is somewhat remarkable that relapses were in a smaller proportion.
>
> This regiment, some parts of the medical history of which I describe, embarked on an expedition to the southward in November, and arrived at its destination in Georgia in the latter end of the year. It remained in the southern provinces and served every campaign until the

capitulation at Yorktown. The same train of observation was continued during this intervening space, and the same influence of the moon seemed in general to prevail.[45]

Georgia

LIEUTENANT COLONEL ARCHIBALD CAMPBELL of the 71st Regiment received orders to lead eight battalions in an invasion of Georgia for the purpose of reestablishing British rule over the rebellious colony. A fleet of at least twenty warships and troop transports set sail on November 26, 1778, to carry Campbell's army from New York to the coast of Georgia.[1]

A wintry trip down the Atlantic coast meant rough sailing. Although the sailors tried to tie down everything, "trunks and portmanteaus were hurled helter-skelter," an officer reported. "The sea was composed of terrific mountains and valleys; the foam looked all the time as if snow were floating about."[2]

"The sick were collected into one ship," reported surgeon's mate Robert Jackson, "which, after a stormy and tedious passage, arrived with the rest of the fleet at Savannah, in Georgia, in the latter end of December. The voyage had an excellent effect on the health of the men. Out of a hundred and twenty convalescents who embarked at New York in the month of November, not a man died and there remained only two who were unfit for the service of the field on the day of our arrival on the Savannah River."[3]

On December 23, the fleet came to anchor off Ossabaw Island, about twenty miles from the mouth of the Savannah River. The next day the fleet entered the river. Campbell sent scouts on two flatboats up the river to find a landing place for his troops. The scouts reported that the only suitable landing place was at Brewton's Hill, a plantation belonging to John Girardeau. "From this intelligence I proposed," Campbell wrote in his journal entry for December 26, "I should push on shore in the middle of the night at Girardeau's plantation with one thousand men, and establish a footing before daylight." His plan was foiled when "the night proved so boisterous, and the wind so contrary, it was impossible to execute this service."[4]

When the weather eventually calmed, Campbell personally led the attack on forty Americans guarding the bluff at Brewton's Hill. "On this bluff a small body of rebels appeared in readiness for our reception," Campbell reported, "having occupied the houses and barns of the plantation and knocked out planks for their firelocks to look through."

A narrow bank with deep ditches on each side crossed a soggy rice field that lay between the landing place and the bluff. The bank was so narrow that only two soldiers could march side by side as they crossed. At dawn on December 29, 1778, a corporal and four Highlanders from the 71st Regiment set out across the bank followed by a sergeant and twelve Highlanders about fifty yards back, followed by Campbell and a light infantry company of Highlanders. Altogether, five hundred British soldiers had landed. When the British approached within one hundred yards of the American position, the Americans opened fire. Campbell launched his company of light infantry in a Highland charge toward the Americans. The Highlanders "rushed on with such rapidity that in less than three minutes we were in possession" of the bluff at Brewton's Hill, Campbell reported. "The rebels retreated with precipitation by the back doors and windows" of John Girardeau's house and barns. "This acquisition was a favorable presage of our future success and were it not for the loss of Captain Cameron, an officer of distinguished merit and bravery, who with three Highlanders were killed, and five Highlanders wounded, nothing could have turned out more fortunate."

As soon as Campbell took possession of Brewton's Hill and secured the landing place, he sent out scouts who reported that the Americans had taken a defensive possession on the southern edge of the Savannah River. Wanting to attack quickly, Campbell led about two thousand troops into battle while the rest of his troops continued to disembark from the troop transports. When Campbell got within eight hundred yards of the enemy, he climbed a tall tree to study the American defenses. A marshy stream separated the British and American forces. One flank of the American army extended to marshes and rice fields beside the Savannah River. The other flank appeared to be protected by swampland.

Campbell, combining his talents as an engineer and a military tactician, looked for a way to maneuver behind the American lines. A slave from a nearby plantation told Campbell that a path led through the swamp that lay beside the right flank of the American army. Campbell sent about six hundred light infantrymen across the path through the swamp while the main body of his command prepared to assault the center of the American position.[5]

The responsibility for defending Savannah fell on about 650 Continental troops from Georgia and South Carolina, about one hundred Georgia militiamen who were even more poorly equipped than the Continental troops, and a small artillery unit.

When the British light infantry emerged from the swamp and attacked Georgia militia at the military barracks inside Savannah, well behind the American defensive position on the edge of town, the American commander ordered the defenders to retreat. The South Carolina brigade withdrew first, the artillery unit went next, and the Georgia brigade covered the rear of the retreat.

The South Carolina brigade moved quickly enough to escape from town before the British light infantry cut off the line of retreat. The Georgia brigade fell behind and came under fire from the British light infantry. Another British detachment cut off the line of retreat along the Augusta Road leading out of Savannah to the west. The Georgians tried to fight through what they considered a weak stretch of the British line in an attempt to escape down the Ogeechee Road to the south. The brigade broke ranks, however, and most of the Georgians fled down the road into Savannah.

The Georgians continued to look for an escape route. When the soldiers reached the bank of Musgrove Creek, however, they could not find a bridge; the creek was at high tide, and if there ever was a bridge then it must have been underwater. They had no choice other than to swim across the tide-swollen creek. Most of the men decided not to take the risk. A few officers and men did manage to swim to the far shore and escape. The 186 remaining soldiers were trapped at the bank of the creek. When British attackers opened fire on the Americans, a Georgia major who had stayed behind because he could not swim raised a white flag and surrendered to a British lieutenant.[6]

Campbell wrote in his journal, "it was flood tide, and such only who could swim effected their escape. Among these, General Robert Howe, Colonels Huger and Elbert were successful, but they left their horses in the mud."[7]

Campbell's well-conceived attack killed eighty-three American defenders, wounded eleven, and took 488 prisoners, while the British lost only seven killed and nineteen wounded. In a single day, Campbell had driven the American forces out of Savannah, seized the American artillery, small arms, shot, gunpowder and other military stores, and occupied Georgia's capital. Campbell bragged that he was the first British officer to tear a stripe and star out of the Continental flag.[8]

Campbell established a network of outposts around the perimeter of Savannah, and stationed the 71st Regiment at Ebenezer. He described Ebenezer and other fortified posts in his journal:

Cherokee Hill is eight miles from Savannah and may of consequence be applied as an intermediary post to support the communication of the great western road and to secure a cross tract to Ogeechee, which enters the great road at this station...

Abercorn is by the road about 9 miles from Savannah, upon the side of a creek, which communicates with the great river, and by which our provisions are happily conveyed and carted from thence to Ebenezer...

Zubly's Ferry is twenty-three miles from the town of Savannah. At this station, the great road communicates to Purrysburg over a long tract of low swamps cut by two considerable creeks, over which the rebels had wooden bridges that are now broken up. The ground on our side of the swamp has from its height an excellent command of this road...

Ebenezer is distant twenty-five miles from the town of Savannah and situated on the bank of the great river between two considerable swamps. As those swamps are only passable over the two wooden bridges, it requires a very great detour for troops to turn them. Here I am constructing some redoubts to shut up the gorge between the two swamps, and I mean to establish this post as the advance magazine for the army. Ebenezer from its happy situation above the town of Purrysburg makes it a post of consequence so long as General Lincoln with the Carolina army, consisting of five thousand men, continues to encamp in the neighborhood [at Purrysburg on the South Carolina side of the river]. The 1st and 2nd Battalions of the 71st Regiment have charge of Ebenezer.[9]

Surgeon's mate Robert Jackson reported that Ebenezer "is situated immediately on the bank of the river Savannah" and "is surrounded by creeks of fresh water. It may not be improper to remark with regard to Ebenezer that few places in America have been observed to be more unhealthful, though such a conclusion probably would not be drawn from a general view of its situation. It occupies a sandy eminence of considerable elevation, and possesses a considerable environ of cleared ground."[10]

AFTER THE CAPTURE OF SAVANNAH, General Augustine Prevost left East Florida and marched up the Georgia coast, capturing the fortified port of Sunbury. General Prevost arrived at Savannah in mid-January of 1779 and immediately took command of the army that Campbell had brought to Georgia.[11]

While Prevost commanded the garrison in Savannah, Campbell led an expedition to capture Augusta, a town at the fall line of the Savannah River that served as the gateway to the backcountry. Campbell's expedition to Augusta set out from Ebenezer at daybreak on January 24, 1779.[12] The expeditionary force contained about a thousand British and loyalist troops. Campbell assigned the 1st Battalion of the 71st Regiment to accompany him, while the 2nd Battalion of the 71st Regiment remained at Ebenezer along with a troop of dragoons "and others to make 800" rank and file soldiers.

On January 25, Campbell sent the light infantry to secure a bridge across Brier Creek. "These troops surprised a body of the enemy," Campbell wrote, "and were in sufficient time to save the bridge, which was actually in flames. Some prisoners fell into our hands on this occasion." Brier Creek, Campbell reported, "is about one hundred feet wide at the bridge, and about eight or ten feet in depth; the current of water is slow, and the bottom muddy." Campbell enrolled several men from the Brier Creek neighborhood into the militia and directed them to "keep within the circle of their respective farms, and to fix upon a place of rendezvous in case of an alarm." He established a post at Brier Creek manned with thirty Carolina loyalists and twenty rifle dragoons. He fortified the post with an abbatis (a defensive structure made of tree trunks and limbs) around houses.

Under Prevost's orders, Campbell reluctantly sent the Florida Rangers under Thomas Brown to attack patriots in Burke County. The patriots defeated the Rangers and wounded Brown.[13]

On January 28, Campbell reported, American soldiers held a position at Telfair's sawmill, about twenty-four miles away from Campbell's army. Campbell set out at four o'clock in the morning to confront the Americans but, by the time Campbell reached Telfair's sawmill, the Americans were no longer there. Campbell sent a spy to "examine General Elbert's situation," referring to Samuel Elbert, who held commissions as a Continental colonel and a Georgia general. Fifty American horsemen pursued the spy close to the lines of Campbell's camp. "By the agility of the spy's horse, he escaped," Campbell reported, "and our dragoons in turn pursued and took two of the rebels, from whom I received confirmation of Colonel Brown's intelligence respecting the junction of General Elbert, Colonels Hammond, Ingram and Few; and that the enemy had taken post at Boggy Gut to dispute our progress."[14]

Campbell hoped to attack Elbert's force. When the British reached Boggy Gut shortly after daybreak on January 29, however, they found nothing but traces of the Americans' campfires. By noon, spies and scouts informed Campbell that Elbert intended to oppose the British advance at a deep, swampy ravine called Macbean's Creek. At two hours before midnight, the British light infantry and Florida Rangers started secretly working their way through the dark woods to a bluff overlooking Elbert's camp. At two hours after midnight, the main body of Campbell's troops started advancing toward Elbert's position. At four o'clock in the morning of January 30, Campbell arranged his troops for battle.

At daylight British artillery pounded Elbert's position. Seeing no response, Campbell sent his infantry across the creek. They found pots of beef and pork on fires lighted so recently that the water in the pots was just slightly warm. They also found blankets, muskets and provisions that had been left behind by the Americans. All the evidence showed that Elbert had abandoned his position in a hurry. Elbert had captured two Florida Rangers searching for plunder who told him of Campbell's plan for a surprise attack. Elbert managed to withdraw from Macbean's Creek just half an hour before artillery fire signaled the start of the attack.[15]

Elbert fell back ten miles along the road to Augusta. At Spirit Creek, his force of two hundred men took shelter in a small stockade called Fort Henderson. On January 30 Campbell placed a howitzer and two six-pounder cannons on a piece of high ground three hundred yards from the stockade. British artillery fire smashed into the stockade and struck several American soldiers. The Americans scrambled out the stockade "in a very precipitate manner," Campbell reported, but remained in battle formation near Spirit Creek. Campbell's army crossed the creek, occupied the stockade, and formed for battle with the right flank against the stockade. Elbert led the Americans in a retreat toward Augusta.[16]

Campbell received intelligence that Elbert's command had been reinforced and lay in ambush at a swamp called the Cupboard. When the British cautiously approached the Cupboard on January 31 they found no resistance, indicating that the intelligence was false or that the Americans had withdrawn.[17]

After reaching Augusta, Elbert crossed the Savannah River and joined forces with Andrew Williamson, a South Carolina brigadier general. American records indicated a combined forced of twelve hundred men, but Campbell thought he faced eighteen hundred men.[18]

CAMPBELL'S ARMY continued toward Augusta and entered the town early in the evening of January 31, 1779, without resistance. Campbell occupied Augusta for two weeks. He deployed his troops in defensive positions and strengthened the town's fortifications. During the occupation an event occurred that would soon have drastic repercussions. A marauding band of patriots killed Sergeant Hugh MacAlister of the 71st Regiment while he protected a patriot family from reprisals by local loyalists. Campbell described the event in his journal entry for February 3:

> The enemy appeared to have no disposition to disturb us, otherways than by sending a number of small parties across the Savannah River to plunder the inhabitants... One of these parties shot and cruelly cut with hatchets one of our most valuable light infantry men (named MacAlister) who had been placed as a safeguard at the house of a rebel major, about one mile from camp. This major was a prisoner of war in my possession, and entreated in pressing terms to grant him a safeguard for the protection of his wife and family.
>
> The barbarity which accompanied this murder was disgraceful in the extreme and I was in hopes that the rebels would have afforded me instant and ample redress, as General Williamson disclaimed the act and, it is said, loaded the perpetrators with irons; but instead of punishing them with promptness according to their deserts, he sent them to General Lincoln at Purrysburg, who directed their irons to be struck off, and there the business ended. The British troops, however, were greatly exasperated by this shameful act of

> injustice; especially the light infantry who had determined to avenge MacAlister's murder on the first favorable occasion.[19]

On February 11 Campbell learned that patriot troops from North Carolina would arrive in the evening to reinforce Elbert and Williamson across the river from Augusta. American officers reported the North Carolinians commanded by General John Ashe numbered from nine hundred to eleven hundred, but Campbell's spies estimated the number at sixteen hundred. Campbell believed that his army of one thousand men faced an American army of 3,800 men. Campbell recognized the risk of remaining in Augusta and on February 14 withdrew toward Savannah.

Campbell's army found security in the fortified British post at Hudson's Ferry, forty-eight miles from Savannah. When his troops reached Hudson's Ferry on the evening of February 20, "to my great concern there was no rum to be had, notwithstanding repeated letters sent to the general and commissary that this detachment was without rum for many days," Campbell grumbled. "To the honor of these brave fellows, they bore the want of rum like good soldiers."[20]

Because Campbell planned to return to England after conquering Georgia, he turned over command of the troops at Hudson's Ferry to Lieutenant Colonel James Mark Prevost, the younger brother of General Augustine Prevost. Campbell wrote in his journal on February 20:

> At this station I met Lieutenant Colonel Prevost, who informed me that he was in the future to command the advance troops and he should be obliged to me for my opinion and advice respecting the intentions of the rebels, which I gave with pleasure by telling him I was well persuaded, if the

> enemy were not disturbed, they would advance as far as Briar Creek, in which case they might be easily surprised by sending some of our troops to amuse them in front while the rest proceeded up the Back Road towards the bridge at Paris's Mills and came round upon their rear. As the colonel had never seen that country, I showed him my sketch of these parts and explained in the fullest manner the nature of the ground lying on each side of the Back Road, and that between the creek and the river.[21]

Leaving Colonel Prevost at Hudson's Ferry, Campbell proceeded downriver to the British post at Ebenezer, where he met with General Augustine Prevost. "I took occasion to mention to the general my ideas regarding the motions of the light troops," Campbell wrote. "The probability of the rebels coming down to Briar Creek, and the facility of getting round into their rear by Paris's Mill. I showed him also my sketch of the country on both sides of Briar Creek, which seemed to give him satisfaction."[22]

When he reached Savannah, Campbell took measures to restore British colonial rule in Georgia. He issued a proclamation for enforcing the laws that governed Georgia in 1775 on the eve of the American Revolution. He restored the civil offices of the British colony and set up a police department for the city of Savannah. At the beginning of his expedition, Campbell had been given a commission as governor of Colonial Georgia and, quite optimistically, as governor of Colonial South Carolina. The plan called for him to be replaced as governor of Georgia by the former colonial governor, James Wright, who had escaped from Savannah when the revolution began. On March 4 Campbell appointed a lieutenant governor pro tempore to serve as the chief civil executive from the time Campbell left Georgia until the time Wright arrived. He chose James Mark Prevost because "being the brother of General Prevost, who was so much attached to his welfare and success that there is not a doubt but harmony and unanimity will take place between the civil and military branches of the government." He sent the commission to Prevost at Hudson's Ferry along with a letter:

> I am happy to have it in my power, before I quit America, to fulfill in great measure the interesting object of His Majesty's Commissioners by re-establishment of legal government in Georgia.
>
> It gives me at the same time great pleasure to reflect that I have it in my power to entrust the commission of Lieutenant Governor into the hands of an officer in whose abilities I place so high a confidence, and who from his knowledge of the country, the temper and inclination of the people, is well qualified to carry into execution the gracious intentions of our Sovereign.[23]

While Campbell was in Savannah restoring colonial rule to Georgia, Colonel Prevost was following Campbell's suggestion for attacking an American army that had, as Campbell predicted, encamped at the junction of Brier Creek and the Savannah River.

The site of the American encampment occupied a large farm field near a fork in Brier Creek, providing the troops with a convenient source of water. The road to Miller Bridge intersected with the road to Augusta at the camp. A vast swamp stretched nearly three miles to the Savannah River on the side of the encampment opposite from Brier Creek.[24]

"The river was very full by reason of the late rains," an American soldier observed, and "the backwater extended up the creek twelve miles at least to where it was fordable from where we lay."[25]

The soldiers in camp could not build defensive works because they did not have entrenching tools. They were not issued ammunition because they did not have cartridge boxes. Supplies were inaccessible because their supply train sat eight miles away at Burton's Ferry.

The American army remained at Brier Creek for four days waiting for reinforcements. General John Ashe, the American commander complained that only 207 mounted soldiers from South Carolina joined him, and only 150 of them were fit for duty.

The American army contained about a hundred Georgia Continentals and militia, nine hundred North Carolinians, a four-pound field piece and a pair of two-pound swivels mounted as field pieces.

On the other side of the Savannah River, South Carolina artillery and a North Carolina regiment of seven hundred infantry arrived at Matthews Bluff. The American plan called for them to cross the river and march three miles to the camp at Brier Creek. Fifty men began building bridges and clearing a road across the swamp from the Georgia side of the Savannah River to the camp at Brier Creek, but they did not complete the job in time for the American plan to take effect.

NEARLY FOUR HUNDRED BRITISH soldiers of the 1st Battalion of the 71st Regiment under the command of Major Duncan Macpherson took a position across Brier Creek from the Americans on March 2. While the Americans watched that battalion, Colonel Prevost led a force of nine hundred British soldiers on a fifty-mile march to come around behind the Americans.

The British force on the march included the 2nd Battalion of the 71st Regiment under the command of Lieutenant Colonel John Maitland. About forty men of the 71st formed a dragoon company using cavalry equipment seized in Savannah. Sir

James Baird commanded two companies of light infantry. The force also included three companies of elite troops of the 60th Regiment, and fifty men of the Florida Rangers.

When the marchers crossed Brier Creek at Paris's Mill, upstream of the American army, they trapped the Americans between Brier Creek and the Savannah River. Meanwhile, on the other side of Brier Creek, Major Macpherson led the 1st Battalion of the 71st Regiment along a causeway toward the American encampment. Within ten minutes after the Highlanders of the 1st Battalion arrived at the head of the causeway, they heard gunfire erupt across the creek.

The British force under Colonel Prevost reached the American camp at 3 p.m. on March 3, 1779, and drove back the pickets. As the Americans scrambled to take defensive positions, the British infantry advanced at the quick step and the British artillery opened fire.[26]

About nine hundred British soldiers attacked the American camp. Captain Baird's light infantry faced the American left flank along the Brier Creek swamp. The 2nd Battalion of the 71st occupied the center. North Carolina provincials and Florida Rangers faced the American right flank. Fifty loyalist riflemen took position to shoot down patriots attempting to flee toward the Savannah River. The grenadiers of the 60th Regiment and dragoons led by Thomas Tawse stood by in reserve. Colonel Prevost placed his five artillery pieces in the center, to the rear of the 2nd Battalion of the 71st Highlanders.[27]

American rosters listed about eleven hundred troops at Brier Creek, but detachments had reduced the number significantly; there may have been as few as six hundred troops in the main encampment. Georgia troops occupied the center of the American line. North Carolina militia from New Bern formed on the left beside Brier Creek, while North Carolina militia from Edenton took position on the right toward the Savannah River swamp. North Carolina militia from Halifax and Wilmington formed the second line.

The entire battle lasted only about fifteen minutes, and most of the Americans fled within five minutes after the initial attack. The Georgians fired two volleys, and the British returned fire. Then, according to Ashe, the Georgians "advanced without orders a few steps beyond the line and moved to the left in front of the regiment from the district of New Bern, which much impeded their firing." The militia from Edenton moved slightly to the right. The combined movements of the Georgians to the left and the North Carolinians to the right created a gap in the American line.[28]

The troops in the center of the British line launched a bayonet charge into the gap. Many of the American militiamen ran away without firing a shot. The Wilmington men and some of the New Bern men fired a few volleys and stood their ground waiting for reinforcements. The militia unit from Edenton fled from the British bayonets, and the rest of the North Carolina militia panicked and joined the flight. A South Carolina soldier said, "We had got to the extremity of the right wing where General Ashe commanded by the time the second fire was made. This was our post, but we had not time to give more than one fire when the general wheeled and fled and the whole wing with him. He was gone about 150 yards or more before our little party followed."[29]

The Georgians realized that the American right wing had evaporated when they discovered British soldiers attacking them from behind their position.[30]

The battle gave the Highlanders in the British force an occasion to avenge the death of Hugh MacAlister, the sergeant whose body had been hacked with hatchets in Augusta. Archibald Campbell, who received second-hand accounts of the battle, wrote in his journal: "...when the light infantry were running up in line to charge the rebels, one of the Highlanders called out – *Now my Boys, remember poor Macalister:* in consequence of which, this corps spared very few that came within their reach."[31]

While the other Americans fled, a band of Continental troops and Georgia militia kept fighting until they were killed, wounded, or captured. Their commander, Samuel Elbert, suffered a gunshot wound before he surrendered.[32]

The Americans fleeing from battle sloshed through three miles of swamp to reach the Savannah River. "General Ashe rode a good horse, left his men, and got round the enemy and made to a ferry above, crossed, and escaped," a soldier said, "while the rest of us were drove into the swamp between the creek and the river. The banks of these were so steep and deep that the horses that went in could not get out again, and some men would have been drowned had not canes been put into their hands and helped them out. We now got into a thick canebreak, and the enemy pursued us no farther. This was late in the evening. Twelve of us got together, and, as it was moonlight in the night, we formed a small raft of driftwood in the mouth of a lagoon, on which three of us with danger and much difficulty got over the river, after being carried above a mile down before we landed."

The Americans who crossed the river continued to suffer. "Many of our men were half-naked, having stripped to swim the river," a soldier remembered. "The third of March we were defeated, and that night there was a light frost, and many suffered in the cold, having nothing on but a shirt or breeches. Here we lay, I know not how long."[33]

THE BRITISH SCORED a decisive victory at the Battle of Brier Creek. Their casualties were relatively light: some sources say one British officer and five privates died in the battle, and ten

British soldiers suffered wounds; nineteenth-century writer David Stewart reports "the loss of the Highlanders being only 5 soldiers killed, and 1 officer, and 12 rank and file, wounded."

The British captured the American artillery—accounts range from two swivel guns to seven field pieces—about a thousand muskets and all of the American supplies, provisions and equipment. One soldier fled so quickly that he left his boots in camp. The panicked Americans discarded hundreds of hats, shirts, canteens and firearms on the banks of the river. Forced to choose between clothes and a rifle, many soldiers chose to keep their rifles as they prepared to plunge into the cold, swift, deep water.[34]

American casualties at the Battle of Brier Creek have been estimated at nearly two hundred either killed in battle or drowned. Exact figures are not available, partly because most of the survivors walked to their homes in North Carolina without stopping anywhere along the way.[35]

Augustine Prevost boasted that "one of their best officers, several more of note, in the whole twenty-seven officers, were taken, with near two hundred men." American casualties, Prevost reported, consisted of "about 150 killed on the field of battle and adjoining woods and swamps; but their chief loss consists in the number of officers and men drowned in attempting to save themselves from the slaughter, and plunging into a deep and rapid river."[36]

The outcome of the Battle of Brier Creek carried significant consequences. British officials continued to implement colonial rule in Georgia, and exiled Governor James Wright returned to Savannah on July 14, 1779, four months after the battle. The British maintained control of Savannah and coastal Georgia until the war was practically finished. From their base in Savannah, the British moved northward, captured Charleston, and set up a chain of posts across the South Carolina backcountry. The

British occupied Augusta from May of 1780 until June of 1781, temporarily exerting control over all of Georgia. Those gains would have been stopped or at least delayed if the American campaign to wrest Georgia from British control had not ended in disaster at Brier Creek.

Stono Ferry

BRITISH AND AMERICAN FORCES continued to struggle over control of Georgia after the Battle of Brier Creek. Continental General Benjamin Lincoln led most of his army up the Savannah River and reached Augusta on April 22, 1779. He intended to hem in the British on the west as well as on the north, and to prevent the British from receiving supplies and reinforcements from the backcountry.[1]

A detachment under General William Moultrie stayed behind at Black Swamp to guard places where the British could cross the Savannah River into South Carolina. About a hundred men under Lieutenant Colonel Alexander McIntosh stood watch at the strategic location of Purrysburg on a bluff above the river.[2]

The British commander in Georgia, Major General Augustine Prevost, took advantage of Lincoln's absence from the coastal area. Facing "the approaching scarcity of every article of provisions in a country so much exhausted on all sides," Prevost reported, "rendered it necessary to adopt a plan that might enable us to procure supplies from Carolina."[3]

Prevost assembled an invasion force at Abercorn, about twenty-five miles up the river from Savannah, and created two divisions. Lieutenant Colonel John Maitland, commander of the 71st Regiment, commanded a division of about two thousand men, including both battalions of the 71st and light infantry. More than a hundred Creek Indians, who had traveled hundreds of miles from their homes on the western frontier, joined the expedition.[4]

Maitland's division boarded flatboats, crossed the Savannah River, and disembarked about four miles below Purrysburg on the evening of April 28. They entered the swamps in the evening and spent the whole night wading through them.[5] Creek Indians guided the troops through the wet wilderness.[6] Robert Jackson, a surgeon's mate with the 71st Regiment, noted that "a part of the army was near five hours in the Purrysburg swamp. The men were always to the middle, sometimes up to the neck in water. The cold and fatigue were both very great, and a fit of intermitting fever was the consequence in a great number of the soldiers."[7]

The Highlanders' perseverance under difficult conditions impressed their commander. "The troops with their usual spirit got over every difficulty," Prevost noted. "But having been detained by the unexpected depth of the water much longer than it was expected, it was ten o'clock in the morning before the light infantry supported by the first battalion of the 71st under Lieut.-Colonel Maitland could make their attack on the detachment the rebels left to guard Purrysburg, consisting of about 300 men, which gave them an opportunity after firing three guns and some musketry to make their escape with the loss of two men killed and of a few prisoners."[8] A Hessian officer reported that the American commander at Purrysburg "retreated in the greatest confusion, whereby it occurred that some of his men who could not follow were scalped by the Indians."[9]

The British waited for floodwaters to subside before bringing the main body of the invasion force across the river along with artillery and provisions. When their full force was assembled, they set out in pursuit of the Americans.[10]

After withdrawing from Purrysburg, the Americans commanded by Lieutenant Colonel McIntosh fell back to the Coosawhatchie River, where they joined the larger force under General Moultrie, and then took up position on high ground beside the Tullifinny River. Moultrie assigned Lieutenant Colonel John Laurens and a force of light infantry and riflemen to protect the American rear guard from being cut off by the advancing British forces. Laurens decided on his own initiative to make a stand on the west bank of the Coosawhatchie River with five hundred Americans against eight hundred British troops—including the 71st Regiment—led by Lieutenant Colonel Maitland. British artillery killed and wounded several Americans. Laurens suffered a wound in the arm and his horse died in the barrage. When Laurens went to have his wound tended, the officer who assumed command retreated to the Tullifinny.[11] "Pursued the Rebels under Gen. Moultrie to Coosawhatchie River," Brigade Major Francis Skelly of the 71st Regiment recorded in his journal entry for May 4. "They crossed the river, burnt the bridge and made a trifling stand on the opposite side. They killed and wounded four of our men. We drove them from thence, waded the river, found a few of their dead, pursued them cross Tullifinny ferry, which we forded, saw their rear at Pocotaligo River, gave them a few cannon shots, they retired towards Charles Town, Col. Maitland with Light Infantry and one Battalion 71st forded the river and took post."[12]

Realizing that twelve hundred Americans could not stop three thousand British troops, Moultrie continued to withdraw. Prevost reported that Moultrie "retreated with all expedition to Charleston, burning and destroying every bridge and putting every impediment in the way with falling of trees across the roads etc. as was in his power without standing to defend them."[13] The British troops further slowed their progress by plundering plantations and sending captured provisions back to their base in Georgia.[14] Moultrie reported "the enemy, with parties of horse and Indians are ravaging the countryside in a barbarous manner, killing people and burning a number of houses as they go on."[15] Moultrie begged General Lincoln to "hasten to our assistance" because "my little army decreases, everyone running to look after his family and property; the enemy carry everything before them with fire and sword; many good houses they have already destroyed, and many more will be consumed before they can be checked."[16]

Referring to the 71st Regiment as "Highlanders," Moultrie said he sent John Laurens "to reconnoiter on the Purrysburg Road...where they saw a field-piece in the road, at the road where the Two Sisters road comes in, with a Highlander sentry standing, [Laurens] endeavored to go round into the wood to make discoveries, but found the sentries of the light troops and Highlanders so far extended on each flank that he could not get near enough; but I think by all appearances it looks as if the enemy intend for Charlestown."[17] Additional reconnaissance convinced Moultrie that the British invaders included 1,300 or 1,500 "Royal Scotch Highlanders."[18]

Major Skelly of the 71st reported that the British army "divided into two columns—the one under Gen. Prevost marched to Bull's, the other under Col. Maitland to near Saltcatcher Bridge which was burnt." British soldiers repaired the bridge the next day, according to Skelly's journal entry for May 7. "Col. Maitland's column marched—halted two miles beyond Fish Pond Bridge which we were likewise obliged to repair. A party of Rebel horse fired at some of our scouts, wounded an Indian and two others, and then rode off. Gen. Prevost's column marched to Combahee Ferry, joined us after dark. The whole marched to near Horseshoe Bridge which was burnt." Skelly noted that the retreating Americans "felled trees and broke up the road to impede our progress. Cap. Moncrief (our chief engineer) with a small group of horse, came up with the negroes who had been employed to do it, and set them immediately at work to clear the road, which they did before the column came up."

The Americans destroyed the bridge over the Edisto River at Jacksonboro and burned all the boats in the vicinity, forcing the British to find a crossing place father upstream.[19] The British forded the Edisto River at Parker's Ferry on the afternoon of May 9, Skelly recorded, and endured a "Violent thunder storm with heavy rain."[20]

On May 11, the 2nd Battalion of the 71st crossed Ashley Ferry—eight miles above Charleston—along with dragoons, grenadiers, light infantry and a battalion of Hessians, and accompanied General Prevost to the outskirts of Charleston. The rest of the British expeditionary force, including the 1st Battalion of the 71st Regiment, remained at Ashley Ferry under the command of Colonel Maitland to intercept the Americans under General Lincoln who were returning from Augusta to Charleston.[21]

With Prevost in position to attack Charleston, the residents panicked. South Carolina's governing officials sidestepped the Continental military commander in an attempt save the city from destruction. State and city officials proposed offering to remain neutral for the rest of the war if the British would leave Charleston in peace. They asked John Laurens, who was both a Charleston native and a Continental officer, to deliver the proposal to the British; hot-headed Laurens vehemently refused to carry a message like that. Alexander McIntosh, who was active in South Carolina politics in addition to serving in the Continental army, also begged to be excused, but eventually was persuaded to deliver the proposal. The British military commander rejected the request from the South Carolina civilians, insisting on negotiating a surrender with the American military commander.[22] General Prevost reported to the British Secretary of State for American Colonies:

> The facility with which the British army had proceeded towards Charleston, notwithstanding the numbers of rivers, creeks and swamps and the natural impediments of the country, added to the repeated suggestions of a few friends of government we met with who assured us positively that Charleston would certainly surrender at our approach, induced me with the advice of all the field-officers of the army to make the attempt, and Lieut-Colonel Prevost who commanded the advance had orders to summons them [on May 12]; but I have the greatest reason to believe that the want of a naval force to cooperate with us, our want of battering artillery, and momentary expectations of a reinforcement and the approach of General Lincoln's army, actuated them in the proposal they made of a neutrality for their province and the refusal of the generous offers made to them if they would surrender.
>
> The numerous artillery mounted on their ramparts, their shipping and galleys covering and flanking their lines, our small numbers, not having more than 2000 fit for duty, and the risk of staking the safety of this small but spirited army and the province of Georgia, induced me and every member of the council of war held on this occasion to resolve to return to the south side of Ashley River.[23]

Meanwhile, General Lincoln hurried back toward Charleston with the main American army of about four thousand soldiers. The British, outnumbered two to one, began a return trip to Savannah along the sea islands. "Colonel Maitland's column marched to James Island," Skelly recorded, and "drove from it a party of Rebels."[24]

The Americans pursued the British, who established defensive positions as they progressed. "Intelligence brought that Lincoln and Moultrie (Rebel Generals) had joined their armies, and taken post in force six miles from our redoubts," Skelly recorded in his journal. "Most of the Army moved and took a position on the Main to defend the redoubts, an attack being hourly expected. Some skirmishing with advanced parties. A man or two killed on both sides."[25] By May 28, most of the British army had crossed to Johns Island.

A rear guard commanded by Colonel Maitland of the 71st Regiment remained on the mainland at Stono Ferry. The rear guard included the 1st Battalion of the 71st Regiment, a battalion of Hessians, some Carolina loyalists, five field pieces and a howitzer. Their defensive works consisted of three hastily-constructed redoubts.[26]

An American colonel described an attempt to dislodge the British rear guard:

> The enemy having established themselves at Stono Ferry, on the mainland, maintained a garrison in their works of about 5 or 600 men. It was of the utmost consequence that it should be in their possession, as it secured the navigation of the Stono River, and facilitated their retreat to Georgia, toward which place all their movements pointed; they had already withdrawn their cavalry to John's Island, where the main body of their army was encamped; their transports had arrived from Savannah, and the baggage was embarking. The season for action was almost exhausted, and the heat of the weather, or the attendant disorders of our summer, would very shortly have put an end to the contention of the two armies, and compelled them to retire into summer quarters...
>
> ...Gen. Lincoln called a council of war on the evening of the 19th of June, wherein it was determined to attack the enemy's post at Stono Ferry on the next morning; the army was in motion at midnight; and having joined the battalion

of light infantry under Lieut. Col. Henderson, which had been advanced towards the enemy's works, we arrived about an hour after daybreak before the works. The front of the enemy was covered by two square redoubts, and a battery between them of three pieces of ordnance, which pointed down the road leading from the ferry over Wallis Bridge to Charlestown; their right was secured by a marsh and a deep creek, over which led a very narrow causeway that was defended by a round redoubt and one piece of artillery; posted on the outside of this last work, a small breastwork on the bank of, and at right angles with, the river, sufficient to cover about 80 or 100, with 2 field pieces, protected the landing; and between this work and their left square redoubts, mentioned before, was almost equidistantly placed a small flank; the river covered their rear; and an abattis surrounded the whole of their works.

Our flanks were covered by the two battalions of light infantry; the left of our line was composed of Continental troops under Gen. Huger, with 4 field pieces; and the brigade of North and South Carolina militia, with 2 field pieces, under Gen. Sumner formed our left. In the rear of this body was posted the Virginia militia with 2 field pieces in reserve, and rather more retired.

The position of the enemy was nearly in the center of an old field (extending about a mile along the river) and was advanced about 200 yards from its margin.

Unfortunately for us, by the misinformation of our guides, we formed our line at the distance of three quarters of a mile from the enemy's works, which retarded the progress of the right of our army very much, as the ground over which they had to pass was very fully wooded with a vast number of pine saplings; the left advanced with more facility, as the ground over which they passed had never been

> cleared and was wooded only with full-grown, tall and stately pines. Our light troops soon drove in their picquets...
>
> ...the battalion commanded by Lieut. Col. Henderson, on our left, in endeavoring to gain his position, fell in with two companies of the 71st Regiment, which had been posted in the woods, with a design of checking those daily attacks that our light troops had been accustomed to make upon them every morning. Lieut. Col. Henderson, who as in column when he first perceived the Highlanders, formed under their fire very deliberately and returned it; then, ordering a charge with bayonets, drove the enemy with great precipitation into their works, nearly half of their men killed or wounded on the field.[27]

Charles Stedman—who served in the British army during the American Revolution but was not present at Stono—compiled an account of the battle:

> An attack made upon the British picquets advanced a considerable distance in front of the works, about seven in the morning, which was attended with a smart firing of musketry, gave the first alarm to lieutenant-colonel Maitland. The garrison was immediately ordered under arms, and two companies of the seventy-first regiment, under the command of captain Campbell, were sent out on the right to feel the strength of the enemy. The highlanders are not the best qualified for such a service: Their impetuosity is apt to hurry them on too far, and their obstinate bravery indisposes them to retreat until it is often too late; and so it happened on the present occasion. This detachment had proceeded only a little more than a quarter of a mile when it fell in with the left wing of the provincial army already formed: An engagement immediately commenced, which was so obstinately

> maintained by the highlanders against so great a superiority of force, that they did not retreat until all their officers were either killed or wounded; and of the two companies, only eleven men were able to make good their retreat.[28]

Robert Jackson, a doctor with the 71st Regiment, credited the Highlanders with heroism derived from their ancestral heritage:

> ...a party of the 71st regiment, consisting of fifty-six men and five officers, was detached from a redoubt at Stono-ferry in South Carolina for the purpose of reconnoitering the enemy, which was supposed to be advancing in force to attack the post. The instruction given to the officer who commanded went no further than to reconnoiter and retire upon the redoubt. The troops were new troops—ardent as Highlanders usually are. They fell in with a strong column of the enemy (upwards of two thousand) within a short distance of the post and, instead of retiring according to instruction, they thought proper to attack—with an instinctive view, it is supposed, to retard progress, and thereby to give time to those who were in the redoubt to make better preparations for defense. This they did; but they were themselves nearly destroyed. All the officers and non-commissioned officers were killed or wounded, and seven of the privates only remained on their legs at the end of the combat. The commanding officer fell and, in falling, desired the few who still resisted to make the best of their way to the redoubt. They did not obey. The national sympathies were warm; national honor did not permit them to leave their officers in the field; and they actually persisted in covering their fallen comrades until a reinforcement arriving from headquarters, which was at some distance, induced the enemy to retire... The

> conduct in the act was heroic, and the authors of it had no skill in the tactics of military skill. The major part of them had been taken at sea on their passage to America, and had only recently been released from prison... The artificial lock-step was not known to them; but heroism of mind and social sympathy locked them together as one man in the hour of danger. They were only peasants of the Scottish mountains—they rank in history with the Spartans who fought at Thermopylae.[29]

When Captain Colin Campbell of the 71st was wounded, an American young man "was left as a safeguard on the field," reported General Moultrie, "to protect Captain Campbell from being killed by our soldiers, but he had nearly been killed by theirs; when we were obliged to retreat, Captain Campbell could scarcely save him. 'Tis an unpleasant situation to be placed as a safeguard on the field of battle, over any one."[30] Campbell said he "will ever retain a most grateful sense" of the Americans' "humanity and goodness" in posting someone to protect him. Another British officer lying wounded on the ground insisted on giving his fine gold watch to an American officer who assisted him; the American accepted it only on condition that he would return it if the British officer survived, because "it was for liberty, not for plunder" that the Americans fought.[31]

The American army advanced to within three hundred yards of the British defensive post, and the opponents exchanged artillery fire for an hour. When the full force of the American army attacked, the Hessians on the British left were pushed back, although they rallied and continued to fight. Maitland threw the 1st Battalion of the 71st Regiment from his right to the left wing to shore up his line.

Unable to dislodge the defenders, the American army withdrew under cover of a cavalry charge. British infantry drove back the American cavalry with volleys of musket fire and a line of bayonets. "The retreat was conducted in an orderly and regular manner," the American commander said, "our platoons frequently facing about and firing by the word of command upon their pursuers, who, however, very soon gave over the chase."[32] British officials reported casualties of three officers killed at Stono, ten officers wounded, twenty-three men killed, and ninety-three men wounded. American losses were 146 killed or wounded and 155 missing.[33]

Brigade Major Skelly of the 71st Regiment described the battle in his journal:

> General Lincoln with his whole Army (five thousand men) attacked at Stono at eight o'clock this morning. He had six pieces of Cannon. We had not above six hundred men. The Redoubts not strong and abattis good for nothing. The action lasted an hour and a half. The Rebels repulsed with considerable loss. Reinforcements arriving from John's Island, we followed them into the woods. They retreated, some towards Jacksonborough, some towards Wallace's Bridge.[34]

Skelly himself earned praise from Charles Stedman, who wrote that "majors McArthur, Fraser, and Skelly in particular distinguished themselves."[35] General Prevost gave a glowing, and possibly exaggerated, report of the battle to his superiors in London:

> ...after every preparation had been made to abandon the post on the main at Stono Ferry and to quit the island of St. John's, the enemy's whole force attacked that post with eight pieces of cannon and five thousand men. Their attack was at first spirited but the good countenance of the troops and the fire of the armed flat that covered the left flank of

> our post, just as the troops were ferrying over to reinforce it, obliged the enemy to retreat. A favorable opportunity of pursuing them and giving them a severe check was lost for the want of the horses who had been sent away two or three days before, and before the troops arrived on the ground the rebels had got too great a distance to expect to come up with them with the foot... Lieut.-Colonel Maitland who commanded there had with him the first battalion, 71st, then much reduced, a weak battalion of Hessians, and the refugees of South and North Carolina, amounting in the whole to about eight hundred men. They all behaved with coolness and bravery.[36]

The rear guard's stand at Stono Ferry stopped the Americans from pursuing the British expeditionary force. The rear guard crossed the Stono River to Johns Island on June 23. By June 27, the whole British force was on Edisto Island. Transporting the army across St. Helena Sound consumed four days. On July 9, the British reached Port Royal Island.

The British and American commanders maintained ongoing correspondence about prisoner exchanges and other military etiquette. Among the officers proposed for exchange was "Ensign McPherson of the 71st Regiment, who was taken sick at Mrs. Heyward's, where it is believed he is still upon parole with his servant," General Prevost noted.[37] A month later, with exchange negotiations continuing, the commander of the 71st Regiment asked an American officer to deliver "a portmanteau containing clothes, and a letter with 3 half joes" to McPherson, "who was left sick at the widow Heyward's."[38]

Throughout the campaign across the South Carolina sea islands, the British soldiers contended with semitropical summer weather. General Prevost commended "the spirit and perseverance with which the troops have borne every hardship to which so difficult a march, the heat of the climate, and the want of many conveniences and necessaries subjected them."[39] Robert Jackson, a doctor with the 71st Regiment, recalled conditions at Port Royal:

> The fever, which usually prevails at this season of the year in all the southern provinces of North America, was then epidemic among the troops who were stationed on this island. The type, however, was still more commonly single tertian here than at Savannah. The beginning of the paroxysms was likewise more generally distinguished by a cold fit, and the intermissions, for the most part, were more perfect and distinct. In a few cases, indeed, marks of malignity were discoverable, yet the disease, upon the whole, was not of a fatal nature, or of obstinate cure; though unless speedily checked by bark, it often degenerated into dysentery or dropsy, which were not only removed with difficulty, but in the circumstances under which we labored, were often of very precarious issue.[40]

The British established a post at Beaufort, "where the advantage of keeping a footing in Carolina," General Prevost said, "and quartering the troops during the great heat of the weather, and the unhealthy season in the best situation, are combined with that of being the most eligible position for effectually covering and securing Georgia from any attempt of the enemy."[41] Skelly recorded:

> Colonel Maitland (whom I had the honor to be with during the whole Campaign as Brigade Major) took the command on Port Royal Island with a troop of Cavalry, the Light Infantry, the 71st Regiment, a Battalion of Hessians, and some Carolinians. The rest of the Army with General Prevost went

to Savannah. We remained in peaceful possession of Port Royal Island till the 12th September 1779 when we quitted it.[42]

Siege of Savannah

THE 71st REGIMENT CONTRIBUTED to the defense of Savannah against American forces and French allies.

Late in the summer of 1779, French Admiral Charles d'Estaing offered to support an attack on Savannah with a fleet of thirty-three naval vessels and four thousand French troops, including about five hundred black soldiers from a French colony in the Caribbean.

The joint operation included the Southern Department of the Continental army under the command of General Benjamin Lincoln. On September 6, Lincoln led the march toward Savannah, leaving William Moultrie in command of the troops defending Charleston. Lincoln's troops crossed the Savannah River on September 12 and took a post at Ebenezer. The next day the Americans brought their artillery and wagons across the Savannah River, and repaired bridges over swampy streams at Ebenezer. On September 14 the Americans arrived at Savannah and encamped at Millen's plantation.[1]

While the Americans were crossing the Savannah River on September 12, the French were disembarking from their ships and setting up camp at Beaulieu, a plantation near the village of Thunderbolt. On September 16, Count d'Estaing demanded that General Augustine Prevost surrender Savannah to King Louis XVI of France; d'Estaing's summons didn't even mention the Americans who were approaching the outskirts of Savannah at that moment. General Prevost answered the summons according to formal European military etiquette, and asked for twenty-four hours to consider the terms of surrender. Count d'Estaing granted the request.

Prevost used the twenty-four hours to finish the fortifications around Savannah and to receive reinforcements who were on their way from Beaufort. Prevost praised officers of the 71st Regiment for preparations to defend Savannah: "Captain Moncrief, commanding engineer, but sincerely sensible that all I can express will fall greatly short of what that gentleman deserves, not only on this, but on all other occasions... We have been greatly obliged to Major Fraser of the 71st, and Quartermaster Jones for his zealous and indefatigable industry in landing and mounting upon the batteries the cannon, stores, etc., and constantly supplying all wants."[2]

Prevost recalled the garrison at Beaufort, which included the 1st Battalion of the 71st Highlanders. A doctor with the 71st reported a fever epidemic "was still acquiring force when the outposts were summoned to the defense of Savannah," and the sickened men included the garrison commander, Colonel John Maitland of the 71st Regiment.[3] Despite his weakened condition, Maitland evacuated Beaufort on September 12 and sailed across Port Royal Sound. He left convalescents suffering in the Southern climate on the southwestern side of Hilton Head and transferred eight hundred relatively healthy soldiers from transport vessels to small boats.

Because the French fleet blocked the open waterway, Maitland had to find an alternate route to Savannah along small creeks through the Savannah River delta. Maitland and the first group of his men reached Savannah at noon on September 16 and more men arrived in groups over the next two days.

Georgia historian Alexander A. Lawrence describes Maitland's startling maneuver:

> ... If the lower South—if America itself was to be saved to the King—Maitland somehow had to get his troops through

twenty miles of marsh and swamp that lay between them and beleaguered Savannah...

At this crucial moment fortune threw some Negro fishermen in the path of Maitland. In their strange Gullah version of the English language they told the British about an obscure waterway behind Daufuskie Island. In serpentining through the marshes a creek looped within a short distance of another. A shallow cut had been dug to connect the two. This passage, which was called Wall's Cut, could be used only at high tide. But once in the creek to which it led, the English with luck and hard work might get into the Savannah above the point to which the French vessels had advanced...

A long stretch of shoal creek lay between Wall's Cut and the Savannah. The men struggled through mud and marsh up to their waists. The boats were dragged through by main force. But suddenly the British were looking out upon the waters of a great river. Along the marsh-bordered banks of the Savannah one could see "multitudes of alligators lying in the mud like old Logs." That was all, for no enemy vessels were that far up the stream...

The English are sometimes accounted an undemonstrative lot, but this was drama to warm the hearts of even the most reserved, the sight of these long-awaited reinforcements—veterans of Brandywine, Fort Montgomery, Brier Creek and Stono Ferry—filing up the bluff and marching off to their posts in the lines. Even rough British tars were so moved that they gave three cheers...[4]

While cheers erupted from the British lines, dismay enveloped the besiegers. French commander Count d'Estaing added these notes to a journal of the siege kept by one of his officers:

> ...I went to Brewton Hill to confirm with my own eyes the report... We saw still crossing the river a string of small boats loaded with troops, a sight so vexatious that I began to bemoan bitterly the impossibility of stopping a reinforcement that was going to give the expedition extreme difficulty...[5]
>
> ... The Scotch troops, transferred from Beaufort and commanded by Colonel Maitland, were the ones the enemy always put in the fore...[6]

Alexander Garden—a patriot officer from Charleston who later wrote about the war—reported that Maitland "reached the garrison before the time allowed for deliberation had expired" and swayed the outcome:

> Entering the Council Chamber where discussions were carrying on, he is said to have approached with hurried step the table, and, striking the hilt of his claymore against it, to have exclaimed, "the man who utters a syllable recommending surrender makes me his decided enemy; it is necessary that either *he* or *I* should fall." So resolute a speech, at a moment so critical, produced the happiest effect on the minds of all. Hope and courage regained their influence in every mind; each individual repaired to his post with alacrity and confidence...[7]

Once the reinforcements began arriving, Prevost defiantly rejected d'Estaing's terms of surrender. As the twenty-four-hour truce ended, rain began to fall. Siege tactics, such as moving artillery forward, became more difficult on the muddy ground. On September 22, the French army in three divisions moved into position east of the Ogeechee Road. The Americans encamped to the left of the French in positions reaching to

McGillivray's Plantation on the Savannah River. Once the ground began drying, d'Estaing opened siege lines on September 23.

The British launched sorties to delay work on the siege approaches. Scottish writer David Stewart says "in the morning of the 24th of September Major Colin Graham, with the light company of the 16th regiment, and the two Highland battalions, dashed out, attacked the enemy, drove them from their outworks, and then retired with the loss of Lieutenant Henry Macpherson of the 71st, and 3 privates killed, and 15 wounded, while the enemy lost 14 officers and 145 men, killed, wounded, and prisoners."[8] A British journal gives this account:

> Sept. 24th. At seven in the morning, saw the enemy very busy entrenching themselves to the left of the barracks. Three companies of Light Infantry made a sortie with great spirit. The enemy being too numerous, obliged them to retreat under the fire of our batteries, with the loss of 21 killed and wounded. Lieut. McPherson, of the 71st, was killed. It is supposed the enemy suffered considerably... A flag was sent to bury the dead, on both sides...[9]

The British journal writer was correct in supposing that his enemy suffered considerably. A French captain described the sortie from his viewpoint:

> ...They decided to make an immediate sortie against us, believing there were few men there. They carried out their maneuver at 8 a.m. Three hundred men ambushed us when we least expected it. They were in front of our trenches before we realized it, and we were caught by surprise. As soon as the enemy was spotted, all the soldiers got out of the trenches in attack formation because the trench's raised

firing platform had not been built. The attack was on our left against three chasseur companies stationed there. They received the first enemy fire. I led my company to that point immediately and counterattacked furiously, making the English fall back. We pursued them back to their own lines; I made this charge with the Gatinois Company; we were not strong enough to go any further. M. O'Dunne, second in command, came out, stopped us, and ordered us to retreat, which we executed with the finest order. At that moment we were exposed to grapeshot charges which killed many of our men. Our two companies regrouped at our trench and the fighting stopped. If my company had not repelled the enemy with its first maneuver, a very large column, outfitted with tools to destroy our trenches, would have approached our right. But they were intimidated when they saw their men repelled and they withdrew.

This skirmish, which lasted less than a half hour, cost us, and especially me, several grenadiers. I lost ten men killed and eleven wounded; my infantry lieutenant, named Blandat, was killed. That officer's death is a cruel loss. He was a 35-year veteran and was to be awarded the Cross of Saint-Louis on November 4th according to a letter of notification from the minister. The Gatinois Company took losses almost as great as ours; its infantry lieutenant was also killed and three officers wounded, two of them seriously. Immediately after the skirmish the enemy sent out an envoy to request a truce for picking up their wounded. It was granted. There was a two-hour cease-fire... Our losses totaled almost 100 men; for although the other companies did not attack, they lost men in cannonade.

After both sides had collected their wounded, we returned to our respective works, recommenced hostilities, and continued for the rest of the day. We lost several more

> men on the path leading to the trench; one of the enemy's batteries had it in range. I was quite happy to come out of the skirmish safe and sound; I looked forward to the hour when I would be relieved. We stayed there until eight o'clock that night and returned to our camp without experiencing a single cannon shot, much to our relief.[10]

Although the French captain perceived that he had been ambushed by three hundred British soldiers, the British commander reported that "97 rank and file" were sent out and the Highlanders were stationed behind the lines to support the rear flank of the attackers.[11]

Three days later, Stewart writes, "Major Macarthur [Archibald McArthur of the 71st Regiment] with the picquets of the Highlanders advanced on the enemy with such caution and address that, after firing a few rounds, the French and Americans, mistaking their object, commenced a fire on each other, by which they lost 50 men; while, in the meantime, Major Macarthur retired silently without loss, leaving the combatants to discover their own mistake at their leisure."[12]

The siege continued with relentless artillery fire. An American officer said:

> ...a more cruel war could never exist than this The poor women and children have suffered beyond description. A number of them, in Savannah, have already been put to death by our bombs and cannon. ...many of them were killed in their beds, and amongst others, a poor woman, with her infant in her arms, was destroyed by a cannon-ball. They have all got into cellars; but even there they do not escape the fury of our bombs, several of them having been mangled in that supposed place of security... We have burnt, as yet,

> only one house; but I expect this night the whole will be in flames.[13]

General Prevost, whose wife and children were in Savannah, noted in his journal entry for October 4, "At day light they open with nine mortars, thirty-seven pieces of cannon from the land side, and sixteen from the water. Continue without intermission 'till eight o'clock without other effect than killing a few helpless women and children and some few negroes and horses in the town and on the common."[14] The colonial Chief Justice of Georgia described the plight of civilians in Savannah:

> ... when all the women and children were asleep, the French opened a battery of nine mortars, and kept up a very heavy bombardment for an hour and a half, in which time those who counted shells found that they fired one hundred, which were chiefly directed at the town. I heard one of the shells whistle over my quarters, and presently afterwards I got up and dressed myself; and as our neighbourhood seemed to be in the line of fire, I went out with a view to go to the eastward, out of the way; but a shell that seemed to be falling near me, rather puzzled me how to keep clear of it, and I returned to the house not a little alarmed.
>
> I then proceeded to the westward, and then the shells seemed to fall around; there I soon joined a number of gentlemen who had left their houses on account of the bombardment, and, like me, were retiring from the line of fire to Yamacraw; here we stayed till between one and two in the morning, when the bombardment ceased...
>
> ...at five I was awakened with a very heavy cannonade from a French frigate to the north of the town, and with a bombardment and cannonade from the French lines in the south, which soon hurried me out of bed; and before I could

get my clothes on, an eighteen-pounder entered the house, stuck in the middle partition, and drove the plastering all about.

We who were in the house now found ourselves in a cross fire; and notwithstanding the rum in the cellar, we thought it less dangerous to descend there than to continue in the house, as the fall of a shell into the cellar was not so probable as the being killed in the house with a cannon ball... After we had descended into it, some shot struck the house, and one passed through the kitchen... Whilst we were in the cellar, two shells burst not far from the door, and many others fell in the neighbourhood all around us. In this situation a number of us continued in a damp cellar, until the cannonade and bombardment almost ceased, for the French to cool their artillery; and then we ascended to breakfast.

...Mr. Pollard, deputy barrack-master, was killed by a shell in that house on the bay which was formerly inhabited by Mr. Moss; and the daughter of one Thomson was almost shot in two by a cannon ball, at the house next to where Mr. Elliot lived. I am told there were other lives lost... Fortunately for us, after breakfast, the town adjutant's wife and myself went over to Captain Knowles, who is agent for the transports, and to whose cellar Mrs. Prevost, the general's lady, and several gentlemen and ladies had retired for security. This house was directly opposite to my quarters, and about thirty or forty feet distant.

The general's lady and Captain Knowles invited us to stay there... and we continued in the cellar, with several others, as agreeably as the situation of matters would admit of, until three o'clock on Tuesday morning. During the whole of this time the French kept up a brisk cannonade and bombardment; the shot frequently struck near us, and the shells fell on each side of us with so much violence that in their fall they shook the ground, and many of them burst with a great explosion...

The guns seemed to approach on each side, and about three o'clock on Wednesday morning a shell whistled close by Captain Knowles's house. Soon afterwards another came nearer, and seemed to strike my quarters, and I thought I heard the cry of people in distress. We all jumped up... my quarters were so much in flames that I could not venture further than the door, for fear of an explosion from the rum... and as soon as the French observed the flames, they kept up a very heavy cannonade and bombardment, and pointed their fire to that object to prevent any person approaching to extinguish the flames.

I retired to Captain Knowles's... Being in the direction of the French fire, I was every moment in danger of being smashed to pieces with a shell, or shot in two with a cannon ball... I thought it safest to... retire to a place of safety...

I had some distance to go before I got out of the line of fire, and I did not know the way under Savannah Bluff, where I should have been safe from cannon balls; and therefore, whenever I came to the opening of a street, I watched the flashes of the mortars and guns, and pushed on until I came under cover of a house; and when I got to the common, and heard the whistling of a shot or shell, I fell on my face. But the stopping under cover of a house was no security, for the shot went through many houses; and Thomson's daughter was killed at the side opposite to that where the shot entered.

At last I reached an encampment made by Governor Wright's negroes on the common between Savannah and Yamacraw, and it being dark I fell down in to a trench which they had dug... I proposed to stop at a house... but a soldier, who was on guard at the Hessian hospital at Yamacraw... conducted me to the house of Mr. Moses Nunez, at the west end of Yamacraw, which was quite out of the direction of the enemy's batteries.

This place was crowded, both inside and out, with a number of whites and negroes, who had fled from the town. Women and children were constantly flocking there, melting into tears, and lamenting their unhappy fate, and the destruction of their houses and property...

The appearance of the town afforded a melancholy prospect, for there was hardly a house which had not been shot through, and some of them were almost destroyed...

Many of the inhabitants went on board the ships in the river, and others retired to Hutchinson's Island, opposite the town, which... is a rice swamp, and very unwholesome, particularly in the fall.

I twice took a stroll to that island, and at Mr. McGillivray's rice barn the ladies told me there were fifty men, women, and children. Other places seemed equally crowded; but neither the ships nor island were places of security, for many shells fell into the river, and some into the shipping...

Most of the houses in the town had banks of earth thrown up, and those that had cellars secured them as well as circumstances would admit of. Captain Knowles, for the security of the ladies in his cellar, had in some places thrown up a bank of sand on the outside, and in other places put large casks filled with sand; he also propped up the floor over the cellar, and put such a quantity of sand on it that it was bomb-proof.[15]

On October 6 Prevost sent a letter to Count d'Estaing containing "Sentiments... of Humanity. The houses of Savannah are occupied solely by women and children. Several of them have applied to me that I might request the favour you would allow them to embark on board a ship or ships and go down the river under the protection of yours until this business is decided. If this requisition you are so good as to grant, my Wife and Children, with a few servants, shall be the first to profit by the indulgence."[16] In his journal, Prevost reported "After three hours and a great deal of intermediate cannon and shells, received an insulting answer in refusal from Messrs. Lincoln and d'Estaing conjunctly."[17]

Lincoln and d'Estaing insulted Prevost because they resented his previous stalling tactics:

> CAMP BEFORE SAVANNAH, October 6th, 1779 – Sir: We are persuaded that your Excellency knows all that your duty prescribes. Perhaps your zeal has already interfered with your judgment.
>
> The Count d'Estaing in his own name notified you that you alone would be personally responsible for the consequences of your obstinacy. The time which you informed him in the commencement of the siege would be necessary for the arrangement of articles, including different orders of men in your town, had no other object than that of receiving succor. Such conduct, Sir, is sufficient to forbid every intercourse between us which might occasion the least loss of time. Besides, in the present application latent reasons might again exist. There are military ones which, in frequent instances, have prevented the indulgence you request. It is with regret we yield to the austerity of our functions, and we deplore the fate of those persons who will be victims of your conduct, and the delusion which appears to prevail in your mind.
>
> We are with respect, Sir,

Your Excellency's most obedient Servants,
B. LINCOLN,
D'ESTAING.[18]

While each side blamed the other for the threat to women and children, the bombardment continued. A teenage woman whose relatives were loyalists gave an account of the events she endured:

> The French and Americans were... constantly cannonading and throwing bomb shells. Fortunately, however, our men were encamped near the trenches, and these deadly shells went a distance over their heads. The streets being sandy and not paved, the shells fell and made great holes in the sand, which often put out the fuse and prevented explosion. Indeed, the colored children got so used to the shells that they would run and cover them with sand, and as we were rather scarce of ammunition they would often pick up the spent balls and get for them seven-pence apiece.
>
> Soon almost every family was removed from the town to an island opposite, where they made use of barns, and taking their bedding and some furniture divided it by portions. In the barn where I was there were fifty-eight women and children, all intimate friends, and who had each one or more near relatives in the lines. My mother-in-law had two sons, I had my father and one very dear to me, my future husband. Only one male friend was with us, Dr. Johnston, too old to fight, though his whole heart was in the cause. Every other house and barn besides the one we occupied was full of females. The General sent a flag to Count D'Estaing to request that he would allow Mrs. Prevost and her children to go on board one of our ships to be in a safe place. The request was refused and she remained in a cellar in Savannah, which was

made bomb proof with feather beds. Fortunately, though their hope was by the incessant fire to burn the town and force a surrender, a merciful God protected us and defeated their intention...

Our men, having few to relieve them, suffered from fatigue and want of rest...[19]

Excerpts from a journal published in *Rivington's Royal Gazette*, a Loyalist newspaper published in New York, give an eye-witness account of the bombardment from the British viewpoint inside Savannah:

Oct. 3d. At 12 o'clock this night, the enemy opened the bomb batteries, and fired warmly into the town, but none into the field.

4th. The enemy still continue their fire from the bomb and other batteries. it was returned by us.

5th. The enemy still cannonading the camp and town. At night a house took fire, but it went out without communicating to any other building...

6th. Enemy still firing on the works, camp and town... the cannonade and bombardment continued all night.

7th. Still continued cannonading and throwing shells on both sides; the enemy throwing most of their fire towards the town, which suffers considerably... At 7 at night the enemy threw several carcases into the town, and burnt one house.

8th. The enemy fired little this morning, but during the night cannonaded and bombarded the town furiously.[20]

Another eye-witness account of the bombardment was given by a British officer in a letter to his wife:

> This morning... they opened one of the most tremendous firings I ever heard; from 37 pieces of cannon – mostly 18-pounders, and 9 mortars, in front, and sixteen pieces of cannon from the river, on our left – mostly 24-pounders. The town was torn to pieces, and nothing but shrieks from women and children to be heard. Many poor creatures were killed in trying to get to their cellars, or hide themselves under the bluff of savannah river. The firing lasted for some hours, and a flag was sent from us to count d'Estaing, to allow time for the women and children to go to an island out of danger. 'Twas savagely refused; and that night they began to fire again, and heave carcasses and red shot, which set two houses on fire, and burnt them down; but some proper persons being appointed to extinguish the bombs, did it very effectually, and prevented any further conflagration.[21]

ALTHOUGH THE SIEGE was still in its early stages, d'Estaing became impatient and decided to launch an attack on Savannah. His strategy called on 3,500 French troops in three columns to lead the attack, supported by 1,500 American troops. He wanted the American and French allies to make a feint at the British left while making an all-out attack against the Spring Hill redoubt near the west end of the British line. He would personally lead the assault.

The defenders of Savannah included–in addition to British army units–militia from Georgia, South Carolina, North Carolina, and New York, as well as armed black men.

A picket of the 71st was placed in front of the British lines on the eastern end of Savannah.

The 1st Battalion of the 71st—a unit that had come through a watery wasteland to reinforce the garrison in Savannah—anchored the east flank. Major Archibald McArthur commanded the battalion because Colonel Maitland, who had led the reinforcements from Beaufort to Savannah was given a greater responsibility.

Maitland, although mortally ill with a fever, was placed in charge of the entire force on the west side of the lines. North Carolina loyalists were located on the extreme west flank of the British defenses with the Savannah River at their backs and Yamacraw Swamp to their right.

The Spring Hill redoubt on the west side of the lines was defended by British regulars of the 4th Battalion of the 60th Regiment and South Carolina Royalists. By special order the defenders at Spring Hill were all under the command of Captain Thomas Tawse, who ordinarily served as an officer in the 71st Regiment.

The 2nd Battalion of the 71st Regiment was positioned behind the Spring Hill redoubt under the command of Major Alexander MacDonald.[22]

As the French and American allies gathered before dawn on October 9, d'Estaing could tell that the Highland Scots of the 71st Regiment defended the exact place he planned to attack. He could tell by the bagpipes. In his notes on the battle, he observed:

> The Scotch troops... evinced the most audacity during the siege. They ordinarily occupied the ground to the left of their barracks, as well as the front before which our siegeworks and batteries were located.
>
> Scotch Highland bagpipes, the saddest and most remarkable of instruments, was the usual band for this corps. Frequently our trench and even our camp heard the mournful harmony; it surprised me that it also taunted us on the day of the attack. At the very moment we came out of the marsh, we were given a serenade which issued from a place quite distant from the one this unit usually occupied. From

> it I concluded that the enemy was not only forewarned but also that he wanted to remind us that his best troops were waiting for us. Undoubtedly the soldiers felt inwardly as I did, for the sound of this band appeared to me to have made a profound impression on their morale.
>
> Certainly when I heard the unexpected sound of these peripatetic bagpipes, I would have decided to call off the attack had we not been so far advanced and had not had the Americans for companions, or rather, for masters.[23]

Just as the sun rose behind the British lines, firing began. French troops swarmed out of the morning mist across open ground toward the British defenses. French grenadiers cut through the abatis with hatchets and broke the British line.

Tawse personally engaged in fierce combat during a stubborn defense on the Spring Hill redoubt. General Prevost reported that Tawse "nobly fell with his sword in the body of the third he had killed with his own hand."[24]

When Tawse was killed, Captain Archibald Campbell assumed command of the troops on the redoubt, writes David Stewart, "and maintained his post till supported by the grenadiers of the 60th, when the enemy's column being attacked on both sides, was completely broken, and driven back with such expedition that a detachment of the 71st ordered by Colonel Maitland to hasten to and assist those who were so hard pressed by superior numbers, could not overtake them."[25]

Faced with such fierce resistance, the French retreated. Count d'Estaing, a French officer in command of the allied operation, rallied his men to charge once again. They became trapped in the entrenchments near Spring Hill redoubt and were cut to pieces by musket balls and grape shot; d'Estaing himself was wounded several times.

John Laurens' light infantry and Francis Marion's 2nd South Carolina Regiment resumed the attack on the redoubt. Under heavy fire, Marion led his regiment across the moat and into the abatis.

A sergeant in the 2nd South Carolina Regiment managed to plant a regimental flag on the redoubt. When the Americans were ordered to retreat, the sergeant retrieved the flag from the redoubt and carried it away.[26]

As the Americans of the 2nd Regiment carried their colors, a French soldier took the fleur-de-lis of France to the walls of the Spring Hill redoubt. The allies could not scale the parapet under fire, and were ordered to retreat. Despite his wounds, Count d'Estaing ordered a drummer to signal the French troops to gather around him for yet another assault.

To repel the repeated allied assaults, the British called in reserves, including the 2nd Battalion of the 71st Regiment. "At this most critical moment," General Prevost wrote, "Major Glasier of the 60th Grenadiers and the marines, advancing rapidly from the lines, charged, it may be said, with a degree of fury. In an instant the ditches of the redoubt and a battery to its right in rear were cleared, the grenadiers charging head long into them, and the enemy drove in confusion over the abatis and into the swamp." Although the 2nd Battalion of the 71st Regiment "advanced with the usual ardor of that corps," Prevost reported, "so precipitate was the retreat of the enemy, they could not close with him."[27]

While the British dislodged allied attackers from the parapet, Casimir Pulaski, a Polish count serving with the Americans, led two hundred cavalrymen on a dash between the British defensive works. Pulaski suffered mortal wounds.[28]

Continental General Lachlan McIntosh led the American reserve column to the foot of the Spring Hill redoubt. D'Estaing ordered McIntosh to move to the left and stay out of the way of the French troops.[29]

The women and children who had sought refuge in barns on an island in the Savannah River heard the sounds of battle and saw clouds of smoke. A 15-year-old girl described her anguish as she pondered the fate of her father and fiancé, who were serving in the loyalist forces with the British defenders:

> Alas, every heart in our barn was aching, every eye in tears! ... Our anxiety to hear about our friends may well be imagined, but we soon had great reason for gratitude and praise. None of our relatives and friends were killed or wounded, though all were much fatigued from many weeks' want of rest, and from that day's action. We had stock of all descriptions, and many a harmless animal and turkey was killed and prepared, to send over to our friends...
>
> When we got into the town it offered a desolate view. The streets were cut into deep holes by the shells, and the houses were riddled with the rain of cannon balls. Winter was now approaching and many houses were not habitable, so Dr. Johnston with his family took a house out of town until his was repaired.[30]

Estimates of British casualties range from sixteen to forty killed and thirty-nine to sixty-three wounded. General Prevost reported that three officers of the 71st Regiment had been killed: Lieutenant Henry McPherson of the 1st Battalion on September 24; Captain-Lieutenant of Dragoons Thomas Tawse of the 1st Battalion on October 9; and Lieutenant of Dragoons Smollet Campbell of the 2nd Battalion on October 9.[31]

The French had 521 men killed and wounded, and the Americans suffered 231 casualties. About one-fourth of the South

Carolinians engaged in the battle were killed. Two hundred bodies were buried around the Spring Hill redoubt.[32]

Count d'Estaing raised the siege on October 18 and evacuated the French forces by sea. General Lincoln led the main American army back across the Savannah River on October 19 and returned to Charleston.

Lieutenant Colonel Maitland of the British 71st Regiment, who had been suffering from a fever throughout the siege, died October 25 at Savannah. Noting that the "fatigues" of the siege damaged Maitland's health, Prevost described Maitland's death as "literally to have happened on Actual Service." Prevost said the loss of Maitland was "very much, and very justly regretted by all who knew him, both as a Gentleman, and as an Officer."[33]

Alexander MacDonald was appointed lieutenant colonel of the 1st Battalion of the 71st Regiment when Maitland died; like Maitland, MacDonald commanded both battalions because the lieutenant colonel of the 2nd Battalion—Archibald Campbell—had left America on personal business.[34]

Siege of Charleston

CHARLESTON, THE MOST IMPORTANT CITY in the South, became the target of British conquest. General Henry Clinton, the British commander in America, personally led an army to augment the units—including the 71st Regiment—that had conquered Georgia and successfully defended Savannah. A hundred ships carrying 8,708 men sailed from New York at the end of December and endured nearly six weeks of rough seas. The hellish voyage took a toll on horses as well as soldiers. When ships sank, men and horses sank with them. Horses suffered injuries and death from being tossed around in the holds of ships. The water and feed that would have nourished horses during a routine ten-day sail to Savannah ran out during the voyage disrupted by wintry storms, and sailors had no choice other than to throw horses overboard. The resulting scarcity of horses would affect the upcoming campaign.

The fleet arrived at Savannah on February 2, 1780. The ships left Savannah on February 9 and arrived the next day at the mouth of the North Edisto River, just south of Charleston. Troop transports carried most of the army into the inlet, where the men boarded longboats and were taken ashore. The fleet proceeded to blockade Charleston Harbor. With Clinton in command and General Charles Cornwallis as second in command, the army moved across Seabrook Island onto Johns Island. Boats in the Edisto and Stono rivers carried supplies for the troops on the island.[1]

On February 28, the British army crossed the Stono River onto James Island across the harbor from Charleston. The 2nd Battalion of the 71st Regiment arrived from Savannah on March

3.[2] On March 7, the British constructed a bridge over Wappoo Cut so that the army could continue to advance.

While the British army marched toward Charleston, the British fleet maneuvered to clear the bar at Charleston harbor. The fleet contended against not only shifting sands, fluctuating tides, and fickle winds, but also the guns of Fort Moultrie and American warships. To deprive the British of navigation markers, the Americans destroyed the beacon and lighthouse, blackened the towering steeple of St. Michael's Church, and removed buoys marking the channel. The British responded by putting three companies of the 71st Highlanders and two cannon on Lighthouse Island to cover their ships while they located the channel and placed new buoys. The Highlanders assisted the sailors in unloading supplies from the ships and bringing them to Lighthouse Island in two transports.[3] The British fleet cleared the bar on March 20, and the next day the American warships withdrew into the Cooper River. On March 22 Clinton sent orders for the Highlanders to leave the harbor and reinforce the army marching toward Charleston.

SHORTLY AFTER ONE BATTALION of the 71st Regiment approached Charleston by sea, the other battalion set out overland. The 1st Battalion under the command of Major Archibald McArthur was part of a 1,500-man brigade under Brigadier General James Paterson. The brigade also included the American Volunteers, consisting of loyalists from the northern colonies led by Patrick Ferguson. The infantry portion of Banastre Tarleton's British Legion joined Paterson while Tarleton led his cavalry to Port Royal Island in South Carolina seeking replacements for the horses that had been lost at sea during the voyage from New York. Paterson's brigade left Savannah on March 5 and marched seventeen miles to Abercorn, where the soldiers spent the night in "disagreeable, rainy weather," reported Lieutenant Anthony Allaire of Ferguson's regiment.[4]

In the morning the brigade marched eight miles to the village of Ebenezer, where the 71st Regiment had been stationed the previous year. Allaire noted that Ebenezer is "situated on the Savannah River" and "contains about twenty houses and a church. The inhabitants are high Dutch. It is garrisoned by our troops, there are four redoubts, but no cannon in any of them." Allaire described the weather on March 7 as "pleasant morning, showery evening and very warm." Allaire also mentioned "Several men taken suddenly ill with pain and swelling of the extremities, occasioned by a weed that poisons where it touches the naked skin, when the dew is on it."

On March 9 the brigade marched out of Ebenezer and "passed a causeway three quarters of a mile in length overflowed with water from two to three feet," Allaire reported. "We marched to a plantation ten miles from Ebenezer called the Two Sisters, situated on the Savannah River. It was formerly a public ferry but at present nobody lives on it. The houses are destroyed."

Ferguson's regiment and the dismounted portion of the British Legion were detached to serve as an advance guard for Paterson's brigade. The detachment went three miles up the river from Two Sisters to a ferry at Tuckasee King.

One division of the brigade crossed the river on March 10 with "the others to follow as expeditiously as possible." Allaire's diary entry for March 11 says: "Crossed the Savannah River; such a fresh that the boats were brought through woods a mile and a half; the water was four to ten feet deep where in a dry time we might have marched on dry ground. The horses were swum over the river—the current sets down very rapid."[5]

Once in South Carolina, a foraging party of dragoons skirmished with an American light horse party. On March 13, "a cool, pleasant day for marching," Ferguson's detachment pushed forward twenty-six miles to secure the crossings of Bee's Creek and the Coosawhatchie and Tulifinny rivers. The next afternoon, the detachment crossed the Tulifinny and continued six miles to Isaac McPherson's plantation. As Ferguson's American Volunteers approached, fifty enemy militiamen rode off from Isaac McPherson's plantation toward John McPherson's plantation in the same neighborhood. A small party of the American Volunteers pursued the Americans as the evening faded into night. At the same time, the British Legion under Major Charles Cochrane chased another group of American soldiers on another road. Cochrane arrived before daybreak in front of Ferguson's picket line. Then a calamity occurred, as described in Allaire's diary entry for March 14:

> He [Cochrane] immediately conjectured we were the party he had been in pursuit of all night. He halted and made a position with an intent to attack as soon as it began to be clearly light; but the alertness of our sentinels obliged them to come on sooner than they intended. He immediately, on their firing, rushed on the picket; they gave the alarm, but were driven to the house, where our men ready for the attack, expecting it was Rebels, a smart skirmish ensued. The sad mistake was soon discovered, but not before two brave soldiers of the American Volunteers and one of the Legion were killed, and several on both sides badly wounded. Col. Ferguson got wounded in the arm by a bayonet, Lieut. McPherson, of the Legion, in the arm and hand.[6]

Ferguson's detachment remained at McPherson's plantation for four days, and sent out foraging parties to provide provisions for the brigade; Allaire observed a "great plenty" of turkeys, fowls and pigs in the vicinity. The main body of Paterson's brigade—including the 1st Battalion of the 71st Regiment—marched along a more direct route toward Charleston. The detachment rejoined the brigade on the south side of the Salkehatchie River, also called Saltketcher. Allaire reported:

> Saturday, 18th. Marched from McPherson's plantation to Saltketcher, a Rebel party consisting of eighty militia, commanded by a Maj. Ladson, placed themselves on the north side of the river to oppose our crossing. They were amused by a company of the Legion returning their fire across the river at the place where the bridge formerly was, whilst the Light Infantry and remainder of the Legion crossed the river below, and came in the rear of them before they were aware of it. Here the bayonet was introduced so effectually that a Capt. Mills and sixteen privates of the Rebels could not exist any longer, and of course gave up the cause. Four were badly wounded, and one taken prisoner that luckily escaped the bayonet. Maj. Graham, of the Light Infantry, and Maj. Wright of the Georgia Loyalists, slightly wounded. The former continued to command his battalion, and the latter continued his march. Two privates of the Light Infantry were also slightly wounded. We remained all night at Ogilvies' plantation, on the side of the river called Indian land. This day's march was very tedious—a disagreeable, rainy, cold day, and through a swamp where the water was from two to three feet deep.
>
> Sunday, 19th. Passed Saltketcher river—where the bridge formerly stood, but has been destroyed since the

> rebellion—in boats, and swam the horses. The causeway on both sides of the river is overflowed with water from two to three feet deep, at the ferry house, about a quarter of a mile from the river. Dr. Johnson dressed the wounds of Maj. Wright and the four Rebels that were bayoneted yesterday.[7]

As the brigade marched on, a detachment remained at the river to load the boats on carriages. A small party of Americans fired on the detachment from across the river and killed three members of the New York Volunteers. The next day the brigade marched three miles on a poorly maintained causeway through a swamp to reach Fish Pond Creek, and halted until evening to repair the bridge. By the time the soldiers crossed the bridge and camped for the night, it was almost ten o'clock. Banastre Tarleton—the British Legion commander who had rounded up horses at Port Royal—joined Paterson's force on March 21. The next day, Allaire reported:

> The army got in motion at ten in the morning and marched as far as Horse Shoe, where we again were detained to repair the bridge. After crossing, continued our march to Jacksonboro, a village containing about sixty houses, situated on Pon Pon, or Edisto River. The most of the houses are very good; the people tolerable well to live; some large store houses for rice, from which they convey it by water to Charleston market. In short, it is a pleasant little place, and well situated for trade, but the inhabitants are all Rebels—not a man remaining in the town except two, one of whom was so sick he could not get out of bed and the other a doctor, who had the name of a friend to Government. The women were treated very tenderly, and with the utmost

civility, notwithstanding their husbands were out in arms against us.

Thursday, 23d. All the army, except the Seventy-first regiment, and greatest part of the baggage, crossed the river in boats and flats, the bridge being destroyed. Col. Tarleton came up with a party of Rebel militia dragoons, soon after crossing the river at Gov. Bee's plantation. He killed ten and took four prisoners...

Friday, 24th. The remainder of the baggage and Seventy-first regiment passed Pon Pon river... This day Col. Ferguson got the rear guard in order to do his King and country justice, by protecting friends and widows, and destroying Rebel property; also to collect livestock for the use of the army, all of which we effect as we go, by destroying furniture, breaking windows, etc., taking all their horned cattle, horses, mules, sheep, fowls, etc., and their negroes to drive them. We had a disagreeable night—very heavy shower, with a great deal of heavy thunder and lightning.[8]

The brigade spent the whole day of March 26 ferrying the baggage and livestock across the Stono River and Rantowles Creek. The next day, three hundred Continental cavalrymen captured a provincial colonel and a British doctor at a house about a mile in front of the brigade's position. British dragoons attacked the Continental cavalrymen, who soon fled. In the skirmish, Allaire said, "Qr. Master Sergeant Mcintosh, of the Georgia Dragoons, badly wounded in the face by a broadsword. Several Dragoons of the Legion were wounded."[9] The skirmish at Rantowles concluded the fighting on the march from Savannah to Charleston; the brigade suffered about a hundred casualties along the way.[10]

Paterson's brigade joined the main British army under General Clinton on March 28 at Ashley Ferry; at this point, both the 1st and 2nd Battalions of the 71st Regiment were with the main body of troops.

THE BRITISH ARMY PREPARED to cross the Ashley River, the last natural barrier separating the British from the Charleston Peninsula. The Americans had posted a light infantry force to guard the river crossing at Bacon's Bridge and a slightly smaller force to guard Ashley Ferry. The British avoided the token American opposition by crossing at Drayton Hall. Longboats carried the first division of the British forces across the river at dawn on March 29. By afternoon the entire force, including the 71st Regiment, was on the Charleston side of the river. The troops then moved into position to lay siege to the town.

On April 2, the British broke ground on their siege works in front of Charleston. The besiegers and defenders began bombarding one another with cannon and mortars. After dark on April 5, the British battery on Fenwick's Point and the galleys in Wappoo Cut opened fire on the town, damaging several houses. Observers in the British lines heard Charlestonians screaming and women wailing. The next night the cannonade continued, killing a carpenter and doing mayhem.

The British commanders, "regretting the effusion of blood, and consonant to humanity towards the town and garrison of Charlestown, of the havoc and desolation with which they are threatened from the formidable force surrounding them by land and sea," issued a summons on April 10. They gave the Americans a chance to surrender, offering the alternatives "of saving their lives and property contained in the town, or of abiding by the fatal consequences of a cannonade and storm." The summons warned:

> Should the place in a fallacious security, or its commander in a wanton indifference to the fate of its inhabitants, delay the surrender, or should public stores or shipping be destroyed, the resentment of an exasperated soldiery may intervene; but the same mild and compassionate offer can never be renewed. The respective commanders, who hereby summons the town, do not apprehend so rash a part, as further resistance will be taken, but rather that the gates will be opened, and themselves received with a degree of confidence which will forebode further reconciliation.[11]

Continental General Benjamin Lincoln refused to surrender, perhaps because the people of Charleston had vilified him for exposing their homes and property to risk in his campaigns of the previous year. He still had the option of evacuating the American army by boat up the Cooper River toward Moncks Corner.

On April 12, Lincoln ordered all officers who were unfit for duty to leave Charleston. Lieutenant Colonel Francis Marion, who had a broken ankle, was carried out on a litter. Marion planned to stay with relatives along the Santee River while he recuperated. British patrols forced him into hiding. He moved from house to house and occasionally hid in the forest. By eluding capture, he created an opportunity to harass British troops, including the 71st Regiment, later in the Southern Campaign.

While the British army besieged Charleston, detachments attacked American positions outside the city. Cavalry under Banastre Tarleton and provincial troops under Patrick Ferguson attacked Americans at Moncks Corner before dawn on April 14. The Americans retreated, and Tarleton captured a herd of badly-needed horses. The loss of Moncks Corner was disastrous to American forces in Charleston, because it cut off their route of escape across the Cooper River and also cut off food and other supplies coming from the backcountry.[12]

The Americans trapped in Charleston tried to negotiate an end to the siege under "honorable terms of capitulation." They wanted their army to be allowed to withdraw from town. They also wanted security for the residents of Charleston and their property. The British commander promptly rejected the terms. That night, British artillery bombarded Charleston "with greater virulence & fury than ever, & continued it without intermission till daylight," observed Continental Brigadier General Lachlan McIntosh. "The killed & wounded lately are so many they cannot be ascertained."[13]

The besiegers continued their relentless approach while the besieged grew more desperate. "Our ration this day ordered to be reduced to ¾ lb. of beef," McIntosh recorded in his journal on April 22. "The Enemy kept up a heavy cannonade, & approach fast on our left in front of the advanced redoubt or Half Moon battery – three men wounded &ca."[14]

The Americans continued to fight back. At daylight on April 24 two hundred Virginians and South Carolinians launched a surprise sortie. Using bayonets, the Americans killed fifty British soldiers inside the siege trenches and took twelve prisoners. Two American privates were wounded and Captain Thomas Moultrie, a brother of General William Moultrie, was killed in the sortie.

That night a rifle ball killed a colonel from Virginia when he looked over the parapet of the Half Moon battery. "Two privates killed also & seven wounded, with several others not known," McIntosh wrote, "having kept an incessant fire of cannon, mortars & small arms on both sides."[15]

Like the Americans in Charleston, British besiegers such as the soldiers of the 71st Regiment endured roaring artillery exchanges, debilitating heat, irritating mosquitoes and enervating sleeplessness. Under these conditions it is not surprising that the fog of war befell the besiegers. One group of British soldiers mistook another group of British soldiers for American attackers and opened fire on their own comrades. A Hessian officer's journal notes that the 71st Regiment was stationed in the British front line and suffered casualties. When the officer mentions "workmen" he means British soldiers assigned to build structures as part of the siege operation:

> The signal that the enemy was making a sortie along the whole line was a threefold "Hurray!" on our side—a fatal signal, indeed! About twenty to thirty of the enemy were seen at the gate-work. Our nearest infantry post on guard gave the signal and fired. Everyone repeated the signal; the workmen ran back; the second parallel saw them coming, heard the "Hurray!" believed they were enemies, and fired. Within a short time there was a tremendous fire of musketry, cannon, and shell on both sides. It was two o'clock in the morning before everyone realized that it was a mistake. We had an officer killed (71st) and more than fifty [men] killed and wounded. Besides, our working parties could accomplish little or nothing during the night.[16]

Another Hessian officer confirmed that one officer of the 71st Regiment was killed, and added that two officers of the 71st were wounded. About twenty noncommissioned officers and soldiers of the 71st were killed or wounded, he reported, while two Hessian grenadiers were killed, and eleven Hessians were slightly wounded.[17]

As British forces advanced downstream on the opposite bank of the Cooper River from Charleston, American units withdrew from that side of the river into the defensive positions in Charleston. The British occupied Lempriere's Point and Haddrell's Point on April 25 and captured Fort Moultrie on May 7. Until then, the Americans had controlled the crossing of the Cooper between Lempriere's Point and Charleston, and had been able to bring beef and other provisions into the besieged city; once the Americans abandoned the opposite side of the Cooper River they faced eventual starvation.

As the siege neared culmination, McIntosh described the inexorable deterioration of the American defenses. "Tar barrels ordered to be fixed before our lines every evening & burn all night to prevent a surprise, as the Enemy are close to the canal, & keep up almost a continued running fire of small arms night & day upon us," wrote McIntosh on April 27. "A picket of a field officer & 100 men of my Militia Brigade ordered every evening to Gadsden's old house, to support a small guard of a sergeant & 12 regulars upon the wharf in case of an attack by the Enemy boats upon that quarter."[18]

With the British siege lines so near the American defensive works, the Americans anticipated an assault. "General Lincoln informed the General Officers privately that he intended the Horn Work as place of retreat for the whole army in case they were drove from the Lines," McIntosh wrote on April 29. "I observed to him the impossibility of those who were stationed at the South Bay & Ashley River retreating there in such case, to which he replied that we might secure ourselves as best we could. A heavy bombardment from the enemy during the night & small arms never ceasing. A deserter from them says they are preparing a bridge to throw over the canal."

The next day McIntosh reported that "severe firing of cannon, mortars & small arms continued on both sides. Lt. Campen & Ensign Hall of North Carolina wounded badly, & Lt. Philips of the Virginians. The number of privates killed and wounded not known because there are so many."[19]

On May 4, McIntosh recorded, rations were reduced to six ounces of poor-quality meat, rice and coffee with sugar.[20]

The Americans surrendered on May 12. American casualties during the siege totaled 89 killed and 138 wounded. British casualties were 99 killed and 217 wounded.

Among the officers of the 71st Regiment, Ensign McGregor and Ensign Cameron were killed and Captain M'Leod and Lieutenant Wilson were wounded. Among the rank and file of the 71st, six were killed, and fourteen were wounded.[21]

Under the terms of the surrender, Continental troops—nearly four thousand men—and sailors would be held as prisoners of war, while members of the militia—about five hundred men—could return to their homes as prisoners on parole. The residents of Charleston also were considered prisoners on parole. The British took possession of the town, fortifications, artillery, public stores, and shipping at the wharves.

More than two hundred Continental officers resided in barracks at Haddrell's Point or in nearby houses while arrangements were made to exchange them for British officers.

Continental enlisted men and non-commissioned officers stayed in barracks near the edge of town. Hundreds of them escaped individually or in groups as large as thirty. In August the British transferred the enlisted men to prison ships in the harbor, where nearly four hundred sickened and died in unsanitary, crowded conditions. By the time prisoners were exchanged more than a year later, the number of enlisted men had been cut in half.[22]

The siege of Charleston inflicted serious harm to the American cause and encouraged the British forces to continue their Southern Campaign. As Captain Charles Campbell of the 71st Regiment wrote to his father, "I have been an actor in two of the most obstinate and most successful contests that the British arms have experienced in this war, the defense of Savannah and the reduction of Charleston."[23]

Cheraw and Camden

FOLLOWING THE FALL OF CHARLESTON, British commander in chief Henry Clinton returned from South Carolina to New York, leaving General Charles Cornwallis in charge of operations in the South. Major Archibald McArthur assumed command of the 71st Regiment when Lieutenant Colonel Alexander MacDonald departed for New York "to solicit leave to go home," Cornwallis reported. "His business in Europe seemed pressing and I did not see any inconvenience in the command's devolving upon Major McArthur, who is an excellent officer."[1]

Within a week after Charleston surrendered, Cornwallis led 2,500 infantry and mounted troops toward Camden, the most important town in the South Carolina backcountry. During the expedition, Cornwallis sent Banastre Tarleton's legion to catch about 350 Continental dragoons under the command of Colonel Abraham Buford who were withdrawing toward North Carolina. On May 29 in the community called the Waxhaws, Tarleton's legion charged Buford's dragoons. When the legion overran the American position, Buford decided to surrender and the Americans lay down their weapons. As the white flag of surrender was being delivered, a musket ball struck Tarleton's horse in the head; the horse collapsed, trapping Tarleton underneath. Tarleton's men responded by resuming their attack, killing more than a hundred Americans and wounding more than two hundred. Only five of Tarleton's men were killed in the battle and only fourteen were wounded.[2]

While Lord Cornwallis was on his way to occupy Camden, British officials ordered loyalist Lieutenant Colonel Thomas Brown to take possession of Augusta, where Brown had been tortured and maimed by patriots at the beginning of the revolution. As Brown approached Augusta, the patriot garrison of 364 men left town without a fight. Brown established British control of Augusta in early June.

British forces also took Ninety-Six—a post in South Carolina within easy communication distance of Augusta—without resistance. The string of posts at Camden, Ninety-Six and Augusta strengthened the British grip on the South Carolina backcountry.

Cornwallis wanted to complete the string with a post near the North Carolina border. He sent the 71st Regiment under Major Archibald McArthur to investigate Cheraw, a trading center at the head of navigation on the Great Pee Dee River, about nine miles downstream from the North Carolina border and about a hundred miles upstream from Georgetown on the coast. Cheraw was located about fifty-five miles northeast of Camden, and about seventy-five miles from settlements at Charlotte and Cross Creek in North Carolina. "At present I cannot form any plan for the disposition of the troops as I don't know what further demands Sir Henry means to make on me," Cornwallis said in mid-June. "I cannot either decide upon the post at Cheraws, which is very important and distant [from the other British posts] and close to North Carolina, until I get an account of it from McArthur."[3]

As he gathered more intelligence on the state of affairs along the North Carolina borderland, Cornwallis decided a post at Cheraw was necessary. "In order to protect the raising of [John] Harrison's corps [about eighty mounted loyalists] and to awe a large tract of disaffected country between the Pedee and Black River," Cornwallis said, "I posted Major McArthur with the 71st regiment and a troop of dragoons at Cheraw Hill on the Pedee."[4] Banastre Tarleton later explained that "Major

McArthur, with the 71st regiment, was stationed at the Cheraws, in the vicinity of the Pedee river, to cover the country between Camden and Georgetown, and to hold correspondence with a friendly settlement at Cross Creek in North Carolina."[5]

On the journey from Camden to Cheraw, "Such was the spirit and activity of the men," observed Robert Jackson, a doctor with the 71st Regiment, "that they performed the march in three days, without fatigue or inconvenience."[6] On the day the regiment reached Cheraw, McArthur reported, "we marched 27 miles without leaving a man behind—the reason was information received that a firing had been heard in this neighborhood, from which I concluded our dragoons, who marched in the night, had met with opposition, but it was only a false alarm, though some attempts had been made to collect the militia for that purpose without effect."[7]

The regiment took possession of Cheraw on June 9. As precautions against the summer weather, the soldiers camped "in an airy situation" and covered their hats with felt cloth.[8] The next morning, McArthur met with local leaders, including Alexander McIntosh, the American officer who had abandoned Purrysburg when the 71st Regiment initiated an expedition into South Carolina in 1779; as a wealthy planter and civic leader in the Welch Neck community near Cheraw, McIntosh subsequently had obtained the rank of brigadier general of militia in the eastern part of South Carolina. McArthur travelled "with all that was mounted to the court house at Long Bluff, sixteen miles down the Pedee, where I met General McIntosh and several of the principal inhabitants, who immediately submitted and gave their paroles. Most of the rebel officers in the militia regiment of this district have come in and given their paroles." McArthur informed Cornwallis:

> I am busy in taking paroles and forming a militia. The country people in general seem desirous to return to their allegiance and form a militia as the only means to prevent plunder from a banditti that are robbing indiscriminately. I have sent an officer's party to the court house to be at hand to support Dr. Mills, whom I have prevailed with to take the command of the militia. He was formerly of the 46th Regiment and is a man of good character... The only obstacle is the want of people proper for officers from the rebellion's having been so universal, for the lower class are all desirous of being enrolled. I shall administer the oath of allegiance to all that are admitted into it. I suppose it will be governed by the militia laws in force during His Majesty's Government before the rebellion broke out. These people have a great avidity for news. Some of the Charlestown papers sent here would produce a good effect.[9]

McArthur also enquired about the arrival of "necessarys for the men, which are much wanted, for, though we fare well enough in point of provisions, no wearables can be procured."[10]

When McArthur's letters reached British headquarters at Camden, Cornwallis responded by sending "all the newspapers I have received" and giving orders "for your being constantly supplied with them." Cornwallis was "much pleased to hear that you had captured a considerable quantity of rum and salt as those articles are not very plentiful at this place, our convoy having been long coming up [from Charleston] and having met with considerable losses on the road. If you should seize any other articles of rebel property that cannot be immediately applied to the use of the troops under your command, you will take the opportunity of any returning wagons to send them to the Commissary of Captures at this place."[11]

Trouble arose immediately after the British arrived a Cheraw. "I am sorry to inform you," McArthur wrote to Cornwallis, "that three of the dragoons deserted in the night of the 9th with their horses—two of them came from Polasky's [Casimir Pulaski's Continental cavalry legion] at Savannah, the 3rd was of Delancey's—and the day after we got here a soldier of the 71st (an officer's servant) was carried off by three lurking villains as he was looking for forage within a mile of the camp."[12] The captors carried the soldier "no further than 20 miles and then allowed him to return, but not the horse."[13]

South Carolina historian Edward McCrady recognized the Highlanders as powerful opponents to the American cause. "Major McArthur with the famous Seventy-first Regiment, which under Maitland had fought so gallantly on the Stono and at the siege of Savannah the year before, and then had taken part in the siege of Charlestown, was stationed at the Cheraws on the Pee Dee," McCrady wrote. "During the occupation of Cheraw by Major McArthur, the Parish Church of St. David's was used as a barrack. According to tradition, McArthur and his officers were not wanting in courtesy to the ladies in the vicinity, and as a consequence were treated with such a degree of civility as the necessities of the case made imperative. The soldiers, however, were not generally restrained, and many persons in the neighborhood were plundered and treated with indignity."[14] Other local historians have said that St. David's Church was used as a hospital, and that several Highlanders who died of disease were buried in the churchyard.[15] McCrady recited an anecdote related to McArthur's attempt to quell disturbances in the community:

Soon after Major McArthur's arrival, he proceeded down the river and made his headquarters for a short time at Long Bluff. While there he offered a reward for the capture of Thomas Ayer. Ayer had made himself conspicuous a short time before as the leader of a company which had been sent out to take some mischievous persons who had rendered themselves obnoxious to the inhabitants by their lawless depredations. Having succeeded in capturing a portion of the band, he secured the country against any more depredations by hanging them all.

The effect of the reward offered for Ayer was his capture by a party of Tory neighbors... [The Tories] hurried him off to the river, intending to take him immediately to Major McArthur, but by the time they reached Hunt's Bluff a severe thunder storm had blown up, and fearing to cross and prosecute their journey through the swamp, they concluded to keep their prisoner in an old unoccupied house on the bank until the morning... But relief was soon to overtake the desperate Ayer.

A few hours after the Tories [captured Ayer], his elder brother Hartwell, with five others, rode up very unexpectedly to the family, and upon learning what had occurred, they at once set out in pursuit, and took the Tory party completely by surprise. Approaching under cover of darkness and storm, they were at the door of the house in which Thomas Ayer was held prisoner before they were discovered. Most of those guarding Ayer were asleep. Shooting first those that were up, they continued to fire and dispatch with the sabre and bayonet until all but one were killed. This one, Asal Johns, the son of his old neighbor, Jonathan Johns, a peaceable man, Thomas Ayer most generously and chivalrously protected with his own body.[16]

Hartwell Ayer and his companions wreaked yet more violence against loyalists. They went to a residence and unleashed "a shower of bullets" on Captain George Manderson, but "though struck with several, the wounds inflicted were slight, and springing through the back door of the house he made his escape to the swamp nearby." Tom Johns "was knocked down with the butt of a musket and pinned to the floor by a bayonet and left for dead. But on the bayonet being removed, he arose and proved to be not seriously injured."[17]

> When informed of the rescue of Ayer and the slaughter of the Tories, McArthur determined in person to take vengeance. Crossing the river with a strong party, he came very near surprising the Ayer family, then consisting of Mrs. Ayer and her sons Lewis Malone and Zaccheus, both of whom were lads. They timely escaped, however, to the swamp, and remained in constant concealment several weeks. McArthur took possession of the deserted premises, killed the stock, and burned all the buildings except a corn crib, which he spared on account of the corn it contained, and which afterwards became the dwelling of the family to the close of the war.[18]

The post at Cheraw served as a refuge for loyalists. Cornwallis reported that "contrary to my instructions" a loyalist force "rose at the forks of the Yadkin under colonel Bryan (driven to it as they said by the most barbarous persecution) and after a long and difficult march joined Major McArthur at the Cheraws to the amount of upwards of 700 men."[19]

The encampment at Cheraw was doomed not by military ineffectiveness but by South Carolina's climate and related diseases. "The Cheraw Hill was a post of great consequence," Cornwallis said, "and had the appearance of being healthy, but it proved so much the contrary and sickness came on so rapidly that in nine days at least two-thirds of the 71st regiment were taken ill of fevers and agues and rendered unfit for service."[20]

McArthur reported "having been some time ill of a fever that does not intermit."[21] Dr. William Henry Mills told McArthur, "I am very sorry to hear of your indisposition, which I apprehend to proceed from the great fatigue you lately took in your incursion up into Anson County."[22]

Analyzing the experience from his perspective as a doctor, Robert Jackson said the situation at Cheraw "proves so clearly the danger of encamping on the banks of fresh water rivers:"

> In June 1780, the first battalion of the 71st regiment was detached to the Cheraws, where it encamped on open ground, within five hundred paces of the river Pedee. The people of the country, taught by experience, suggested the propriety of drawing back the encampment into what is called the Pine-barren, assigning as the cause of their advice, that the distance, as well as the cover of the wood, might be a security against the damps of the river, which were observed to be extremely noxious in that climate. A position in wood, accessible on all sides, would not perhaps have been military, so that no alteration was made.
>
> The other battalion of the regiment arrived in July. It arrived in perfect health, and encamped likewise on open ground, but still nearer the river. In a fortnight the intermitting fever began to make its appearance, and in less than three weeks, more than two thirds of the men were ill, whilst scarcely one of the officers had escaped. The officers, it must be remarked, encamped in the rear of the men, and

> immediately on the bank of the river, the course of which was uncommonly slow at this place, while its banks, though high, were oozy and foul. There are few instances on record, perhaps, where a degree of sickness greater than the present has been observed in so short a space of time.
>
> The first battalion, however, did not suffer in the same proportion. The ground of encampment was not only at a greater distance from the river, but being also nearer to a wood, many of those who were not confined by their duty to a particular spot, found a convenient shelter in its shade from the powerful heat of the sun. These, I must not omit to mention, were the least sickly of the whole encampment.[23]

In describing symptoms, Jackson said "the anxiety and restlessness were intolerable, bilious vomitings and purgings were frequent and excessive."[24]

"The salvation of the 71st regiment as well as every other consideration" required abandoning Cheraw in search of a healthier site.[25] The regiment could not round up enough wagons to carry off all the sick men in addition to provisions and supplies, "so that no other resource was left than to convey some part of them to Georgetown by water," Jackson reported.[26] Jackson recalled that "about forty of those who were least likely to be soon fit for service were sent down the river in boats," but another British officer reported "upwards of one hundred sick men" went aboard.[27] The British commander at Camden said that McArthur's "men fell sick so fast at Cheraw that, not being able to bring off all his invalids, he sent no less than ninety of them by water to Georgetown."[28] South Carolina historian Edward McCrady gave this account:

Major McArthur was directed to draw nearer to Camden, and on the 24th [of July] he moved to a position on the east branch of Lynch's Creek. Knowing of no enemy within many miles, he ventured to send about one hundred sick in boats down the Pee Dee to Georgetown, under the care of Lord Nairne [Lieutenant Nairne of the 71st Regiment] and the escort of a detachment of the Royal militia under Colonel William Henry Mills...

Hearing of the projected expedition down the river, a party of Whigs under the lead of James Billespie collected... and determined to surprise it. As they went on, their numbers increased, the command being assigned to Major Tristam Thomas... The Whigs fixed upon Hunt's Bluff, a point about twenty-five miles below Cheraw... for intercepting the expedition. A battery of wooden guns was hastily constructed and placed immediately on the bank in a sudden bend of the river. In due season, as the slowly moving flotilla appeared, a most imposing demonstration was made by the gallant Thomas, and unconditional surrender demanded. The British authorities charge that there was absolute treachery on the part of the Loyal militia, who, they say, rose in mutiny upon Colonel Mills; the American accounts admit that it was not improbable that there was an understanding with some of the leading men of the party. However this may have been, no resistance was attempted, and the capture was effected. At the same time a large boat coming up the river from Georgetown, well stored with necessaries for Major McArthur's force, was seized for the use of the American army. Colonel Mills succeeded in getting away, and made his escape to Georgetown. The other new-made British officers of the militia with the rest of the party were taken prisoners.[29]

Among the British authorities who supported the "absolute treachery" charge, Banastre Tarleton said:

> ...the militia mutinied, and securing their own officers and the sick, conducted them prisoners to General Gates in North Carolina. This instance of treachery in the east of the province followed the perfidious conduct of Lieutenant-colonel Lisle on the western border, and strongly proved the mistake committed by the British in placing confidence in the inhabitants of the country when acting apart from the army.[30]

The British commander at Georgetown reported the incident to Cornwallis, who was in Charleston at the time:

> ...Colonel Mills of the Cheraw militia is just now arrived here. He tells me that on Sunday the last the 71st Regiment fell back towards Camden, that on Monday their sick (upwards of 60) embarked in boats to come to this place. On Tuesday a party of militia from North Carolina in conjunction with several of Colonel Mills' people, who had just before taken the oaths of allegiance, intercepted and took the whole party prisoners with a Lieutenant Nairn and the surgeon. The number of the rebels was betwixt two and three hundred. Colonel Mills was pursued by different parties until he got to within a few miles of this place. By all accounts Mr. Cassillis is likewise taken. In short, the whole country is in confusion and uproar. All the friends of Government have been plundered of their Negroes and of every thing they have worth taking.[31]

"I cannot conceive how McArthur could have been so off his guard about his sick," Cornwallis replied. "I dare say Colonel Mills has rather seen things in the blackest light."[32] Writing to the British commander in Camden concerning "the disaster of McArthur's sick" and "the confusion and terror of Colonel Mills's district," Cornwallis said "It is a very unpleasant business, but we must expect many mortifications in our trade. I cannot help lamenting that McArthur was not better informed. This blow certainly might have been avoided."[33] Reporting to his superior officer in North America, Cornwallis said:

> Colonel Mills, who commanded the militia in the Cheraw District, though a very good man, had not complied with my instructions in forming his corps, but had placed more faith in oaths and professions and attended less to the former conduct of those whom he admitted. The instant that this militia found that McArthur had left his post... they seized their own officers and the hundred sick and carried them all prisoners into North Carolina... The whole country between Pedee and Santee has ever since been in an absolute state of rebellion.[34]

While the sickest men were being evacuated from Cheraw by boat, most of the men set off on foot. "I have the satisfaction to add that not a man died of those who retired to Camden by land," Jackson said, "and that after the third day scarcely a fever was left." Jackson attributed the men's recovery to "a change that accidentally happened in the state of the weather." He noted that the weather "during the time we remained at the Cheraws was uncommonly hot," but "became unexpectedly cool after the march was begun; together with the rain, from which the sick men had nothing to shelter themselves." As a medical observer, Jackson reached what he admitted was a "paradoxical" conclusion that the cool rain, "which continued for two or three days without intermission," helped, rather than hurt, the sick men. He also cited "removal from a situation where the fumes of the disease were in a very concentrated state" and "the mere exercise of travelling."[35]

THE CONTINENTAL CONGRESS cobbled together a new Southern army to replace the one that had been captured at Charleston, and placed General Horatio Gates in command. As the Americans advanced toward Camden, they fell prey to many of the ills afflicting their opponents. The American army contained more than four thousand men, but only three thousand were fit for duty.

On the British side, Lieutenant Colonel Francis Rawdon commanded the troops in the vicinity of Camden while General Cornwallis lingered in Charleston solving administrative problems. Rawdon later explained why he established posts to prevent the Americans from launching a direct attack on Camden:

> I therefore detached [James] Webster [of the 33rd Regiment], a good and gallant officer, to the east branch of Lynch's Creek, and I reinforced a post which I had at Hanging Rock. As soon as I had made the necessary arrangements at Camden, I followed Webster... My object in taking this forward position was to retard the progress of Gates until Lord Cornwallis should collect force from other parts of the Province, or to reduce the enemy to hazard an action where my peculiar advantages of situation would compensate for my disparity in numbers. I had 1100 men with me, all regulars or provincials; the detachment at Hanging Rock consisted of 400 provincials and 800 militia. ...there

> was no turning my right flank without going fifty miles down Lynch's Creek, there was no turning my left by a shorter process than heading the Creek and getting into the other road above Hanging Rock. Lynch's Creek runs through swamps of perhaps a mile in breadth on each side; impenetrable except where a causeway has been made at the passing-places on the great road. The thick woods of those swamps prevented us from seeing each other's encampments across the Creek. ...Gates had a post at the outlet of this causeway on his side, but he appeared never to have discovered a pass which came out about two miles from his camp, communicating with a ford on the Creek, from which there was a path into the causeway on my front. By this track I used to send out and receive my spies.[36]

When the 71st, 23rd and 33rd regiments and the Volunteers of Ireland assembled at at Lynch's Creek, the troops were "in general sickly," Cornwallis noted, "the 71st so much so that the two battalions have not more than 274 men under arms."[37] Robert Jackson of the 71st Regiment observed "The weather was excessively hot, and fevers were frequent—sometimes malignant and dangerous."[38] British officers at Lynch's Creek "performed the arduous task of removing the sick of the 71st Regiment to Camden."[39]

A few days after the 71st reached Lynch's Creek, McArthur complained to Cornwallis of longstanding logistical problems:

> I think it my duty to represent to your Lordship that the 71st Regiment has not been settled with since the 25th of October 1778 owing to the commissary's not giving in their demands for provisions, though Lt Colonel McDonald [who preceded McArthur as commander of the regiment] and

> myself frequently demanded these accounts of them, but I apprehend nothing but a positive order from your Lordship will procure them, which I hope you will think proper to issue with a menace that, if they are not immediately given in, they will not be paid. If our men were not the most patient creatures of any, they would before now have broke out, and as it is, we frequently overhear conversations among them on this subject reflecting on their officers for not doing them justice. This is to all the officers very distressing and will lose to us the confidence of our men. 'Tis only your Lordship can relieve us from this disagreeable situation...
>
> Lieutenant Murchieson sets off this day and will wait on your Lordship for an order for a vessel to bring our cloathing and baggage from Savannah.[40]

In response to American maneuvers, Rawdon withdrew from Lynch's Creek and concentrated his force at Camden. Cornwallis, meanwhile, hurried from Charleston to personally supervise affairs at Camden. On the night of August 15, Cornwallis and Rawdon led more than two thousand British troops out of Camden in an attempt to surprise the American army. "The town, the magazine, the hospital, and the prisoners were committed to the care of Major McArthur with a small body of provincials and militia, and the weakest convalescents of the army," reported Banastre Tarleton.[41] With McArthur remaining in Camden, the 71st Regiment's highest-ranking officers on the march were captains. Sickness prevailed among the seven hundred men in the regiment, and only 230 of them were fit to fight. A field return indicated the 1st Battalion of the 71st had two captains, four lieutenants, one ensign, an adjutant, a quartermaster, a mate, fourteen sergeants, six drummers, and 114 rank and file. The 2nd Battalion had one captain, three lieutenants, three ensigns, nine sergeants, and ninety-four rank and file.[42]

At the same time when Cornwallis attempted to surprise the Americans, the American commander attempted to surprise the British. Gates had ordered more than three thousand American troops on a night march to Camden. At two o'clock in the morning of August 16, the British advance party ran into the American advance party about nine miles out of Camden. The British infantry moved up and exchanged fire in the dark with the Americans for fifteen minutes. Then, Tarleton observed, "a silent expectation ushered in the morning."[43] Cornwallis issued a report on the ensuing battle:

> At the dawn, I made my last disposition and formed the troops in the following order: the division of the right consisting of a small corps of light infantry, the 23rd and 33rd Regiments under the command of Lt. Colonel Webster; the division on the left consisting of the Volunteers of Ireland, infantry of the Legion, and part of Lt. Colonel Hamilton's North Carolina Regiment under the command of Lord Rawdon, with two six and two three pounders which were commanded by Lieutenant McCloud. [John Macleod]. The 71st Regiment with two six pounders was formed as a reserve, one battalion in the rear of the division on the right, the other of that of the left, and the cavalry of the Legion in the rear and (the country being woody) close to the 71st Regiment with orders to seize any opportunity that might offer to break the enemy's line and be ready to protect our own in case any corps should meet with a check
>
> This disposition was just made when I perceived that the enemy, having persisted in their resolution to fight, were formed in two lines opposite and near to us, and observing

a movement on their left, which I supposed to be with an intention to make some alteration in their order, I directed Lt. Colonel Webster to begin the attack, which was done with great vigour, and in a few minutes the action was general along the whole front. It was at this time a dead calm with a little haziness in the air, which, preventing the smoke from rising, occasioned so thick a darkness that it was difficult to see the effect of a very heavy and well supported fire on both sides. Our line continued to advance in good order and with the cool intrepidity of British soldiers, keeping up a constant fire or making use of bayonets as opportunities offered, and, after an obstinate resistance for three quarters of an hour, threw the rebels into total confusion and forced them to give way in all quarters. At this instant I ordered the cavalry to complete the route, which was performed with their usual promptitude and gallantry, and after doing great execution on the field of battle, they continued the pursuit to Hanging Rock, 22 miles from the place where the action happened, during which many of the enemy were slain, a number of prisoners, near 150 wagons (in one of which was a brass cannon, the carriage of which had been damaged in the skirmish of the night) a considerable quantity of military stores, and all the baggage and camp equipage of the rebel army fell into our hands.

The loss of the enemy was very considerable: a number of colours and seven pieces of brass cannon (being all their artillery that were in the action) with all their ammunition wagons were taken; between eight and nine hundred were killed...; and about one thousand prisoners, many of them wounded, of which number were Major General Baron de Kalb, since dead, and Brigadier General Rutherford.[44]

Despite being placed in reserve, the 71st Regiment faced artillery fire, and followed the front line into battle. The 1st Battalion of the 71st supported the 33rd and 23rd regiments in chasing away patriot militiamen and fighting Smallwood's brigade of Marylanders, all the while enduring barrages of grape shot and case-shot. The 2nd Battalion supported the Volunteers of Ireland and the Legion infantry in checking an advance by the Second Maryland Brigade and the Delaware regiment.[45] Casualties for the 1st Battalion of the 71st Regiment were: Lieutenant Archibald Campbell and four rank and file killed; Captain Hugh Campbell, Lieutenant John Grant, a sergeant, and twenty-two rank and file wounded. Casualties for the 2nd Battalion were: one sergeant and four rank and file killed; one sergeant and eight rank and file wounded.

Among those who died in all the British units combined were one captain, one lieutenant, two sergeants and sixty-four rank and file; those wounded included two lieutenant colonels, three captains, eight lieutenants, five ensigns, thirteen sergeants, one drummer, and 213 rank and file; two sergeants and nine rank and file were reported missing.[46]

CORNWALLIS DEPENDED ON TARLETON to conduct scouting missions and inflict rapid strikes against elusive American forces. Cornwallis noted that a troop of seventy light infantrymen from the 71st Regiment was detached to Tarleton's Legion, and he proposed that about twenty men be designated for cavalry duty with the 71st Regiment. Cornwallis suggested that Captain Charles Campbell, who at the time was stationed at Ninety Six in command of the light companies of the 71st Regiment, "will be the properest man to command the troop of that regiment. Without good cavalry we can do nothing in this country. I would have it of as good a species as possible."[47]

Shortly after the Battle of Camden, Cornwallis sent Tarleton after Thomas Sumter's partisans. In the relentless heat of August in South Carolina, Sumter's eight hundred men were resting on the banks of Fishing Creek or splashing in the water when Tarleton's 160 men launched a surprise attack. The British killed 150 partisans, wounded many more and took three hundred prisoners. Sumter himself escaped. The raid recovered a supply convoy of forty-four wagons that Sumter's men had captured, rescued a hundred British prisoners of war, and released more than a hundred Americans with loyalist views.

"Captain [Charles] Campbell, who commanded the light infantry, a very promising officer, was unfortunately killed in this affair," Cornwallis said. "Our loss otherways was trifling."[48] McArthur informed Campbell's father that "Capt. Campbell advancing at the head of his men with his usual intrepidity received a musquet ball in his breast & instantly expired, much regretted not only by the 71st Regiment, but by the whole Army as a very spirited and intelligent officer. He was decently interred that evening on the field of Battle."[49]

Charlotte and Winnsboro

GENERAL CHARLES CORNWALLIS CONCEIVED a strategy of invading North Carolina to consolidate British control over Florida, Georgia, and the Carolinas. He expected support from recent immigrants from the Scottish Highlands who had settled in a region called Cross Creek. He intended "to get as soon as possible to Hillsborough and there assemble, and try to arrange, the friends who are inclined to arm in our favour and endeavor to form a very large magazine for the winter of flour and meal from the country and of rum, salt etc from Cross Creek, which I understand to be about eighty miles' carriage."[1] Since the soldiers of the 71st Regiment had abandoned their Highland woolen plaids in favor of linen overalls in the Southern climate, Cornwallis proposed giving the plaids to the immigrants at Cross Creek. "The only serviceable regiment I expect to raise in North Carolina will be the Highlanders under Governor Martin," Cornwallis observed. "I intend to purchase for them some plaids of the 71st which they do not want and which, McArthur tells me, are ordered from Savannah to Charles Town."[2]

Cornwallis left Camden on September 8 on his way to North Carolina with 2,200 men. He camped about forty miles from Charlotte at the Waxhaws for two weeks "to live on the flour of this rebellious settlement until the 71st should be in a condition to join me, as a great number of their men who had missed the fever for some time were still too weak to march." In addition to the Highlanders, "every captain of [Tarleton's] Legion, and indeed every officer but one of the cavalry, is left sick at Camden." On September 19, Cornwallis "had the infinite mortification to hear that Lt. Colonel Tarleton, instead of having marched [from Fishing Creek to Charlotte] was very dangerously ill, and for two days I have been in the greatest anxiety for him. His fever has now intermitted and the surgeons think him out of danger."[3] "I am very anxious for the next accounts of Colonel Tarleton," Cornwallis told Lieutenant Archibald Campbell—who commanded a detachment of the 71st Regiment serving with the Legion—and begged for news "twice a day at least."[4]

The men of the 71st who were not disabled by wounds or disease marched from Camden to join Cornwallis at the Waxhaws. Cornwallis noted that the Highlanders "are beginning a little to recover."[5] The 71st took post on September 21 about two miles away from Cornwallis's encampment. Lieutenant John Macleod of the Royal Artillery accompanied the 71st and brought up the artillery stores.[6] Robert Jackson, a doctor with the 71st Regiment, reported a phenomenon that he called "curious and important."

> Between thirty and forty of the men of the regiment entered upon the service of the campaign in so weak a state that they were unable at first to carry their arms. They however gained strength speedily as they proceeded on the march, and seldom forgot to mention that they felt a new accession of vigour after every accidental relapse. But I must further observe that, together with the above changes which happened in the progress of the season, the epidemic showed a remarkable tendency to degenerate into dysentery or dropsy in the months of September and October. The gripings in this species of dysentery were often severe... Indeed the intermittent, the dysentery, and even the dropsical swellings so often alternated with one another as evidently showed that they all depended upon the same cause.[7]

Meanwhile, an American officer named William Richardson Davie set out with 150 men to avenge "havoc and destruction" inflicted by Tarleton. Davie mistook a few companies of volunteer militia for Tarleton's Legion, and prepared to attack their camp at Wahab's Plantaton, about two miles away from the rear of Cornwallis's encampment. After taking "a considerable circuit to avoid the patrols of the enemy," the Americans eventually got around the British main encampment. At sunrise on September 21, Davie attacked the militia camp. Cornwallis reported that the militiamen "contrived this morning to be totally surprised and routed by a Major Davy, who is a celebrated partisan in the Waxhaws." Davie said his men killed fifteen or twenty loyalists, and wounded forty; he had given the order to take no prisoners "because of the vicinity of the British quarters, and the danger of pursuit." Davie said the militia camp "was overlooked by the camp of the 71st Regiment," although he may have mistaken some other regiment for the 71st just as he had mistaken the militia companies for Tarleton's Legion. When battle noise erupted from the militia camp, the British regiment marched "briskly to attack," Davie said, "as they entered one end of the lane, the Americans [went] out of the other in good order." The owner of the plantation rode off with Davie and "had the mortification to see [his family's] only hope of sustenance wrapt in flames."[8]

Cornwallis proceeded toward Charlotte, leaving the 71st Regiment at a staging area on Waxhaw Creek. The British Legion, led by Major Charles Hanger while Tarleton recuperated from fever, served as the advance guard for the British army. Davie's partisans beat the British to Charlotte and set up a defensive position around the courthouse. When the British arrived on September 26, the Legion charged the Americans. At sixty yards, Davie's men fired a volley that broke up the charge.

The British infantry joined the battle, and Cornwallis personally came to the front lines and ordered the British Legion to charge once more. With no chance of halting the large British army, the small patriot band retreated in good order. A captain in the 71st light infantry named Campbell [probably Patrick Campbell] was wounded in the battle, reported Cornwallis, "but we hope not dangerously."[9]

After capturing Charlotte, Cornwallis asked Major Archibald McArthur to send the 2nd Battalion of the 71st Regiment with a six-pounder, ammunition wagons, and convalescents who had recovered enough to rejoin their regiments. Cornwallis instructed McArthur "to remain on Waxhaw Creek with the First Battalion and try to form a little magazine of flour for the regiments as they come up."[10]

During this time, an American surgeon's mate asked Cornwallis to approve a prisoner exchange involving the 71st Regiment. "I understand the surgeon's mate of the 71st Regiment who was lately captivated is come to [Camden] on parole and is extremely desirous of being exchanged" the American said.[11]

PATRICK FERGUSON COVERED the western flank during Cornwallis's incursion into North Carolina. Ferguson—a Scottish gentleman with more than twenty years of military experience—officially held the rank of a major in the 71st Regiment. Although his corps of about nine hundred men consisted entirely of provincial troops and loyalist militia, he signed his letters "Pat Ferguson, Major 71st Regiment," and Cornwallis addressed a letter to him as "Major Ferguson, 71st Regiment."[12]

Cornwallis harbored misgivings about Ferguson's strategy. "Ferguson is going to advance with some militia and his own miserable naked corps," Cornwallis observed. "I think it rather hazardous."[13] When Cornwallis planned to send Tarleton's

Legion to protect Ferguson's loyalists, Ferguson complained that Tarleton, as a lieutenant colonel, would outrank Ferguson. "If your Lordship should be pleas'd not to supersede me by sending a superior officer," Ferguson told Cornwallis, "it will be an addition to the obligations I owe you."[14] Because Tarleton was too ill to travel to the western flank, Cornwallis's back-up plan was to send the Highlanders who had remained in the Waxhaws.

"I desire that you will march with the 1st Battalion of the 71st Regiment to Armer's Ford," Cornwallis ordered McArthur on October 5, "where you will please to take post and inform me of your arrival. It is possible that you may meet with, or hear of, Ferguson... You may march either on the 7th or 8th."[15] At the same time, Cornwallis ordered Ferguson to rendezvous with McArthur at Armer's Ford, a location described as lying just below the forks of the Catawba River.[16]

Ferguson, meanwhile, wrote Cornwallis on October 3 that "I shall fall behind Little Broad River towards Cherokee Ford, take a strong ground till I know exactly the amount of the several detachments of the enemy that are join'd, and, if they insist, at any rate rather give than receive an attack." Cornwallis answered, "I received your letter of the 3rd and am still of opinion that you should come to Armer's Ford, to which place Major McArthur has orders to proceed from Waxhaw. If the enemy should presume to come down to the lower part of Tryon County, Tarleton shall pass at some of the upper fords and clear the country. For the present both he and his corps want a few days' rest."[17]

On October 5, the day that Cornwallis sent letters ordering McArthur and Ferguson to join forces, Ferguson wrote to Cornwallis that "I am on my march towards you by a road leading from Cherokee Ford north of King Mountain."[18] The next day, Ferguson wrote, "I arrived today at King Mountain and have taken a post where I do not think I can be forced by a stronger enemy than that against us."[19] When Cornwallis received the letter two days later, he advised Ferguson to "come to this side of the Catawba unless you feel yourself perfectly secure and see any reason for continuing a few days longer where you are," and added, "I shall order McArthur to join me here [Charlotte], as I now consider you perfectly safe."[20] That was the final correspondence between Cornwallis and Ferguson. The next letter to Cornwallis came from a provincial officer serving in Ferguson's corps:

> I am sorry to acquaint your Lordship that the 7th instant Major Ferguson was attacked near King Mountain by a body of the enemy. Their numbers enabled them to surround our post, and ours was only sufficient to form a single line on the top of the hill.
>
> The action lasted an hour and five minutes, when the North Carolina militia who were entirely commanded by their own officers on the right gave way, which not only discouraged the other regiments but drove them down the hill before them. Our little detachment of soldiers charged the enemy with success and drove the right wing of them back in confusion, but unfortunately Major Ferguson made a signal for us to retreat, being afraid that the enemy would get possession of the height from the other side. The militia being ignorant of the cause of our retreat, it threw the few that stood their post under the officers from Ninety Six in disorder, though the officers cut some of them down. They intermixed themselves with our detachment and broke us in such a manner that we could no longer act, being then reduced to 2 sergeants and 20 rank and file.

> The left, on seeing us broke, gave way, got all in a crowd on the hill, and, though every officer used his endeavors to rally the men, as nothing now offered but to make a breach through the enemy, I am sorry to say was not able to get a man to follow them, the chief part being without ammunition, excepting four men that followed Major Ferguson while the other officers were doing their best amongst the crowd to collect more to follow them; but I am sorry to say that Major Ferguson was killed before he advanced 20 yards. Ensign MacGinnes of Colonel Alan's corps was also killed soon after the action commenced, which rendered the militia he commanded almost useless. In this situation, and the small body of soldiers we had being cut up, and finding it impossible to rally the militia, I thought proper to surrender as the only means of saving the lives of some brave men still left.[21]

THE DEFEAT OF FERGUSON coupled with resistance from residents convinced Cornwallis to withdraw from Charlotte. "This county of Mecklenburg is the most rebellious and inveterate that I have met with in this country," Cornwallis complained, "not excepting any part of the Jerseys."[22]

By the time the army left Charlotte on October 14, the fever that had sickened so many British soldiers debilitated Cornwallis himself, who delegated command of the withdrawal from Charlotte to Lieutenant Colonel Francis Rawdon. The withdrawal took place at night to elude enemy pursuit. A local guide treacherously led the army down the wrong road, where the marchers stumbled among steep hills punctured by deep ravines. To thread their way through the woods, the soldiers separated into small groups. Despite shouting "halloo" to keep in contact with one another in the darkness, they wandered miles apart by midnight. The soldiers in small, disconnected groups feared being ambushed in the dark. They abandoned forty wagons and other possessions. When daylight came, they began to assemble about seven miles from Charlotte, with small groups trickling in until noon.[23]

Charles Stedman, an officer serving with Cornwallis, observed that conditions remained hazardous:

> In this retreat the king's troops suffered much, encountering the greatest difficulties; the soldiers had no tents; it rained for several days without intermission; the roads were over their shoes in water and mud. At night, when the army took up its ground, it encamped in the woods, in a most unhealthy climate; for many days without rum.
>
> Sometimes the army had beef, and no bread; at other times bread and no beef. For five days it was supported upon Indian corn, which was collected as it stood in the field, five ears of which were the allowance for two soldiers for twenty-four hours. They were to cook it as they could, which was generally done by parching it before the fire... The water that the army drank was frequently as thick as puddle. Few armies ever encountered greater difficulties and hardships; the soldiers bore them with great patience, and without a murmur...
>
> The continual rains had swelled the rivers and creeks prodigiously, and rendered the roads almost impassable. The wagon and artillery horses were quite exhausted with fatigue by the time the army had reached Sugar Creek. This creek was very rapid, its banks nearly perpendicular, and the soil, being clay, as slippery as ice. The horses were taken out of some of the wagons, and the militia, harnessed in their stead, drew the wagons through the creek...[24]

While on the march, the British commanders sought a suitable destination. "I am very much obliged to you, my dear Sir, for the pains which you have taken in looking out for a position for us," Rawdon told Tarleton, "The supplies of rum and other stores which we must receive from Camden, would make it eligible not to strike off too wide from that post."[25]

The officers chose the pleasant town of Winnsboro, about thirty miles north-west of Camden. "Winnsboro is the most eligible post for us at present," Rawdon told the commanding officer at Camden, "as our communication with you and Ninety Six will be easy, we shall cover Congarees, and may be readily and plentifully supplied with flour or meal."[26] Tarleton described the search process:

> ...the next object was to look out for a proper position to cover South Carolina. Immediate attention was given to procure intelligence of the state of the country between the Catawba and Broad rivers, and of the situations that would allow safe and direct communication with Ninety Six and Camden. Several movements were made before a regular camp was established... Before the end of October, Earl Cornwallis fortunately recovered from his indisposition, and about the same period a proper encampment was discovered. After minute inquiry and examination, Winnsboro presented the most numerous advantages. Its spacious plantations yielded a tolerable post; its centrical situation between the Broad River and the Wateree afforded protection to Niney Six and Camden; and its vicinity to the Dutch forks, and a rich country in the rear, promised abundant supplies of flour, forage, and cattle. As soon as the army arrived on this ground, the sick were conveyed to the

> hospital at Camden; rum and other stores were required from that place, and communication was opened with Ninety Six.[27]

The main part of the army arrived at Winnsboro on October 29, while Tarleton's Legion and light infantry conducted patrol duty. Cornwallis set up headquarters at Winnsboro, and Rawdon resumed command at Camden. Cornwallis told his superior officer that Winnsboro "is a healthy spot, well situated to protect the greatest part of the northern frontier and to assist Camden and Ninety Six."[28] Despite relocating to a healthy spot, the Highlanders suffered relapses of the sickness that had plagued them since their assignment at Cheraw. Jackson reported:

> In the months of October and November relapses were numerous, and original attacks, though rare, were dangerous and alarming when they happened.
>
> Some instances of a disease were now observed of a more serious nature than any that had hitherto appeared. Instead of distinct intermissions, which prevailed during the preceding months, the smallest traces of remission were scarcely perceptible; the countenance was dusky, and of a greasy appearance, the tongue was constantly dry and parched; the head was often much affected, and gangrenous spots sometimes appeared on the extremities. The duration of this disease often did not exceed seven days; sometimes it continued a fortnight, or even longer. It was generally of a fatal nature; and where it happened to people who had been subject to the intermitting fever in the preceding months, it for the most part effected such a change on the constitution as destroyed the tendency to relapse.

> But besides this unusual species of disease, which sometimes appeared in the months of October and November, it was likewise observed that relapses of the fever, which preserved the distinct intermitting character, were not only less frequent, but commonly less alarming, in proportion as the weather turned cooler. Relapses were often remarked in this season to terminate of their own accord, in a very short time; and frequently to leave the body in a state of greater vigor than they found it.[29]

"Our surgeon's mate at Camden informs me there are a considerable number of men of the 71st that are capable of doing garrison duty but very unfit for a winter campaign," McArthur told Cornwallis. McArthur suggested sending the men to Charleston or "Sullivan's Island, where they would be more out of harm's way—and probably in the spring they may be fit for active service."[30] Cornwallis replied, "I have no objection to your plan for the convalescents who will not be equal to the winter campaign," and recommended that they garrison Fort Moultrie at Sullivan's Island.[31]

The Highlanders had worn out their clothing by the time they reached their winter encampment. The logistics of transporting new clothing upriver from Charleston toward Winnsboro proved to be troublesome. Cornwallis told McArthur that "the necessaries for the 71st, 33rd and Volunteers of Ireland were embarked at Nelson's Ferry [on the Santee River] on the 11th [of October]. I hope they were come safe, but I had much rather have heard of their coming by land."[32] Rawdon told Cornwallis, "I think the navigation of the Santee seems at present tolerably secured, but I think you will have difficulties on account of the very bulky articles which are now embarked upon it. I wish to know whether the clothing of the 71st Regiment should stop at McCord's [an important ferry on the Congaree River about forty miles upriver from Nelson's Ferry] or should come up in the boats to this place [Camden]. From either there will be much labor in conveying it by land to Winnsboro."[33] Cornwallis promptly replied, "In regard to the clothing coming up I can only say that the regiments are in the utmost want of it. Therefore the safest and speediest method will be the best. The 71st," Cornwallis stressed, "are quite naked."[34] The next day Cornwallis reiterated "In regard to the clothing, you know the great importance it is to us. If it was to be lost, the 33rd and 71st Regiments would be rendered totally unfit for service." Wondering whether the army had enough wagons to transport all the supplies, Cornwallis said "we must send as much as we can at once."[35]

Rawdon seemed to have good news on November 26 when he wrote, "the necessaries for the 33rd and 71st are arrived and shall be forwarded as soon as possible."[36] Cornwallis responded, "I have sent 5 wagons for the clothing of the 71st to McCord's this evening and hope to send 3 or 4 more tomorrow." Cornwallis told McArthur, "I expect some necessaries for your battalion this day or tomorrow, which shall be immediately forwarded to you, and I will use every endeavor to get up your clothing, which I believe is by this time at McCord's Ferry. If you can press any wagons in your neighborhood [Brierley's Ferry] for the purpose of bringing your clothing from McCord's, you may promise them 13s. a day and a discharge as soon as that service is performed."[37] McArthur replied, "I have got four wagons in readiness to set off tomorrow morning for McCord's Ferry to bring the clothing of the 71st. I send a serjeant with them. They go down the west side of the river and I have ordered them to cross at Camden and leave clothing there for the sick and convalescents of the regiment."[38] Cornwallis responded, "Camden is vastly out of the way for the wagons and must make a difference of at least fifty miles, and the road is much worse."[39]

The clothing, however, had not reached McCord's Ferry. Cornwallis told Rawdon on December 1, "I cannot get any certain account of the clothing of the 71st. I have seen an officer of that corps to McCord's to assemble the nine wagons which I sent and take care of them and to send forward to find out where the clothing is. As soon as that is ascertained, I have directed him to proceed with the wagons and bring up the clothing by land."

Two days later, Cornwallis reported, "I find that five of the wagons which I sent for the clothing of the 71st are returning with that of the 33rd, and 71st's clothing not being arrived at McCord's." Cornwallis sent four more wagons from Winnsboro and McArthur sent four wagons from his camp at Brierley's Ferry. Cornwallis "directed the officer when those wagons arrived at McCord's, if the clothing was not there, to find out where it was and proceed with the wagons to greet it... The 71st is in the greatest want of their necessaries. I should be much obliged to you," Cornwallis told Rawdon, "if you could find out where they are and get them conveyed to the regiment by the most expeditious means, otherwise I am much afraid it will soon be unfit for service."[40]

Cornwallis sent McArthur some good news and some bad news: "I have ordered your necessaries with some rum to be forwarded to you. The clothing of the 71st was nor arrived at McCord's. I have sent the best directions I could to the officer to expedite that business."[41] The next day Cornwallis reported "The twelve wagons return tomorrow to McCord's in quest of the 71st clothing and anything else that may offer."[42]

Finally, on December 11, Cornwallis reported a successful conclusion: "The clothing of the 71st is arrived and every regiment here has received its winter appointments."[43]

AMERICAN MILITIA BANDS continued to harass British forces in the South Carolina backcountry during the late autumn of 1780, and British General Charles Cornwallis attempted to subdue them. Cornwallis sent Banastre Tarleton with the British Legion after Francis Marion, and sent Major James Wemyss with most of the 63rd Regiment after Thomas Sumter. On November 9, Wemyss attacked Sumter at Fishdam Ford on the Broad River. Wemyss was wounded in the arm and knee, and was taken prisoner. Sumter crossed the Broad River, gathered reinforcements, and threatened the British post at Ninety-Six.

In response to Sumter's maneuvers, Cornwallis sent Major Archibald McArthur of the 71st Regiment with the 1st Battalion of his regiment, the 63rd Regiment, a few cavalrymen, and a few cannon to Brierley's Ferry on the Broad River. "The detachment "is good and respectable in point of numbers," Cornwallis said. "McArthur's battalion is strong."[44] Cornwallis reported to his superior officer that he had detached McArthur's corps to the Broad River "in order to cover our mills and to give some check to the enemy's march to Ninety Six."[45] The commander at Ninety Six agreed that "Major McArthur's situation will awe in some measure the [American] Colonels Clark, Thomas, Brandon, Candler etc."[46]

McArthur's detachment arrived at Brierley's Ferry on the morning of November 13. He estimated that his position was nine miles from the nearest ford on the Enoree River, a tributary of the Broad, and seventeen miles from a mill on the Tyger River, another tributary of the Broad. At Brierley's Ferry, the British took possession of two flat boats capable of carrying 30 men each and two canoes. McArthur assigned guards to a nearby mill, where "there was a considerable quantity of meal ground and two wagons ready to receive it," he said, but the wagons "could not proceed for want of casks or bags to contain it. I sent them some casks... and hope they went off in the night. The cattle that were to be sent with us by Colonel Philips's people have not yet appeared. However, we have had no want. The ferryman here has a little rum, which I have secured for the detachment, but as he is a true friend, it costs very dear."[47] On November 14, Cornwallis was "a little uneasy for fear the enemy should attempt a blow at McArthur."[48]

Cornwallis ordered Tarleton to abandon his pursuit of Marion and take up pursuit of Sumter. Tarleton's route took him by Brierley's Ferry. On November 18 McArthur reported that "a party of rebels having come within two miles of the ferry this morning, I was just going to pass over with 150 men when Colonel Tarleton arrived at nine o'clock, and I countermanded my party." McArthur continued:

> The rebels had the audacity, in half an hour after, to come close to the river and fire at our men who were washing in the flats. Luckily the most of them had retired before the firing began, so there was only one soldier of the 63rd wounded slightly and a wagon horse hurt. They blackguarded us a great deal, but no return was made them except one shot by a militia man without orders. At two o'clock the infantry of Tarleton's corps passed this ferry and only one shot was fired at them, which hurt nobody, for care was taken to fire several cannon shot across, which dispersed the enemy... Tarleton has left his baggage here and taken the cannon I had with me, it being in better condition than his own, which he has left with me...[49]

While the infantry crossed the river at Brierley's Ferry, "Care was taken to conceal the green uniform of the cavalry from the view of an enemy's detachment," Tarleton said. "This precaution was necessary in order to throw the Americans off their guard, and continue their belief of the absence of the British Legion, which Sumter supposed still employed on an expedition against Marion. The appearance of the 63rd and 71st in red clothing tended to corroborate the enemy's information, and lull them into security."[50] The Legion cavalry and the 63rd Regiment crossed the river three miles downstream from Brierley's Ferry late in the evening. The various portions of Tarleton's force assembled later that night.

Tarleton's Legion cavalry and a portion of the 63rd Regiment collided with Sumter near nightfall on November 20 at Blackstock's plantation on the Tyger River. In heavy fighting, Sumter was wounded. Darkness stopped the fighting, and Sumter withdrew across the Tyger River. Sumter's force suffered three killed and five wounded. Tarleton lost about fifty killed and wounded; Lieutenant John Money—commander of the 63rd Regiment—suffered a wound that would lead to his death twelve days later.

When Cornwallis learned of the battle, he ordered McArthur to advance with the 1st Battalion of the 71st Regiment to Kelly's Ford on the Enoree River. Cornwallis told McArthur to bring "the baggage of Colonel Tarleton's corps and send an express to Colonel Tarleton to let him know that you will forward the baggage from thence with an escort of a captain and 50 men, but if he wishes your battalion to follow, you will do it with the utmost expedition. In the meantime, let the baggage and escort go on... If Tarleton does not want your battalion, I would have you return to Brierley's Ferry."[51] Cornwallis permitted Tarleton to summon McArthur's battalion if necessary but added "of course

I had rather have it within reach of me."[52] Tarleton ordered McArthur to come to Blackstock's not only to guard the British supplies but also to protect the wounded British soldiers and transport them to safety in wagons.[53]

While the 1st Battalion of the 71st Regiment moved farther afield, the 2nd Battalion remained at Winnsboro with the 23rd and 33rd regiments, for a total of about six hundred soldiers.[54] With the 1st Battalion so far away, Cornwallis wanted reinforcements sent to Winnsboro. "Tarleton has sent to McArthur to come to him," Cornwallis told Francis Rawdon—the commander at Camden—on November 24. "I have sent Manley to get him back as soon as he can be spared, but as this is uncertain and I feel myself very weak, I wish you could lend me the 7th Regiment for a few days. If you can do this, I beg you would lose no time. You may depend on their being returned and the march will do the men good."[55] The next day, Cornwallis told Tarleton "I hope soon to hear of McArthur's being on his way toward us."[56] On November 28, Tarleton informed Cornwallis "All affairs in the district are settled. McArthur is a day and a half march on his return. I march this day."[57]

Tarleton "returned to the Broad River," Cornwallis reported on December 3, "where he at present remains as well as Major McArthur in the neighborhood of Brierley's Ferry." Meanwhile, the garrisons at Camden and Ninety Six improved their fortifications, and a regiment came from Charleston to provide security to transportation along the Santee.[58] The string of military posts accomplished its mission, Tarleton reported:

> Since the period of their establishment, neither the encampment at Winnsboro nor its communication with the magazine at Camden has ever been disturbed or interrupted. Meal, flour, cattle, and forage were peaceably supplied by

> the inhabitants; and the convalescent and sick men were daily recovering on the neighboring plantations. The 1st battalion of the 71st regiment continued to occupy Brierley's ferry on Broad River in order to cover the country between Winnsboro and that place. The vicinity of the British Legion and light infantry to that post afforded support to Major McArthur, protection to the mills in the Dutch fork, and security to all the districts in the rear. Many confiscated estates yielded great supplies to the royal army, which, in its present position, could enjoy the greatest plenty with the strictest economy of public money.[59]

On December 22, an aide-de-camp relayed orders sending McArthur's corps on a reconnaissance mission:

> Lord Cornwallis having received intelligence that Colonel Campbell is near King's Mountain with a considerable body from the back of the mountains, his Lordship therefore desires you will be pleased to march tomorrow morning and take post at Owens' plantation and do every thing in your power to procure intelligence, and that if you are informed by creditable authority that there is any considerable force within 50 miles of you, you will be pleased to march and join his Lordship, but without hurry or any appearance of retiring, which might discourage the country.[60]

McArthur complied promptly; "I sent out several people for intelligence the moment I received the order," he said. His battalion maintained a guard at the mill, which was as close to Owens's plantation as it was to Brierley's Ferry, while militia guarded the ferry. "Half a dozen of rebels came within three miles of the ferry," McArthur reported. "They fired at one man, who is much wounded in the body, took his gun and rode off."[61] In investigating a report that thirty or forty shots had been fired on Christmas Eve, McArthur discovered that the commotion resulted from "a company of militia who began so early to celebrate Christmas by firing their pieces, and I have learned from the men sent that the militia had got plenty of rum, which made them feel bold."[62] On Christmas Day, high wind blasted the region, and McArthur lamented "We lost a man yesterday, killed outright by the fall of a tree at our quarter guard in the great squall."[63]

As the year came to an end, McArthur tended to administrative matters. He told Cornwallis that George Harvey—a sergeant major with the 2nd Battalion of the 71st who had deserted at Bonhamtown, New Jersey, and subsequently had served as a cavalry officer with the Americans—had been captured aboard a privateer and jailed in Charleston. McArthur mentioned that several officers of the 71st were in Charleston and could conduct a court martial.[64]

Cowpens and Guilford Courthouse

THE SEVENTY-FIRST Regiment faced new opponents and renewed warfare when a new year opened. At the beginning of 1781, the British held South Carolina and Georgia with a network of strategically located posts. They maintained an administrative headquarters at Charleston, where the port provided for reinforcements and supplies to pour in from the sea. They also held the other ports in South Carolina, at Georgetown and Port Royal, and in Georgia, at Savannah and Sunbury. In the backcountry, they established strongholds in South Carolina at Ninety Six and Camden, and in Georgia at Augusta.

General Charles Cornwallis's army, including the 2nd Battalion of the 71st Regiment, encamped at Winnsboro in the backcountry of South Carolina while the 1st Battalion of the 71st encamped nearby at Brierley's Ferry on the Broad River. The British Legion, commanded by Banastre Tarleton, patrolled the neighborhood surrounding Brierley's Ferry.

Although the British army remained vastly superior, the Southern Department of the Continental Army came to life under new leadership. The American commander in chief, George Washington, chose General Nathanael Greene to succeed Horatio Gates as commander of the Southern Department, and Greene chose Brigadier General Daniel Morgan as his second in command. Greene led half of his army from Charlotte to Cheraw, and sent Morgan with a select detachment toward the British post at Ninety Six.

Cornwallis learned of Morgan's movement on New Year's Day of 1781. "I immediately ordered Tarleton to cross Broad River with the Legion and 1st Battalion of the 71st and to proceed with the utmost dispatch to the relief of Ninety Six or pursuit of Morgan," Cornwallis said.[1] A courier told Major Archibald McArthur of the 71st Regiment that "if Lt Colonel Tarleton judged it necessary to pass the river, that you would likewise pass with the 1st Battalion 71st Regiment at Brierley's Ferry. Lt Colonel Tarleton proposes moving immediately," the courier said at 8:30 a.m. on January 2, "and will join your battalion at the ferry. Lord Cornwallis desired you would leave your heavy baggage at the encampment of the Legion."[2] Tarleton crossed the Broad River with his cavalry and infantry, the 1st Battalion of the 71st Regiment, and two three-pounder cannon.[3]

Shortly after the Legion and the Highlanders departed, Cornwallis sent the 7th Regiment to Brierley's Ferry, observing that the ferry was "on their road to Ninety Six, and, if I cannot conveniently send the Legion 3 pounder to Camden, shall direct them to take it with them to Ninety Six." The 7th Regiment also would bring the baggage for Tarleton's troops.[4] "The two hundred men of the 7th regiment, who were chiefly recruits, and designed for the garrison at Ninety Six, and fifty dragoons of the 17th regiment, brought the wagons from Brierley's to camp," Tarleton noted. Instead of sending the newcomers on to Ninety Six, Tarleton incorporated them into his expedition.[5] Tarleton's force contained: 249 enlisted men in the 1st Battalion of the 71st Regiment; sixty-nine men in a light company selected from the two battalions of the 71st Regiment; 451 in the British Legion; 167 in the 7th Regiment; and fourteen in the 16th Regiment. Counting officers, sergeants, and drummers, Tarleton commanded about 1,150 soldiers.[6]

Expecting to be joined by reinforcements marching up from Charleston, Cornwallis remained temporarily in Winnsboro while planning to lead his troops in support of Tarleton within a few days. "You will contrive to correspond with me,"

Cornwallis told Tarleton, "keeping on my left flank, either east or west of Broad River as you will judge best according to the intelligence you may receive. McArthur will of course march with you."[7]

When Tarleton closed to within six miles of Morgan's position, Morgan hurriedly broke camp and put some distance between the opposing forces. Later that day, Tarleton's men took possession of Morgan's abandoned campground because, Tarleton observed, "it yielded a good post, and afforded plenty of provisions, which they had left behind them, half cooked, in every part of their encampment."[8] Tarleton's delight at finding Morgan's provisions implies that Tarleton's men needed food. Roderick Mackenzie of the 1st Battalion of the 71st Regiment reported "The detachment, by fatiguing marches, attained the ground which Morgan had quitted a few hours before; this position was taken about ten o'clock on the evening of the 16th of January. The pursuit recommenced by two o'clock the next morning."[9]

Morgan managed to move only twelve miles over rain-ravaged roads through the rough terrain of upstate South Carolina in midwinter weather. Late in the afternoon, Morgan arrived at a landmark known as the Cowpens. Patriot militia groups joined him at the traditional backcountry gathering place throughout the day and night; some of the men who joined Morgan had previously assembled at the Cowpens before proceeding to fight Patrick Ferguson's loyalist troops at Kings Mountain. As the backwoodsmen continued to arrive at the Cowpens, Morgan's force grew to somewhere between eight hundred and a thousand men.[10]

With guidance from local men, Morgan surveyed the terrain of the Cowpens. Taking into account Tarleton's temperament as well as the lay of the land, Morgan decided on a disposition of his troops. He conceived a new way of using militia in battle, an innovation so successful that American commanders continued to take advantage of it for the rest of the war. Morgan's innovation sprang from knowing the strengths and weaknesses of militiamen. Bitter experience had exposed their glaring weakness: they would not stand and fight against the bayonets of advancing infantry or against the sabers of charging cavalry. The most valuable strength of the backwoodsmen who gathered at Cowpens was their accuracy in shooting a rifle, honed from a lifetime of hunting, defending their homes from Indian raids, and choosing to participate in certain battles during the American Revolution, especially when war raged near their homes. To take advantage of their skill with a rifle, Morgan placed the best sharpshooters in the front lines. After aiming and firing, the sharpshooters would be free to run for cover behind the patriot lines.

Under Morgan's plan, the next line after the sharpshooters consisted of militia units. The militiamen were instructed to fire two well-aimed volleys with their rifles or muskets. After that, they would not be expected to stand and face the British bayonet charge; they would withdraw in good order to safety behind the Continental infantry. The militia units were expected to regroup for further service as needed, but the men also knew where their horses were kept in case they felt obliged to flee. Morgan, however, knew there was no escape because the Broad River flowed behind the battlefield.

The next line in Morgan's plan consisted of Continental infantry, trained and experienced in fighting conventional warfare. Morgan's force included several hundred Continental soldiers who had fought valiantly under De Kalb at Camden. The force also had a couple of hundred veteran riflemen from Virginia.

As a reserve force, Morgan placed cavalry in a swale behind a low ridge. The force included a group of South Carolina horsemen and fewer than a hundred Continental dragoons.

Morgan explained his plan to his troops in person. He fit right in with the militiamen; being a backwoodsman and former wagoner, he talked like them and acted like them, and they considered him to be one of them. Morgan was recovering from malaria in cold, rainy, midwinter weather. His chronic sciatica flared up again, hurting him so badly that he could not ride his horse faster than a walk. As he visited with the soldiers at the Cowpens, he wanted to show them the scars on his back, but his rheumatism kept him from raising his shirt and he had to ask someone to raise it for him.

During the long, cold January night at Cowpens, Morgan moved through the camp, explaining his battle plan and exhorting the men to valor in battle. An eye-witness, teenaged partisan Thomas Young of South Carolina, described Morgan's conversations with his men:

> He went among the volunteers, helped them fix their swords, joked with them about their sweet-hearts, told them to keep in good spirits, and the day would be ours. And long after I had laid down, he was going about among the soldiers encouraging them, and telling them that the old Wagoner would crack his whip over Ben (Tarleton) in the morning, as sure as they lived. "Just hold up your heads, boys, three fires," he would say, "and you are free, and then when you return to your homes, how the old folks will bless you, and the girls kiss you, for your gallant conduct!" I don't believe he slept a wink that night![11]

Twelve miles away, the British set out toward the Cowpens in the middle of the night. Slogging across rain-swollen creeks and trudging along muddy paths, the British had to cross the same rugged terrain that Morgan's men had crossed earlier, but the British had to do it in the darkness of a midwinter night.[12] Mackenzie said the nighttime march "was rapidly continued through marshes and broken grounds till daylight, when the enemy were discovered in front."[13]

Scouts alerted Morgan that Tarleton was on the way. Knowing that the British had a long march ahead of them, Morgan let his men sleep awhile longer. At about an hour before sunrise, Morgan woke up the men and told them to cook breakfast.[14] After eating, the men took their battle stations, Morgan shored up their resolve by going to their positions and speaking to them.[15]

The British arrived at the Cowpens around sunrise. Tarleton immediately launched an attack. "Without delay of a single moment, and in despite of extreme fatigue, the light legion infantry and fusiliers were ordered to form in line," recalled Mackenzie. "Before this order was put into execution, and while [the commander of the fusiliers] was posting his officers, the line, far from complete, was led to the attack by Lieutenant Colonel Tarleton himself. The Seventy-first regiment and cavalry, who had not as yet disentangled themselves from the brushwood with which Thickety Creek abounds, were directed to form and wait for orders."[16]

Fifty dragoons drew their sabers and charged the sharpshooters positioned in Morgan's first line. The riflemen aimed and fired, and fifteen dragoons fell from their horses; the survivors galloped back to the cover of the British infantry.

Holding the 1st Battalion of the 71st Regiment in reserve, Tarleton ordered the main body of his infantry to advance. The infantrymen yelled as they charged, prompting Morgan to tell his men, "They give us the British halloo, boys, give them the Indian whoop."[17]

When the British came within range, the militiamen set their sights on the officers and sergeants, following Morgan's instructions to "Look for the epaulets! Pick off the epaulets!"[18] The militiamen fired a volley. The advancing British infantry slowed down but kept coming. The American militia fired a second aimed volley, and withdrew as instructed by Morgan.

When Tarleton saw the units leave, he thought the militia had broken as it so often had in the past. He ordered fifty cavalrymen to pursue what he thought were panic-stricken men in flight. American cavalry drove Tarleton's cavalry away, and covered the withdrawal of the militia.

As American officers tried to convince the militia units to regroup and reload, Morgan rode up, sword in hand, and shouted, "Form, form, my brave fellows!"[19]

The British infantry continued to advance, but because it had lost so many officers it did not stay in formation. The line of Continental infantry Morgan had placed near the crest of a ridge fired a volley that stopped the British in their tracks. The disciplined, veteran foes exchanged fire at point-blank range.

Tarleton then called on his reserves, the 1st Battalion of the 71st Highlanders. "The reserve, which as yet had no orders to move from its first position, and consequently remained near a mile distant, was now directed to advance," Mackenzie remembered. "When the line felt the advance of the Seventy-first, all the infantry again moved on; the Continentals and backwoodsmen gave ground; the British rushed forwards."[20]

Tarleton ordered the reserves to execute a flanking movement against Morgan's right. The Highlanders fired a volley that created confusion among the Americans. As the Americans maneuvered into position to oppose the flanking movement, some of them misunderstood the maneuver, and soon the whole line was moving in order away from the British attackers.

The British assumed that Morgan's entire army was in retreat, and gave chase. Because they were charging at a run through a stand of trees, and because they had lost many of their officers, the usually well-disciplined British troops disintegrated into a mob as they pursued their foes. The British, however, did not overrun the Americans, mostly because the British were physically exhausted. The Americans had rested throughout the previous night and had eaten breakfast, while the British had been on the march through the night in cold, wet weather across rugged terrain. The British not only did without breakfast but also had been on meager rations for several days. When the Highlanders had been called into action, they trotted three hundred yards uphill toward the American right flank. When the Americans withdrew, the Highlanders charged another hundred yards in pursuit. Mackenzie observed that "not less than two-thirds of the British infantry officers had already fallen, and nearly the same proportion of privates; fatigue, however, enfeebled the pursuit more than loss of blood."[21]

The Highlanders closed to within ten to thirty yards before the Americans turned to fight some more. Morgan's men remained in formation as they marched toward the rear. Morgan picked a place to make a stand, and ordered them to halt. "Face about, boys!" Morgan told them. "Give them one good fire, and the day is ours!"[22] The Americans fired point-blank at their pursuers. Bodies of the killed and wounded covered the battlefield; among the casualties were nearly half the men of the 1st Battalion of the 71st Regiment. The Highlanders kept fighting hand-to-hand. Continental infantry charged the 71st Highlanders with bayonets while American horsemen attacked the Highlanders from their left flank and rear. American militia charged the Highlanders' right flank. The Highlanders began to retreat; many of them ran for their lives. "In disorder from the pursuit, unsupported by the cavalry, deprived of the assistance of the cannon, which in defiance of the utmost exertions of those who had them in charge were now left behind," reported Mackenzie, "the advance of the British fell back, and communicated a panic to others, which soon became general: a total rout ensued."[23]

Surrounded and without hope of relief, the Highlanders surrendered. Of the sixteen officers of the 71st who fought at the Cowpens, six were taken prisoner. Two lieutenants—Macleod and Chisholm—were killed, and seven lieutenants—Grant, Mackintosh, Flint, Mackenzie, Sinclair, Forbes and Macleod—were wounded.[24] The only soldiers of the 71st who escaped from the Cowpens were a few who had been left behind to guard the baggage train.

When the Highlanders surrendered, they expected their American captors to take revenge for Tarleton's numerous acts of cruelty. A high-ranking American officer—John Eager Howard—described a Highlander's apprehension:

> ...In the pursuit I was led towards the right, in among the 71st, who were broken into squads, and as I called to them to surrender, they laid down their arms, and the officers delivered up their swords. Captain Duncanson [Robertson Duncanson of the 1st Battalion of the 71st Regiment] gave me his sword and stood by me. Upon getting on my horse, I found him pulling at my saddle, and he nearly unhorsed me. I expressed my displeasure and asked him what he was about. The explanation was that they had orders to give no quarter, and they did not expect any; and as my men were coming up, he was afraid they would use them ill. I admitted his excuse and put him into the care of a sergeant...[25]

Another American soldier recalled that "the Highlanders of the 71st plucked the feathers from their caps and cried, 'Dear, good Americans, have mercy upon us! We were ordered to take no prisoners, except a few Continentals.' 'We wish,' it was replied, 'that this had been known a little sooner.'"[26]

McArthur surrendered to James Jackson, the brigade major of the American militia.[27] Humiliated by defeat, McArthur vented his fury not on the Americans but on Tarleton:

> Major McArthur very freely entered into conversation, and said that he was an officer before Tarleton was born; that the best troops in the service were put under *"that boy"* to be sacrificed; that he had flattered himself the event would have been different, if his advice had been taken, which was to charge with all the horse at the moment we were retreating.[28]

Tarleton, watching his infantry surrender and most of his dragoons flee, rallied fifty loyal horsemen for a last desperate charge. American riflemen recognized Tarleton and fired at him; he was not hit but his horse fell beneath him. Mounting another horse, Tarleton charged into the thick of the fighting. The American cavalry met the charge and drove off the British dragoons. The commander of the American cavalry—William Washington, who was kin to George Washington—took up pursuit of Tarleton. Washington was alone ahead of his men when Tarleton and a few of his horsemen turned to fight. In hand-to-hand combat, Washington broke his saber at the hilt. Washington's 14-year-old black servant raced to his rescue and shot Washington's opponent in the sword arm. Another British officer attacked Washington, but an American sergeant arrived in the nick of time and deflected the officer's sword. Tarleton himself charged in and swung his saber at Washington, who blocked it with his broken saber. Tarleton fired his pistol, missing Washington and wounding Washington's horse. As Washington's cavalry caught up with him, Tarleton galloped away. Morgan sent a company of mounted infantry and cavalry commanded by Washington to pursue the remnants of Tarleton's detachment. Washington broke off the chase after riding twenty-four miles without overtaking the British.[29]

Tarleton and the remnant of his command withdrew down the road to the place where the British baggage had been left with a small guard under Ensign Fraser of the 71st Regiment. Tarleton and Cornwallis claimed that a detachment of American troops had captured the baggage, and that Tarleton's dragoons "retook the baggage of the corps, cut the detachment who had it in possession to pieces, destroyed the greater part," and carried away the survivors as prisoners.[30] An officer of the 71st Regiment disputed that story. When the British soldiers guarding the baggage learned that their comrades had been defeated, the officer contended, Fraser destroyed the baggage that could not be carried off and retreated to Cornwallis's position with the baggage wagon and all the horses without ever seeing any American troops.[31] Morgan reported that the British left behind thirty-five wagons filled with supplies. Morgan made no mention of Tarleton having retaken any baggage, and no American troops reported being attacked by Tarleton in an attempt to retake the baggage.[32]

Morgan reported the aftermath of the Battle of Cowpens in a letter to Greene:

> ...As I was obliged to move off the field of action in the morning to secure the prisoners, I cannot be so accurate as to the

> killed and wounded of the enemy as I could wish. From the reports of an officer whom I sent to view the ground, there were one hundred non-commissioned officers and privates and ten commissioned officers killed and two hundred rank and file wounded. We have now in our possession five hundred and two non-commissioned officers and privates prisoners, independent of the wounded, and the militia are taking up stragglers continually. Twenty-nine commissioned officers have fell into our hands. Their rank, etc., you will see by an enclosed list. The officers I have paroled; the privates I am conveying by the safest route to Salisbury...
>
> Two standards, two fieldpieces, thirty-five wagons, a travelling forge and all their music [bagpipes of the 71st Regiment] are ours. Their baggage, which was immense, they have in a great measure destroyed.[33]

About a dozen Americans were killed in the fighting at the Cowpens. Reports of the number of Americans wounded range from sixty to more than a hundred.

The Battle of Cowpens started at sunrise and was over within an hour. By noon, Morgan moved out, and by nightfall his division had crossed to the north side of the Broad River. Before dawn the next morning, the division continued its rapid retreat and marched until sundown. Morgan detached a force to take the prisoners into Virginia, and led the rest of his division across the Catawba River. He had covered a hundred miles and crossed two rivers in six days. Once encamped on the Catawba, Morgan stayed in bed in his tent, suffering from sciatica and a high fever.

After the Battle of Cowpens, the Highlanders never relented in their animosity toward Tarleton. Roderick Mackenzie later wrote a book ridiculing Tarleton's claims of military expertise. Mackenzie wrote:

> The first error of judgment to be imputed to Lieutenant Colonel Tarleton, on the morning of the 17th of January, 1781, is, the not halting his troops before he engaged the enemy. Had he done so, it was evident that the following advantages would have been the result of his conduct. General Morgan's force and situation might have been distinctly viewed, under cover of a very superior cavalry; the British infantry, fatigued with rapid marches, day and night, for some time past... might have had rest and refreshment; a detachment from the several corps left with the baggage, together with batt-men, and officers' servants, would have had time to come up, and join in the action. The artillery all this time might have been playing on the enemy's front, or either flank, without risque of insult; the commandants of regiments, Majors M'Arthur and Newmarsh, officers who held commissions long before [Tarleton] was born, and who had reputations to this day unimpeached, might have been consulted, and... time would have been given for the approach of Earl Cornwallis...
>
> The second error was, the un-officer-like impetuosity of directing the line to advance before it was properly formed, and before the reserve had taken its ground; in consequence of which, as might have been expected, the attack was premature, confused, and irregular.
>
> The third error in this ruinous business was the omission of giving discretional powers to that judicious veteran M'Arthur, to advance with the reserve, at the time that the front line was in the pursuit of the militia, by which means

> the connection so necessary to troops engaged in the field was not preserved.
>
> His fourth error was, ordering Captain Ogilvie, with a troop, consisting of no more than forty men, to charge, before any impression was made on the continentals, and before Washington's cavalry had been engaged.
>
> The next, and the most destructive, for I will not pretend to follow him through all his errors, was in not bringing up a column of cavalry, and completing the rout, which, by his own acknowledgment, had commenced through the whole American infantry...[34]

Tarleton claimed in his memoirs that "an unaccountable panic extended itself" along the whole British line at Cowpens, and reprinted a letter written to him by Cornwallis two weeks after the battle saying "the total misbehavior of the troops could alone have deprived you of the glory which was so justly your due."[35] In response, Mackenzie wrote that the best "criterion to judge the conduct of these corps, upon whom Lieutenant Colonel Tarleton has stamped the charge of 'total misbehavior'" would be "an examination of the state of discipline they were then under, of their general conduct upon every former occasion, and of the loss which they sustained" at Cowpens. Mackenzie then described the 71st Regiment's distinguished history, focusing on the 1st Battalion because it was the battalion at the Cowpens:

> The first battalion of the 71st regiment, who had landed in Georgia in the year 1778, under the command of Sir Archibald Campbell, had established their reputation in the several operations in that province, at Stono Ferry, at the sieges of Savannah and Charlestown, and at the battle of Camden.

> Now... they were led by an officer of great experience, who had come into the British service from the Scotch Dutch brigade: Out of sixteen officers which they had in the field [at Cowpens], nine were killed and wounded.
>
> The battalion of light infantry had signalised themselves separately on many occasions. ...those of the seventy-first regiment were distinguished under Sir James Baird at the surprise of General Wayne in Pennsylvania, of Baylor's dragoons in New Jersey, at Briar Creek in Georgia, at the capture and subsequent defense of Savannah, and at the battle near Camden under Earl Cornwallis...
>
> Such were the troops whom [Tarleton] has so severely stigmatised. Few corps, in any age or country, will be found to have bled more freely... I am not without my feelings as an individual for so wanton an attack on characters and entire corps, whose conduct had been, till then, unsullied. There is not an officer who survived that disastrous day, who is not far beyond the reach of slander and detraction; and with respect to the dead, I leave to Lieutenant Colonel Tarleton all the satisfaction which he can enjoy, from reflecting that he led a number of brave men to destruction, and then used every effort in his power to damn their fame with posterity.[36]

THE MAIN BRITISH ARMY UNDER CORNWALLIS threatened the much smaller force under Daniel Morgan that had defeated Banastre Tarleton at Cowpens. Cornwallis wanted not only to eliminate Morgan's division of the American army but also to retrieve the British soldiers who had been taken prisoner. "The late affair has almost broken my heart," Cornwallis confided. "Morgan is at Gilbertown. I shall march tomorrow with 1,200 infantry and the cavalry to attack or follow him to the banks of the Catawba. General Howard remains at Cherokee Ford with all baggage, knapsacks included, ready to meet us at Ramsour's. I was never more surrounded with difficulty and distress, but practice in the school of adversity has strengthened me."[37]

Cornwallis came up with a scheme to make his army mobile enough to keep up with Morgan. He ordered the destruction of cumbersome baggage, provisions, rum and personal possessions. Then he set out after Morgan as a light rain fell on the morning of January 28. The rain fell harder as the day went by and continued through the next day. By the time Cornwallis reached the Catawba, the river was too swollen to cross. As the army waited for the river to recede, the soldiers sought shelter under trees because their tents had been destroyed with their baggage.

With Morgan on the run and Cornwallis in pursuit, Greene prepared to reunite the two divisions of his army. Greene instructed General Isaac Huger to lead one division from Cheraw to North Carolina, where it would rendezvous with Morgan's division. Greene himself set out on January 28 to join Morgan on the Catawba. With only a five-man escort, Greene traveled more than a hundred miles through no-man's land and arrived at Morgan's camp on January 30. Greene sent Morgan's division marching toward Salisbury, a major supply center, while a force of several hundred riflemen guarded the fords of the Catawba.

Before dawn on February 1, the British waded through chest-high water to cross the Catawba at Cowan's Ford while American militiamen fired upon them from the far bank. As Cornwallis rode across the river, his horse was hit by several musket balls but managed to carry Cornwallis across before collapsing. Once across the river, the British fired a volley at the militiamen. Most of the militiamen fled when their commander,

General William Lee Davidson, was killed. British casualties, according to Cornwallis, were four killed and thirty-six wounded but, according to local residents, more than a dozen bodies of British soldiers washed downstream.

Even after the two divisions of the American army met at Guilford on February 6, the Americans were still outnumbered; Cornwallis led three thousand men, mostly British regulars, in pursuit of fourteen hundred Continentals and six hundred militiamen. Once the American divisions had reunited, Morgan left the army in Greene's hands. Fighting and marching in cold, wet weather had aggravated Morgan's ailments so that he could no longer ride a horse. He was carried on a litter when he began his journey home to Virginia.

Greene continued to withdraw before Cornwallis. The British and American armies marched northward for four days through cold rain and snow, skirmishing along the way. Greene had arranged for boats to be waiting at the Dan River, and during the night of February 13 the Americans crossed into Virginia. The British were close behind but could not follow the Americans across the river because there were no boats left on the bank. Cornwallis withdrew to Hillsboro, where his men could forage for provisions.

On February 18, Greene sent a force back across the Dan to keep Cornwallis from consolidating British control of North Carolina, and two days later sent another force. Three days later, Greene led the Southern army back into North Carolina. Greene had been receiving reinforcements that boosted his army to more than four thousand men, including Continental infantry, Continental cavalry, Continental artillery, and militia units from Virginia and North Carolina. Many of the militiamen bore Scottish names such as McDowell, Stuart, and Campbell, and wore hats imported "from home," meaning from

Scotland.[38] Two officers in the North Carolina militia—Brigadier General Thomas Eaton and his cousin Colonel Pinkatham "Pink" Eaton—had been at the Battle of Brier Creek in Georgia in 1779, where the 71st Regiment had contributed to a convincing British victory.[39]

On March 6, Cornwallis reported, "I moved to Wetzell's Mill on Reedy Fork east of Buffalo, where we fell in with five or six hundred of his militia and light troops, who were obliged to retire with precipitation."[40] The 2nd Battalion of the 71st Regiment participated in the action. "The 23rd and 71st moved forwards to the creek without any great impediment," Tarleton reported, "and the ardent bravery of the 33rd and the light company of the guards soon dislodged them [the Americans] from their strong position. The infantry mounted the hill above the creek, and dispersed the Americans so effectually that the cavalry could only collect a few stragglers from the woods in front."[41]

While the American army gathered reinforcements, the British army dwindled. Exhaustion and desertion—blamed partly on the lack of rum—reduced the British army to about two thousand men. Following the loss of the 1st Battalion of the 71st at Cowpens and attrition during the campaign across the Carolinas, the 71st consisted of one battalion with fewer than 250 men. The battalion had dwindled from 237 rank and file on January 15 to 194 on March 15. With no lieutenant colonel or major in the field, the regiment was led by three captains, six lieutenants, five ensigns, a staff officer, and twenty-five sergeants, assisted by ten drummers.[42]

On March 14, Greene prepared for battle at Guilford Courthouse. Greene stationed the militia in front of the Continental troops, similar to Morgan's disposition at the Cowpens. Greene, like Morgan, rode up and down the line inspiring the militiamen with themes of honor and liberty, and asking them to fire two volleys and then withdraw from the front line.

In another echo of the Cowpens, the British awakened before dawn on March 15 and, without taking time to eat breakfast, marched twelve miles to confront the Americans. As the British neared Guilford, Tarleton's dragoons skirmished with American cavalrymen.[43]

At Guilford, the 71st Highlanders were paired with a Hessian musketeer regiment called the Von Bose to form Leslie's brigade, under the command of Major General Alexander Leslie. The command of the 71st Regiment fell to the senior captain—Robert Hutcheson—and the regiment was deployed in two wings, each commanded by a captain and each consisting of three companies led by lieutenants. Leslie's brigade took its position in a wooded area on the British right; the 71st was on the south side of the main road to Guilford Courthouse and the Von Bose was farther to the right. On the north side of the road, the British left was held by Webster's brigade, under the command of Lieutenant Colonel James Webster, a son of a prominent Edinburgh minister. The 23rd and the 33rd regiments made up Webster's brigade. The 23rd Regiment, known as the Royal Welch Fusiliers, was across the road from the 71st, and the 33rd Regiment was on the British left flank farther from the road.[44]

By noon the armies were exchanging artillery fire. In the early afternoon, Cornwallis deployed the British for battle. The British soldiers beside the road moved out of the woods into a clearing, while the soldiers farther to the left and right remained in wooded terrain. The Highlanders in the clearing faced hundreds of American soldiers positioned behind a rail fence. The Highlanders and their Hessian brigade-mates advanced across a recently-plowed field that had been turned to mush by rainy weather. They had to cross a fence on the edge of the clearing where they started the advance, and cross another fence a couple of hundred yards away from the American line.[45]

As the attackers approached, American riflemen in flanking parties picked their targets, particularly British officers. The commander of a local militia regiment saw a "British officer with his sword drawn driving up his men;" and told a rifleman to "take him down, which he did;" the doomed officer presumably was Ensign Archibald McPherson of the 71st Regiment.[46] When the British reached the "killing range" of a musket, American militiamen in the front line fired a volley. Ensign Dugald Stuart of the 71st reported the damage inflicted by Scots-Irish militiamen deployed on the American first line: "In the advance we received a very deadly fire from the Irish line of the American army, composed of their marksmen, lying on the ground behind a rail fence."[47] The regiment lost as many as thirty men in the assault, reducing its number to fewer than two hundred men.[48] The British returned fire as they continued to advance—the American who had killed Archibald McPherson was wounded in the thigh and abdomen. Threatened by the onrushing British line of bayonets, most of the American militiamen ran for their lives. As the British overran the American position, they bayoneted the man who had killed McPherson.[49]

As the British pursued retreating Americans, a gap opened between the 71st and 23rd regiments; Cornwallis sent reserves to fill the gap. The battle broke up into various encounters spread across a long front through woods and across ravines. Cornwallis himself led a charge on the north side of the road; his horse was shot from under him, and soon afterwards the replacement horse also was shot from under him.

The Highlanders continued to advance on the south side of the road; the British artillery moved forward on the road beside the Highlanders, followed by cavalry. The Highlanders crashed into the second line of American defenders, who fired so many rounds that their gun barrels became almost too hot to handle. Fierce fighting killed the horse Cornwallis rode onto the scene, then killed the horse that replaced it, in addition to wounding Brigadier General Charles O'Hara.[50] The Virginia regiments held their ground until one of their commanders was wounded and gave the order to retreat. Hard fighting continued to the south of the Highlanders' position, and the British formations continued to be stretched farther southward.[51]

The 33rd Regiment led the British attack on the American third line. Continental infantry and artillery drove the 33rd back to a strong position on high ground. The 2nd Battalion of Guards attacked next, routed their Continental opponents, and captured the American artillery. Other Continental units counterattacked. In hand-to-hand fighting, Continental Captain John Smith killed British Lieutenant Colonel James Stuart, the son of a Scottish lord. In an exchange of volleys, General O'Hara was shot in the chest—the second wound he suffered during the battle—and fell from his horse. Continental and militia horsemen including Colonel William Washington's light dragoons supported the counterattack and took back the American artillery pieces. The 71st Highlanders eventually reached the American third line, after maneuvering in heavily wooded, deep ravines while exchanging fire at close range with Americans among the trees. Cornwallis reported:

> The 71st Regiment and Grenadiers and 2nd Battalion of Guards, not knowing what was passing on their right and hearing the fire advance on their left, continued to move forward, the artillery keeping pace with them on the road, followed by the cavalry... The enemy's cavalry was soon

> repulsed by a well directed fire from two three-pounders just brought up by Lieutenant Macleod, and by the appearance of the grenadiers of the guards, and of the 71st regiment, which having been impeded by some deep ravines, were now coming out of the wood on the right of the guards, opposite to the courthouse.[52]

With the British pressing the American third line, General Greene decided it was more important to save his army than to win the battle. He ordered the Americans to withdraw from the field with one regiment of Continentals covering the withdrawal. The 71st Highlanders and the 23rd Royal Welch Fusiliers emerged from the ravines and came out of the woods opposite the courthouse as the Americans were leaving.[53] Cornwallis ordered the 71st and 23rd to pursue the retreating Americans. As at Cowpens, fatigue became a factor. The British, who had not eaten anything all day, had been fighting for nearly seven hours counting the skirmishes on the march toward Guilford Courthouse. Since their arrival at Guilford Courthouse, they had advanced uphill and had engaged in combat for more than two hours.[54] "The fatigue of my troops," said Cornwallis, "and the great number of wounded put it out of my power to pursue beyond the Reedy Ford in the afternoon of the action."[55] The British wounded, he said, were "dispersed over an extensive space of country" and "required immediate attention."[56]

Cornwallis claimed "a signal victory" because he held the field at the end of the day, but victory came at a terrible cost.[57] He had lost at least a fourth of his army. He reported casualties of ninety-three killed, 413 wounded, and twenty-six missing.[58] Tarleton's wounds resulted in the amputation of his fore finger, his middle finger, and part of his right hand.

Three ensigns in the 71st Regiment were killed at Guilford Courthouse: Malcolm Grant, Archibald McPherson and Donald McPherson. Total casualties of the 71st were thirteen killed and fifty wounded.[59]

American casualties at Guilford Courthouse were seventy-nine killed and 184 wounded. More than a thousand Americans were reported missing, but they were mostly militiamen who had simply gone home.

The aftermath of the battle presented more hardships to the British troops, partly because they had destroyed their tents with their baggage earlier in the campaign. "The night succeeding this day of blood was rainy, dark and cold;" a veteran of the battle reported, "the dead unburied, the wounded unsheltered, the groans of the dying and the shrieks of the living shed a deeper shade over the gloom of nature. The victorious troops, without tents and without food, participated in sufferings which they could not believe. The ensuing morning was spent in performing the last offices to the dead and in providing comfort for the wounded. In executing these sad duties, the British general regarded with equal attention friends and foes."[60]

General O'Hara, who was wounded twice in the fighting at Guilford Courthouse, described the battle in a letter:

> ...every part of our army was beat repeatedly on the 15th March, and were obliged to fall back twice. The Rebels were so exceedingly numerous as to be able constantly to oppose fresh troops to us, and be in force in our front, flanks and r- s impossible to say too much in praise of our officers in a conflict that lasted near two hours. Though so outnumbered, their spirit and constancy never n, and at length crowned their manly exertions

> with victory. I never did, and hope I never shall, experience two such days and nights as those immediately after the battle. We remained on the very ground on which it had been fought covered with dead and dying and with hundreds of wounded, Rebels as well as our own. A violent and constant rain that lasted above forty hours made it equally impracticable to remove or administer the smallest comfort to many of the wounded.[61]

Cornwallis informed the British command in New York "that our military operations were uniformly successful and the victory at Guilford, although one of the bloodiest of this war, was very complete." He said it was "impossible to follow the blow the next day" because of "the want of provisions and all kinds of necessaries for the soldiers."[62] In a report to the Secretary of State for the American Colonies, Cornwallis said:

> The conduct and actions of the officers and soldiers that compose this little army will do more justice to their merit than I can by words. Their persevering intrepidity in action, their invincible patience in the hardships and fatigues of a march of above 600 miles in which they have forded several large rivers and numberless creeks, many of which would be reckoned large rivers in any other country in the world, without tents or coverings against the climate and often without provisions, will sufficiently manifest their ardent zeal for the honour and interests of their Sovereign and their country.[63]

The British transported their wounded soldiers—along with a surgeon, a mate, and a wagonload of medicine and supplies—to the New Garden Quaker Meeting House. Among the sixty-four wounded men were six members of the 71st Regiment. One of them, John McKuhan, died ten days after the battle of wounds in the body and lungs. Two members of the regiment were listed in "Doubtful" condition: John McCoy, who was wounded in the arm and side; and Rory McKenzie, who was wounded in the left side and breast. Another two members were listed as "Recovering:" Daniel McCallam, with a wound in the thigh; and Alexander Campbell, with wounds in the thigh and side. The sixth member, John Wallace, suffered from a fractured leg that was mending.[64]

Yorktown

AFTER THE BATTLE of Guilford Courthouse on March 15, 1781, the opposing armies went in separate directions. The British army led by General Charles Cornwallis, including the 71st Regiment, sought food and supplies. "This part of the country is so totally destitute of subsistence that forage is not nearer than nine miles and the soldiers have been two days without bread," Cornwallis reported. "With a third of my army sick and wounded, which I was obliged to carry in wagons or on horseback, the remainder without shoes and worn down with fatigue, I thought it was time to look for some place of rest and refitment." Cornwallis decided to withdraw toward the coast of North Carolina where British ships could bring supplies into port. He envisioned "approaching our shipping by easy marches that we may procure the necessary supplies for further operations and lodge our sick and wounded where proper attention can be paid to them."[1] He expected the Continental army commanded by Nathanael Greene to pursue him, but Greene moved southward, knowing that the British outposts in South Carolina had been left vulnerable when Cornwallis departed.

Cornwallis planned his route through the Cross Creek country, where emigrants from the Highlands of Scotland—some of them with ancient clan connections to some of the soldiers in the 71st Regiment—maintained allegiance to the British government. "Notwithstanding the cruel persecution the inhabitants of Cross Creek had constantly endured for their partiality to the British, they yet retained a great zeal for the interest of the royal army," said Lieutenant Colonel Banastre Tarleton. "All the flour and spirits in the neighborhood were collected and conveyed to camp, and the wounded officers and soldiers were supplied with many conveniences highly agreeable and refreshing to men in their situation."[2] General Charles O'Hara had a different impression, saying "we fell back by easy marches upon Cross Creek, a very large settlement at the head of Cape Fear River, chiefly inhabited by Scotch, who were said to a man would join us, but that has proved like the other Government dreams."[3] Cornwallis admitted that the Highlanders were "not equal to my expectations." Upon arrival at Cross Creek, he reported, "I found to my great mortification, and contrary to all former accounts that it was impossible to procure any considerable quantity of provisions and that there was not four days' forage within 20 miles."[4]

Cornwallis also discovered that his army could not rely on supplies coming up the Cape Fear River from the coast to Cross Creek. "The navigation of Cape Fear, with the hopes of which I had been flattered, was totally impracticable, the distance from Wilmington by water being 150 miles, the breadth of the river seldom exceeding one hundred yards, the banks generally high, and the inhabitants on each side almost universally hostile." Cornwallis decided to keep moving from Cross Creek to the port of Wilmington.[5]

At the beginning of April—when the army halted at Cross Creek—a report showed 163 rank and file present and fit for duty in the 71st Regiment. A report two weeks later—while the army rested at Wilmington—listed 183 rank and file present and fit for duty. The regiment also had 108 men sick, thirty-seven wounded, and thirty-five men assigned outside the district. Additionally, 123 men—presumably the soldiers captured at Cowpens—were listed as "prisoners with the rebels." Still lacking any high-ranking officer, the regiment contained three captains, six lieutenants, five ensigns, an adjutant, a quartermaster, a surgeon, a medical mate, twenty-two sergeants, and nine drummers. A report on the first of May showed 175 rank and file.[6]

Bureaucratic problems interfered with supplies for the 71st Regiment, which consisted of only the 2nd Battalion after the 1st Battalion was destroyed at Cowpens. While at Wilmington, Captain Robert Hutcheson asked Cornwallis to grant a temporary warrant providing money to the battalion's paymaster "in order that the battalion be supplied without loss of time with such necessaries as they want."[7]

During the lull in action at Wilmington, O'Hara wrote to a political ally in England about the state of Cornwallis's army:

> The Gazette will acquaint your Grace with our success on the 15th March near Guilford Court House. I wish it had produced one substantial benefit to Great Britain. On the contrary, we feel at this moment the sad and fatal effects of our loss on that day, nearly one half of our best officers and soldiers were either killed or wounded, and what remains are so completely worn out, by the excessive fatigues of the campaign in a march of above a thousand miles, most of them barefoot, naked and for days together living upon carrion, which they had often not time to dress, and three or four ounces of Indian corn, has totally destroyed this army—entre nous, the spirit of our little army has evaporated a good deal. No zeal or courage is equal to the constant exertions we are making.[8]

The British general commanding at Chesapeake Bay shared O'Hara's general sentiments. William Phillips said the campaign in the Carolinas had been a "tale of many difficulties and distresses, great perseverance and resolution, and honour," but he feared the Battle of Guilford Courthouse had been "that sort of victory which ruins an army." He continued, "The face of affairs seems changed, and the Carolinas, like all America, are lost in rebellion."[9]

Cornwallis decided to leave Wilmington and march into Virginia, reasoning that if the British conquered Virginia they would exert control over all the southern colonies. His battered army of 1,780 men, including the 71st Regiment, could receive supplies and reinforcements by sea through the ports of coastal Virginia and could expect support from British troops operating out of Norfolk. The army marched 225 miles in twenty-five days. When Cornwallis reached Petersburg on May 20, he received reinforcements of 1,700 rank and file sent from New York, and joined forces with about 3,500 troops already stationed in Virginia.[10]

In in early June, Cornwallis sent 250 cavalry and mounted infantry under Tarleton to disrupt a meeting of the Virginia General Assembly at Charlottesville. Virginia Governor Thomas Jefferson escaped from his home Monticello near Charlottesville five minutes before British soldiers arrived; the soldiers drank some of Jefferson's wine in a birthday toast to their king.[11] The initial plan for the raid on Charlottesville provided for Tarleton's force to include the 71st Regiment under the command of Captain Robert Hutcheson. The Highlanders, however, had not forgiven Tarleton for leading their comrades to death or capture at Cowpens. An officer who served with Cornwallis reported that when the 71st received the order to accompany Tarleton to Charlottesville, "the officers drew up a remonstrance, and presented it to Lord Cornwallis, stating their unwillingness to serve under Tarleton, from a recollection of his conduct at the Cowpens, where the other battalion of the 71st was taken by

Morgan. In consequence of this remonstrance, the 71st regiment was attached to Colonel Simcoe."[12]

Cornwallis had proceeded to Williamsburg when he received orders from Sir Henry Clinton, the commander of British forces in America, to send units from the army in Virginia to reinforce British headquarters at New York. Cornwallis felt that he could not defend Williamsburg with his smaller army, and made plans to establish a post at Portsmouth, where his army could be supported by the British navy.

The British army left Williamsburg on July 4 and camped near a plantation called Green Spring. The Marquis de Lafayette, commander of the American army in Virginia, attacked the British camp. In forming the British line of battle, Cornwallis placed the 2nd Battalion of the 71st Regiment and Tarleton's Legion in the rear.[13] The Americans advanced along a causeway through marshes toward the British position on high ground. The British used their advantageous position to inflict about three hundred casualties on the Americans while suffering only seventy-five casualties themselves.

The next morning, Cornwallis crossed the James River and marched toward Portsmouth. The British units bound for New York under Clinton's orders boarded ship at Portsmouth, but did not depart because a new order from Clinton told them to stay with Cornwallis.

Having been commanded by a captain for six months, the 71st Regiment received higher-ranking officers. Duncan Macpherson of Cluny—who had served as a major in the 71st until transferring to another regiment in 1779 as a lieutenant colonel—arrived at Portsmouth on July 12 to take command of the 71st.[14] James Campbell of the 33rd Regiment was promoted to major at the urging of Cornwallis, and transferred to the 71st Regiment. "Captain Campbell of the 33rd has commanded the regiment in two important actions," Cornwallis had said after the Battle of Guilford Courthouse, and "on both occasions he behaved with the greatest bravery and distinguished himself very much. He is an old captain and very deserving of a share in the promotion occasioned by the death of his late lieutenant colonel."[15]

Clinton instructed Cornwallis to establish a post that could protect British naval vessels anchored at Hampton Roads in Chesapeake Bay. Cornwallis chose to fortify Yorktown and Gloucester on opposite banks of the York River. Writing from Yorktown on August 2, Cornwallis informed O'Hara at Portsmouth:

> After a passage of four days we landed here and at Gloucester without opposition. The position is bad, and you know that every senior general takes without remorse from a junior and tells him that he has nothing to fear. I send nine boats for the Regiment of Prince Hereditaire, and as your Portsmouth boats must by this time be put to rights, I wish you would send me the 71st or, if that regiment is too strong for the boats, either the 23rd or the 33rd. You will judge how many trips may be absolutely necessary for the horse vessels; the first must be the Legion. Pray send them as soon as possible; we are in great want of them. The cattle drivers are absolutely necessary; we cannot do without them. We are likewise in the greatest want of engineer's tools and labouring Negroes. [In another letter, Cornwallis said he was "in great want of Negroes to work, as the heat is too great to admit of the soldiers doing it."] The transports will be sent as soon as possible for the removal of every thing. Adieu, my dear Charles. I shall be happy to embrace you on the delightful banks of York River.[16]

"I send you the Hereditary Prince's Regiment with their guns and the 71st Regiment," O'Hara replied. "We have been able to send you 50 Negroes only, as I am obliged to keep about 50 more to assist in embarking the victualling and other stores, which I am afraid will be a very heavy, tiresome business. What will you have done with the hundreds of wretched Negroes that are dying by scores every day?"[17] On August 6, Cornwallis told O'Hara that the "boats with the two regiments are just arrived safe."[18] Responding to O'Hara's question, Cornwallis said "It is shocking to think of the state of the Negroes, but we cannot bring a number of sick and useless ones to this place. Some flour must be left for them and some person of the country appointed to take charge of them to prevent their perishing."[19] Cornwallis informed Clinton of his progress:

> I embarked the 80th Regiment in boats and went myself on board of the *Richmond* very early in the morning of the 29th [of July], but we were so unfortunate in winds as to be four days on our passage. The 80th landed on the night of the 1st at Gloucester, and the troops which were on the transports on the morning of the 2nd at this place [Yorktown]. I have since brought the 71st and Legion hither and sent the Regiment du Prince Hereditaire to Gloucester. The works on the Gloucester side are in some forwardness and I hope in a situation to resist a sudden attack. Brigadier General O'Hara is hastening as much as possible the evacuation of Portsmouth. As soon as he arrives here I will send to New York every man that I can spare consistent with the safety and subsistence of the force in this country.[20]

A FRENCH FLEET ENTERED Chesapeake Bay on August 20. When a British fleet arrived outside the entrance to the bay on September 5, the French sailed out to do battle; the naval action inflicted 346 British casualties and two hundred French casualties. The French fleet returned into Chesapeake Bay, while the British fleet departed for New York on September 9. As a result, enemy forces isolated the British army under Cornwallis at Yorktown, with the French fleet preventing relief from the sea and Lafayette's Continental troops cutting off escape routes over land.

Meanwhile, General George Washington led an allied army on a march from near New York to Virginia. By September 24, Washington commanded a force of 7,800 French troops, 8,845 Continental soldiers, and 3,200 Virginia militiamen at Williamsburg. The American and French allies commenced a siege of Yorktown on September 28. The 71st Regiment had endured the siege of Savannah from the inside and the siege of Charleston from the outside; once again the regiment was subjected to incessant cannonading, nerve-wracking periods of enforced inactivity, and scarcity of provisions. Cornwallis praised "the patience of the soldiers in bearing the greatest fatigues, and their firmness and intrepidity under a persevering fire of shot and shells that I believe has not often been exceeded."[21] An American observed that shot and shell passing overhead turned the sky into one continuous blaze.[22]

The British force included about seven thousand troops in Yorktown, and a smaller post across the river at Gloucester.[23] The 71st Regiment took up a position on the left side of the outer defenses of Yorktown. The regiment helped cover an arm of Wormley Creek ravine near the junction of Goosley Road and Hampton Road. When the British later withdrew from the outer defenses, the 71st occupied a post on the eastern flank of the inner defenses.[24]

During the siege, a remarkable reunion occurred. It involved a boy who had served as a drummer in the 71st Regiment until he was captured at Cowpens. He subsequently joined the American army. When his unit was positioned outside Yorktown, he escaped and made his way to the British lines. As fate would have it, the 71st Regiment was maneuvering on the front lines at the time, and the boy found refuge in the piquet commanded by his father.[25]

By the beginning of October, the British at Yorktown depleted the feed for their horses and were forced to kill the animals or turn them loose in the no-man's land between the besiegers and the besieged. Facing the same shortages across the river at Gloucester, the garrison commanded by Tarleton killed more than a thousand horses, a decision that destroyed the capacity of the British to conduct cavalry maneuvers.

On the night of October 14, American and French assault parties attacked two redoubts a short distance in advance of the post defended by the 71st Regiment. The troops defending the redoubts included selected soldiers from the 71st and five other regiments.

About four hundred Americans attacked Redoubt 10—perched on a cliff above the York River—where Major James Campbell of the 71st Regiment commanded sixty to seventy men. The British fired their muskets and slashed with blades but could not prevent the Americans from overwhelming the position. The combat killed nine American soldiers and eight British soldiers, and wounded twenty-five Americans. When the British attempted to withdraw, they encountered a detachment of eighty Americans blocking the escape route. The Americans captured Major Campbell, three other officers, and seventeen soldiers while their comrades fled to the British lines.[26]

Simultaneously, four hundred French troops assaulted Redoubt 9, where Lieutenant Colonel Macpherson commanded about 130 British and Hessian troops. The French cut through defensive works, crossed a ditch and climbed the wall of the redoubt while the defenders countered with musket fire and bayonet charges. Inside the redoubt, the enemies engaged in vicious hand to hand fighting. Fifteen French soldiers died in the assault and seventy-seven suffered wounds; eighteen British soldiers were killed and about forty were captured. Macpherson escaped with the rest of his command.[27]

A British sally before dawn on October 16 caused seventeen casualties among French and American troops, but failed to stop the allied advance. Later that morning, the allies came within rifle range of the British lines, and marksmen exchanged fire throughout the day. The allies placed howitzers on captured redoubts and inflicted close-range shelling on the British garrison.

Cornwallis decided to evacuate the garrison by boat across the river to Gloucester, starting late in the night of October 16. While the evacuation was underway, a storm arose and stopped further attempts to cross the river. When the weather improved, the troops that had landed in Gloucester were recalled to Yorktown.

The besiegers opened fire at daylight October 17 with more than a hundred pieces of artillery. The British responded feebly because most of their artillery had been damaged and they had exhausted their supply of shot and shell. Cornwallis realized that he had to surrender, and during the morning of October 17 he asked Washington for a cease fire.

The 71st Regiment lost three officers at Yorktown: Lieutenant Thomas Fraser (who had guarded Tarleton's baggage at Cowpens), Lieutenant Angus Cameron, and Ensign John Grant.[28] Other casualties in the 71st at Yorktown were nine soldiers killed, nineteen soldiers wounded, and three drummers wounded. A major and ten rank and file were listed as missing.[29]

On October 19, the British army marched out of Yorktown and proceeded along a road lined with French soldiers on the west and American soldiers on the east. General O'Hara told Washington that he represented Cornwallis, who was too ill to attend. Washington, aware of rank and status, asked O'Hara to deal with General Benjamin Lincoln; the general who had surrendered an American army at Charleston was designated to accepted the surrender of a British army at Yorktown.

The British soldiers continued marching into a field surrounded by French hussars on horseback. Many of the humiliated British soldiers cursed, and a few cried, as they laid down their weapons.[30]

Officers in the 71st Regiment who surrendered were a lieutenant colonel, a major, a captain, eleven lieutenants, four ensigns and cornets, a quartermaster, a surgeon, a surgeon's mate, twenty-eight sergeants, nine drummers, and 242 rank and file. Some officers could expect to be exchanged, but the other officers and soldiers of the 71st Regiment would be prisoners of war for more than a year.[31]

Losing an army at Yorktown dissolved the will of the British people to wage war in America. The political process of peacemaking progressed slowly while fighting continued in South Carolina and Georgia. British and American commissioners signed preliminary peace terms on November 13, 1782, and British forces evacuated Charleston a month later. The final peace treaty between Great Britain and the United States of

America was ratified in September of 1783, and British troops left New York on November 25, 1783. The soldiers of the 71st Regiment sailed to Scotland and received their discharge at Perth.[32]

Part 2: Additional Information

About the 71st Regiment

BRITAIN RECRUITED SOLDIERS to quell rebellion in America, raising troop strength from 48,000 to 110,000 in six years. In 1775 officials augmented existing regiments and authorized a new regiment designated as the 71st Regiment of Foot. Responsibility for raising the new regiment fell on a dependable, experienced organizer, Simon Fraser of Lovat. In the past, he had raised a regiment of Scottish Highlanders who distinguished themselves in fierce fighting against the French in Canada before being disbanded in 1763. The new regiment, like its predecessor, became known unofficially as Fraser's Highlanders.[1]

A typical regiment contained four hundred to five hundred men organized into ten companies, including a grenadier company and a light infantry company in addition to eight line companies. Although the size of a company varied as circumstances demanded, a typical company consisted of 38 privates, six noncommissioned officers, and three officers; usually a captain commanded a company. The 71st Regiment was twice as large as a typical regiment, so it was subdivided into battalions; each battalion contained about the same number of men and officers as a typical regiment.[2]

The Highlands of Scotland provided fertile recruiting ground for the British army on the brink of the American Revolution. By the time the 71st Regiment assembled at Stirling, it boasted a strength of 2,340.[3] Among the inducements was an offer of land in America at the end of the war. "For a society still shaped by the contours of land as the basis for success," points out Matthew Dziennik, "the provision of cheap or free land without rents proved an effective means of encouraging

Highlanders to acquire colonial lands. The limited evidence available from the rank and file soldiery suggests that promises of land were a key part of their conception of military service." William Mackenzie, who served in the 71st as a piper, told a relative in Argyll that he hoped to obtain "200 acres of free ground of my own" in America. A recruiting poster distributed for the 71st Regiment promised:

> They [the soldiers of the 71st Regiment] are to go to America, and by his Majesty's royal and most gracious proclamation, they will be entitled to a full discharge at the end of three years [or the end of] the present American rebellion. Now, considering that the British army will be from forty to fifty thousand strong, there, in spring next it cannot in all probability fail to be entirely quelled next summer. Then, gentlemen, will be your harvest, and the best one too you ever cropt. You will each of you, by visiting 'This' New World, become the founders of families. The lands of the rebels will be divided amongst you, and every one of you became lairds.[4]

Under a system called "raising for rank," an influential man could obtain the rank of captain by raising a company for the 71st Regiment rather than by purchasing a commission.[5] David Stewart—a nineteenth-century military officer who enquired into the history of the Highland regiments—notes that when Fraser raised his regiment, "The completion of this numerous corps must, no doubt, have been accelerated by the exertions of his officers, of whom six besides himself were chiefs of clans, and all of respectable families, or sons of gentlemen tacksmen." Stewart composed the following list of officers:

FIRST BATTALION

COLONEL: The Honourable Simon Fraser of Lovat, died in 1782, a lieutenant general.

LIEUTENANT COLONEL: Sir William Erskine of Torry, died in 1789, a lieutenant general.

MAJORS: John Macdonell of Lochgarry, died in 1789, colonel. Duncan Macpherson of Cluny, retired from the foot guards in 1791, died in 1820.

CAPTAINS: Simon Fraser, died lieutenant-general, 1807. Donald Chisholm of Chisholm. Colin Mackenzie, died general in the army, 1818. Francis Skelly, died in India, lieutenant-colonel of the 94th regiment. Hamilton Maxwell of Monreith, died in India, lieutenant-colonel of the 74th regiment, 1794. John Campbell, son of Lord Stonefield, died lieutenant-colonel of the 2nd battalion of the 42nd regiment, at Madras, 1784. Norman Macleod of Macleod, died lieutenant-general, 1796. Sir James Baird of Saughtonhall. Charles Cameron of Lochiel, died 1776.

LIEUTENANTS: Charles Campbell, son of Ardchattan, killed at Catauba [the Catawba River near Charlotte, North Carolina]. John Nairne. William Nairne of Nairne. Charles Gordon. David Kinloch. Thomas Tawse, killed at Savannah. William St. Claire. Hugh Fraser. Alexander Fraser. John Macdougall. Colin Mackenzie. Alexander Fraser. Thomas Fraser, son of Leadclune. Dougald Campbell. Robert Macdonald, son of Sanda. Roderick Macleod. John Ross. Patrick Cumming. Thomas Hamilton.

ENSIGNS: Archibald Campbell. Henry Macpherson. John Grant. Robert Campbell. Allan Malcolm. John Murchison. Angus Macdonell. Peter Fraser. Chaplain: Hugh Blair, D.D. Professor of Rhetoric, Edinburgh College.

Adjutant: Donald Cameron. Quartermaster: David Campbell. Surgeon: William Fraser.

SECOND BATTALION

COLONEL: Simon Fraser.

LIEUTENANT COLONEL: Archibald Campbell, died lieutenant-general, 1792.

MAJORS: Norman Lamont, son of the Laird of Lamont. Robert Menzies, killed in Boston Harbour, 1776.

CAPTAINS: Angus Mackintosh. Patrick Campbell. Andrew Lawrie. Aeneas Mackintosh of Mackintosh. Charles Cameron, son of Fassafearn, killed at Savannah. George Munro, son of Culcairn. Boyd Porterfield. Law. Rbt. Campbell [presumably abbreviated form of Lawrence Robert Campbell].

LIEUTENANTS: Robert Hutchinson. Alexander Sutherland. Archibald Campbell. Hugh Lamont. Robert Duncanson. George Stewart. Charles Bon. Mackenzie. Dougald Campbell. Lodk. Colquhoun, son of Luss. John Mackenzie. Hugh Campbell. John Campbell. Arthur Forbes. Patrick Campbell. James Christie. James Fraser. Thomas Fraser. Archibald Balnevis, son of Edradour. Archibald Maclean. David Ross. Robert Grant. Thomas Fraser.

ENSIGNS: William Gordon. Charles Main. Archibald Campbell. Donald Cameron. Smollet Campbell. Gilbert Waugh. William Bain. John Grant. Chaplain: Malcolm Nicholson. Adjutant: Archibald Campbell. Quartermaster: J. Ogilvie. Surgeon: Colin Chisholm, Physician in Bristol.[6]

Ed Brumby provides a wealth of biographical information in *71st Fraser Highland Regiment in the American War of Independence*, published in 2012 by Anchorprint.

SEVERAL TRANSPORTS sailed into Boston Harbor in June of 1776 with the crews not knowing that the Americans had taken control of Boston. The following members of the 71st Regiment became prisoners of war: Lieutenant Colonel Archibald Campbell; captains George McKenzie, Lawrence Campbell, and Hamilton Maxwell; Lieutenant and Adjutant Archibald Campbell; lieutenants Archibald Balnevis, Hugh Campbell, Colin McKenzie, Robert Duncanson, Archibald Maclean, Lewis Colhoun, Charles Campbell, a Fraser whose first name was not listed, and another lieutenant whose entire name was not listed; Ensign Peter Fraser; Quartermaster William Ogilvie; Surgeon's Mate David Burns; acting Sergeant-Major Patrick McDougal; seven volunteers; fifteen sergeants; sixteen corporals; eight drummers; and 363 privates.[7]

SINCE COLONEL FRASER had remained at home, and Lieutenant Colonel Campbell was a prisoner of war, command of the regiment passed to Lieutenant Colonel William Erskine of the 1st Battalion. When the regiment was subdivided temporarily into three battalions in 1776, Erskine received an appointment as brigadier general in command of all three battalions. Under Erskine's command, the regiment fought in the Battle of Brooklyn in August of 1776 with Lieutenant Colonel John Maitland in command of the 1st Battalion.[8] In October of 1776, Erskine took responsibility as quartermaster of the army at New York, and in 1777 transferred to the 80th Regiment as a colonel.[9]

Campbell was released in a prisoner exchange in 1778 and was in command of the 71st Regiment in the summer of 1778.[10]

Late in 1778, Campbell led an expeditionary force—including both battalions of the 71st Regiment—that sailed to Georgia, captured Savannah, and made excursions into the backcountry. As the expedition set off, Campbell assigned duties to several officers in the 71st Regiment: Lieutenant Colonel Maitland as Deputy Adjutant on the Expedition; Major Simon Fraser as Deputy Quartermaster General; Captain Francis Skelly as Major of Brigade; Lieutenant Dougald Campbell as Aid de Camp; and Lieutenant James Christie as Major of Brigade for the Hessians.[11]

Lieutenant Colonel Maitland of the 1st Battalion assumed command of the regiment after Campbell left Georgia in March of 1779 to attend to personal affairs.[12] Under Maitland's leadership, the regiment fought valiantly at Stono Ferry. During the Siege of Savannah, Maitland commanded all forces on the west side of the line—where the fighting was bloodiest—despite being mortally ill with a fever.

When Maitland succumbed to his illness in October of 1779, Alexander MacDonald was appointed lieutenant colonel of the 1st Battalion and effectively commanded both battalions in the absence of Campbell. After the British captured Charleston in 1780, MacDonald sought permission to go home; command of the regiment rotated to Major Archibald McArthur, an experienced and respected professional officer.[13] McArthur led the regiment during the campaign in the Carolinas in 1780. In January of 1781, the 2nd Battalion of the 71st Regiment remained with Cornwallis while the 1st Battalion under McArthur's command went out under Banastre Tarleton to confront the Americans at Cowpens. The soldiers of the 1st Battalion who survived the fighting surrendered to the victorious Americans, and McArthur became a prisoner of war. The 2nd Battalion—all that was left of the regiment—had suffered so much attrition during the campaign that its highest-ranking officer at the Battle of Guilford Courthouse was its senior captain, Robert Hutcheson.[14]

Shortly before the surrender at Yorktown, Duncan Macpherson of Cluny—who had served as a major in the 71st until transferring to another regiment in 1779 as a lieutenant colonel—arrived at Portsmouth on July 12, 1781, to take command of the 71st.[15]

In addition to Duncan Macpherson of Cluny, there was at least one other officer named Duncan Macpherson who served, briefly, in the 71st Regiment. This officer had served in the 42nd Regiment before being promoted to major and transferred to the 2nd Battalion of the 71st Regiment on December 31, 1780.[16]

James Campbell of the 33rd Regiment was promoted to major and transferred to the 71st Regiment during the Virginia campaign.[17]

Officers in the 71st Regiment who surrendered at Yorktown were a lieutenant colonel, a major, a captain, eleven lieutenants, four ensigns and cornets, a quartermaster, a surgeon, a surgeon's mate, twenty-eight sergeants, nine drummers, and 242 rank and file. Some officers could expect to be exchanged, but the other officers and soldiers of the 71st Regiment would be prisoners of war for more than a year.[18]

In apparently purely administrative moves, Sir Thomas Stirling held the title of commanding officer of the 1st Battalion from 1781 to 1784, and Alexander Lindsay, 6th Earl of Balcarres, held the title of commanding officer of the 2nd Battalion from 1782 to 1784.[19] Simon Fraser, the titular commander of the 71st Regiment, died in 1782, and Stirling was promoted to the position of colonel of the regiment.[20]

At the end of the war, the Highlanders returned to Scotland and received their discharge at Perth; of the 2,693 soldiers sent to America to serve with the 71st Regiment, only 863 returned home.[21]

BRIEF BIOGRAPHICAL NOTES on the following members of the 71st Regiment are given in *The Cornwallis Papers*, edited by Ian Saberton:

David Burns, volume 3: page 318, note 13.

Donald Cameron, 2: 283, n. 64.

Archibald Campbell, one of three lieutenants in the 71st who bore his name, 2: 284, n. 65.

Charles Campbell (c. 1755-1780), 1: 227, n. 57.

Colin Campbell, Patrick Campbell, or Lawrence Robert Campbell, 2: 99, n. 78.

James Campbell, 4: 112, n. 18.

Colin Chisholme, 2: 361, n. 84.

Robertson Duncanson, 3: 330, n. 30.

Arthur Forbes, 2: 361, n. 83.

Alexander or Edward Fraser, 3: 327, n. 24.

Simon Fraser (1737/8-1813), 2: 357, n. 76.

John or Robert Grant, 3: 327, n. 25

Robert Hutcheson, 4: 136, n. 21.

Alexander McBean, 1: 135, n. 26.

Alexander MacDonald, 1: 178, n. 36.

Angus or Robert McDonald, 3: 324, n. 23.

Lieutenant McKensie, perhaps Roderick MacKenzie, 5: 189, n. 60.

Donald MacPherson, 5: 276, n. 9.

Donald McPherson, 3: 240, n. 158, and also 3: 360, n. 77.

Duncan MacPherson (1748-1817), 5: 124-25, n. 81.

Magnus Murchieson, 1: 365, n. 4.

John Nairne or William Nairne, 1: 320, n. 17.

John Stewart, 2: 284, n. 66.

EIGHT WOMEN PER COMPANY accompanied the regiment to America.[22] Under the British military system of the time, the women—supposedly wives of soldiers, although details may not have been scrutinized too closely—drew rations and accompanied the soldiers in camp. The women did laundry and other chores, and often nursed sick or wounded soldiers. During the campaigns of 1776 and 1777 under General William Howe, the troops—including the 71st Regiment—were allowed only six women per company.[23] Lieutenant Colonel Archibald Campbell of the 71st Regiment mentioned women in his orders of disembarkation at Savannah:

> GENERAL ORDERS 24th December 1778 at Tybee
> When a Yellow Pendant is hoisted at the Maintop Gallant Masthead, the Senior Officer of each Transport will order three Days Provisions to be immediately cooked for the Troops on Board of his Transport.
>
> On a White Flag with a Red Cross being displayed at the Foretop Gallant Masthead, the Army will prepare themselves for Landing, each Man to be completed to 60 Rounds of Ammunition and 2 Spare Flints.
>
> The Soldiers are to carry nothing on Shore with them, exclusive of their Ammunition, but a Blanket, 3 Days Provisions, and one Day's Rum.
>
> One careful soldier to be left in Charge of the Baggage on Board of each Transport, and no Man to be left behind that is able to do his Duty.
>
> No Woman to be permitted to land before it is expressly authorized in General Orders; such who are found on Shore previous to that period, are to be immediately confined in the nearest Guard.[24]

THE UNIFORMS OF THE 71ST REGIMENT evolved as wartime conditions changed. Like other British regiments, the Highlanders wore red coats made of wool broadcloth.[25] While Simon Fraser was raising the regiment in 1775, he was told the uniform would include "Highland kilts." Additional details included: "Facings, white; buttons numbered 71; lace, white with a red worm."[26] The plaid of the Highland regiments—the 42nd Regiment and the 71st Regiment—was described as "Government Set," now called the Black Watch Tartan. Along with the kilt, the Highlanders wore red-and-white checkered stockings. The headgear of the two regiments also reflected Scottish customs and was described as a stiffened Kilmarnock bonnet; the line companies of the 71st wore blue bonnets with black ostrich feathers, and the light companies wore a bright red hackle. Lt. Colonel Campbell ordered in 1778, before the expedition to Georgia, that trousers made of the Government Sett would be worn on campaigns, guard duty, and picket duty, but the kilt would be worn in garrison.[27]

The kilt proved unsuitable for warfare in America, and the Highland regiments switched to trousers or overalls. An inspection report for the 42nd Regiment in 1782 said that the Highlanders "could not appear in their full uniform for want of plaids, etc., which the C.O. [Commanding Officer] thought proper annually to dispose of during the late War, to purchase a more commodious dress for the American service, with the approbation of the Commander-in-Chief. The regiment appeared remarkably clean dressed—the men had on white strong ticken [a closely woven linen or cotton fabric] trousers with short, black cloth gaiters."[28] The 71st Regiment apparently quit wearing kilts sometime after arriving in Georgia at the end of 1778. In the autumn of 1780, General Charles Cornwallis planned to provide the unused kilts to a provincial regiment recruited among Scottish Highlanders who had recently immigrated to the Cross Creek country of North Carolina. "I intend to purchase for them," Cornwallis said, "some plaids of the 71st which they do not want and which, McArthur tells me, are ordered from Savannah to Charles Town."[29] The 71st Regiment wore white linen trousers in the sultry southern summers and sometimes wore brown wool trousers. While on the march, soldiers of the 71st carried a blanket, a musket, a sheathed bayonet, a water flask, and a knapsack stuffed with about fifty pounds of ammunition, food, and utensils.[30]

Several artists have depicted the uniforms of the 71st Regiment. Jeff Trexler shows the 71st Regiment at the Battle of Brier Creek in a painting titled "One Gallant Stand;" prints are available from the artist's website *Trexler Historical Art*, and the art was published on the cover of *Georgia Historical Quarterly* 100.2 (Summer 2016).

Don Troiani features a soldier in the 71st Regiment on page 44 of *Don Troiani's Soldiers of the American Revolution* (Mechanicsburg, PA: Stackpole Books, 2007); Troiani gives the following description:

> This soldier of Captain Aeneas Mackintosh's company in the 2nd Battalion is dressed as he would have appeared during the winter campaign of 1780-81 in North Carolina. His uniform coat is worn and patched, though his white waistcoat is in slightly better condition, redone with new woolen from that autumn. He wears tartan gaiter-trousers or "trews" made from his old plaid, although new brown trousers of wool had also been issued to his company. Spare clothing is rolled in his blanket, which is worn slung over the left shoulder in lieu of the red-painted knapsack usually worn for such

> purpose. Arms and accoutrements have been minimized to the belly-mounted cartridge box bearing its regimental "ornaments" of cast brass. On the opposite shoulder from the blanket roll is carried the haversack and tin water flask. His bonnet is trimmed according to regimental practice, with the two black ostrich plumes above his cockade denoting his status as a battalion company private.[31]

AN ARTIFACT OF THE 71ST REGIMENT is on display at The Charleston Museum in South Carolina. The coppery metal badge once was attached to a cartridge box, which was a leather pouch carried by soldiers to hold their ammunition. The badge displays a thistle—an emblem of Scotland—and the regiment's motto, "Quicquid aut facere aut patee," meaning "Whatever is to be performed or endured." Jack Boineau, a former member of the museum's board of trustees, discovered the badge in 1966 on the northeast end of Edisto Island along the North Edisto River. Presumably, a soldier in the 71st Regiment lost the badge during General Augustine Prevost's expedition to Charleston in 1779. After the British withdrew from Charleston and fought a battle at Stono Ferry, the army camped from June 28 to July 4 at the spot where Boineau found the badge 187 years later. The owner of the property donated the badge to the museum. Two similar badges have been found in South Carolina; one at the Camden battlefield and in the other in the Savannah River.[32]

PRIMARY SOURCES related to the 71st Regiment are preserved in institutions such as the national archives in Edinburgh and London. Ed Brumby cites an impressive array of primary sources in *71st Fraser Highland Regiment in the American War of Independence*, published in 2012 by Anchorprint.

The Tain & District Museum has an orderly book of the 71st Regiment covering from June to August 1783, at the end of the war when preparations were being made to disband the regiment. The catalog number is 1209.002; for information, see https://www.tainmuseum.org.uk/object.php?id=557

The Huntington Library has two orderly books of the 71st Regiment of Foot. One of them covers the summer of 1778 when the regiment was encamped at New York, and is available only in the reading room; the call number is mssHM617, and the link to the record is
https://catalog.huntington.org/record=b1702361
The other orderly book is from April 27 through June 15, 1779, and is available online at
https://cdm16003.contentdm.oclc.org/digital/collection/p15150coll7/id/17692

The Dallas Historical Society has two items related to the 71st Regiment in the Coit collection: A.35.77.9 – McIntosh's reports 1778-1779, and A.35.77.11 – A Weekly State of Capt. Angus McIntosh's Company Feb 1778 – June 1779. Robert S. Davis cited one of these sources in "Augusta in the Center: The Revolutionary War Battles of Kettle Creek and Shell Bluff," *Augusta Richmond County History* vol. 49, no. 1 (Spring 2018), page 29, note 19; the citation is: Angus McIntosh order book, 1778-1779, pp. 40-40a, J.T. Coit Family Papers (A3577), Dallas Historical Society, Dallas, TX. The captain who wrote these reports may have died in the autumn of 1779. A story on the siege of Savannah published two months after the battle in *Rivington's Royal Gazette* announced the death of Eneas McIntosh, Paymaster of the 71st Regiment, without specifying whether his death was a direct result of the battle. A correction in a subsequent paper gave the Paymaster's name as Angus McIntosh. Another officer named Eneas McIntosh was reported to be still at Savannah.[33]

AN ARCHAEOLOGICAL PROJECT discovered the remains of an enlisted man of the 71st Regiment on the site of the Battle of Camden, and the soldier received a dignified burial in 2023. The South Carolina Institute of Archaeology and Anthropology coordinated the project with funding from the South Carolina Battleground Protection Trust and assistance from the South Carolina Department of Natural Resources, the Richland County Coroner's Office, the Historic Camden Foundation, Kershaw County, the Columbia office of the TRC consulting company, and other organizations and individuals.

Archaeologists excavated seven graves and discovered the remains of fourteen soldiers. The member of the 71st Regiment was the only British soldier whose remains were found. Evidence of a gruesome skull injury indicates that he suffered a mortal wound in hand-to-hand combat. His comrades had laid his body out with his hands placed over his waist and had buried him about two feet deep. Because he had been buried in his uniform, archaeologists determined he had served in the 71st Regiment when they recovered pewter "71" buttons and the brass hardware from a sword belt.[34]

Three days of ceremonies culminated in the reburial of the soldiers. A procession carried their flag-draped coffins to Camden, where they lay in state at Historic Camden. On April 20, 2023, a funeral cortege featuring horse-drawn caissons proceeded to the grounds of historic Bethesda Presbyterian Church, where Anglican and Presbyterian clergymen conducted a funeral for the soldiers. The events culminated in a burial honors ceremony at the Camden Battlefield.

A bearer party from the 2nd Battalion of the Royal Regiment of Scotland served as pall bearers for the soldier from the 71st Regiment. "Remembering our fallen is a fundamental part of life in the military," commented Colonel Alcuin Johnson, a military attaché at the British Embassy in Washington. "I feel humbled to be able to represent both the British Defense Staff in the United States and the British Army at this important ceremony."[35]

Accusations of Atrocities

ATROCITIES THAT COULD be considered war crimes have been attributed to the 71st Regiment on several occasions, starting with their first battle at Long Island, New York, in August of 1776. An officer in the 71st Regiment whose name was not recorded wrote this letter:

> Rejoice, my friend, that we have given the rebels a d—'d crush. We landed on Long Island the 22d ult. without opposition. On the 27th we had a very warm action, in which the Scots regiments [the 42nd and the 71st] behaved with the greatest bravery, and carried the day after an obstinate resistance on the rebel side. But we flanked, and overpowered them with numbers. The Hessians and our brave Highlanders gave no quarters; and it was a fine sight to see with what alacrity they dispatched the rebels with their bayonets after we had surrounded them, so that they could not resist.
>
> Multitudes were drowned and suffocated in morasses, a proper punishment for all rebels. Our battalion outmarched the rest; and was always first up with the rebel fugitives. A fellow they call Lord Sterling one of their Generals, with two others, is prisoner, and a great many of their officers, men, artillery and stores.
>
> It was a glorious achievement, my friend, and will immortalize us, and crush the rebel colonies. Our loss was nothing. We took care to tell the Hessians that the rebels had resolved to give no quarters to them in particular, which made them fight desperately, and put all to death that fell into their hands. You know all stratagems are lawful in war

> especially against such vile enemies to their kind and country.
>
> The island is all ours and we shall soon take New York, for the rebels dare not look us in the face. I expect the affair will be over this campaign, and we shall all return covered with American laurels, and have the cream of American lands allotted us for our services.[1]

Another British officer claimed to be "greatly shocked at the massacre made by the Hessians and Highlanders after victory was decided."[2] A twenty-first century historian, however, asserts "There was also talk of massacres and blood-letting on a huge scale, particularly by the Hessians, but, although there were incidences of soldiers being killed while trying to surrender, there was no large-scale butchery. Most modern historians favor an assessment of around 1,000 total losses on the American side, with only 200 or so killed or wounded."[3]

Sir James Baird—an aristocratic Lowlander Scot who led the light troops—often appears in the accusations. When one accuser says "Sir James Baird of the 71st... is known in the northern part of America, as well as in these for his unfeeling heart and relentless cruelty" he may have been referring, notes William E. Cox, "to an incident that supposedly happened in a little village in Jamaica, New York." Cox explains:

> The story is that General Woodhull and two companions were captured in an inn by a party of British under Sir James Baird. Tradition says that Baird ordered Woodhull to shout "God save the King!" and because he shouted "God save us all," Baird struck him with his broadsword and would have killed him if Major Delancey, who accompanied Baird, had

not interfered. Woodhull later died from the blows delivered by Baird.[4]

Another historian believes the tale involving Woodhull is untrue or only partly true:

> There is a tradition that when Sir James Baird's men captured General Nathaniel Woodhull on Long Island, the Scotch officer ordered him to shout, "God save the King!" The American having cried instead, "God save us all!" Baird struck him with his broadsword, mangling Woodhull's arm. (B.J. Lossing. *The Pictorial Fieldbook of the Revolution.* 2 vols., New York, 1860: II, 811 n.) The tale is at best doubtful. It seems more likely that the New York patriot was wounded in attempting to escape. During a night attack in New Jersey Baird's troops butchered a number of Americans trapped in a farm house, an affair described as "one of the most disgraceful" of the Revolution (*New York Archives – Newspaper Extracts,* 1778: III, 457 n.)[5]

"It has been said that [Baird] was the officer who attacked and mortally wounded Brigadier General Nathaniel Woodhull after the latter's capture on Long Island, August 28, 1776," writes Colin Campbell. "All commentators on the matter seem to have ignored the fact that Baird was still in England, and about to set out for America, on June 14, 1776."[6]

Baird's dubious reputation in the North followed him to the South. His men were accused of rioting and pillaging after the capture of Savannah. Mordecai Sheftall described Baird's treatment of civilians:

> I endeavored, with my son Sheftall, to make our escape across Musgrove Creek... But on our arrival at the creek, after having sustained a very heavy fire of musketry from the light infantry under the command of Sir James Baird during the time we were crossing the common, without any injury to either of us, we found it high water. And my son not knowing how to swim, and we with about 186 officers and privates being caught as it were in a pen, and the Highlanders keeping up a constant fire on us, it was thought advisable to surrender ourselves prisoners, which we accordingly did and which was no sooner done than the Highlanders plundered every one amongst us except Major Low, myself and my son, who, being foremost, had an opportunity to surrender ourselves to the British officer, namely Lieutenant Peter Campbell, who disarmed us as we came into the yard formerly occupied by Mr. Moses Nunes.
>
> During this business Sir James Baird was missing but, on his coming into the yard, he mounted himself on the stepladder which was erected at the end of the house and sounded his brass bugle horn, which the Highlanders no sooner heard than they all got about him, when he addressed himself to them in Highland language, when they all dispersed and finished plundering such of the officers and men who had been fortunate enough to escape their first search.[7]

A teenage girl who lived in Savannah at the time of the battle reported:

> ...the Americans as they retreated wantonly fired on the 71st Regiment of Highlanders, without attempting a regular stand. This exposed the inhabitants to the fury of the British

soldiers, who then felt as though they were taking the place by storm. In consequence, before the officers could have time to stop them they committed much outrage, ripped open feather beds, destroyed the public papers and records, and scattered everything about the streets. Numbers of the enemy were taken in a swamp a few miles from Savannah. While Mr. Johnston was with his [loyalist] company in the pursuit he saw his father at his own door, and had only time to go up to Colonel Maitland [of the 71st Regiment] and request that he would put a guard at his father's house to secure his safety from the enraged troops, who knew not friend from foe. Colonel Maitland had been the early friend and college companion of my father-in-law Dr. Johnston, in Edinburgh, and meeting with his son at New York was like a father to him and did all he could to serve him. He, of course, placed a guard there.

My father in a few days sent a passport for myself and my aunt to come to town. I was then in my fifteenth year, and new to scenes of the kind, and having to stop within a mile of Savannah that the Hessian officer on duty there should examine our pass, I was dreadfully frightened. He soon allowed us to go on; and what a sight did the streets present of feathers and papers!

The meeting with my father I scarce need add was joyful...[8]

Although the British commander at Savannah reported "few or no depredations occurred," other witnesses claimed that British soldiers not only stole property, destroyed public records, and smashed fine furniture, but also stabbed defenseless Americans repeatedly with bayonets.[9]

In a report delivered to Congress, the governor of Georgia claimed: "the spirit of Rapine Insolence and Brutality indulged in by the soldiery, exceeds Description... People who have got out of Town since the Action say [the British commanders] profess great humanity, and totally disavow many horrid Acts committed by their People... for my Part I wish to leave nothing to their Humanity and as little to their Justice."[10]

There were horror stories about British treatment of civilians in Savannah: "Robbery, incendiarism, rape and murder were the fruits of that unhappy day," wrote a witness.[11]

At Brier Creek, Archibald Campbell's assertion that Baird's light infantrymen "spared very few that came within their reach" is balanced by Augustine Prevost's report that the British took two hundred prisoners.[12]

An anonymous account—based on information from someone who visited Brier Creek after the battle was over—accuses Baird's troops of murder and torture:

> ...Many parties of the Americans finding the day lost, threw down their arms and begged for quarter; but alas! they found none.
>
> The merciless 71st and light infantry boasted of sheathing their bayonets in the bosoms of these poor supplicants.
>
> The gentleman who gave this detail saw the next morning on the field and adjoining many clusters of Americans who had been massacred on their knees praying for quarter, most of their bodies disfigured with reiterated gashes and stabs.
>
> Sir James Baird of the 71st, whose name is known in the northern parts of America, as well as in these for his unfeeling heart and relentless cruelty, vaunted [or recounted] of having put to death nearly a dozen of these supplicants with

his own hands, and eventually [?] showed their blood oozing out of the touchhole of his fusee.

But what particularly added to the horrors of the field was that portion of the 71st in the night, after plundering the camp set afire (through sport) to the booth [brush?] hut where the American sick were, and where a number of the wounded had crawled to by way of sanctuary from the highlanders as well as to screen themselves from the inclemency of the night. Their half consumed, their parched and blackening bodies joined the next morning in offering a sight such perhaps as the sun seldom rises upon among the civilized nations. His nature (said the gentleman) sickened at the sight of so many spectacles of cruelty, and he turned with disgust from the scene.

His humanity soon after must have received an additional shock which language indeed can but weakly describe. It was about 14 or 15 wounded Americans that had been brought together under a pine tree, by some of the humane English in order, as he supposed to have their wounds dressed; but alas! they never experienced the Doctor's Aid. Twas 1 o'clock when the shade having moved from off them, they were exposed to a very burning sun, at the same time come up a 71st officer, and his party passing, stopped likewise to view them; several were just expiring and others appeared to be in the agonies of death. The rest that were able to speak joined in supplicating their pity and begged the soldiers for a little water from their canteens. Can it be believed that their piteous situation, their gaping wounds, their convulsed frames and agonizing tears, moved not these men's pity. Their prayers were answered with damns and wishes that all rebels were in the same predicament; and the party

> marched off without giving a drop of water to cool their parched lips.[13]

After the British Parliament heard accounts of Sir James Baird's conduct, he was recalled from the American field of action. He returned to Europe in the summer of 1779, a few months after the Battle of Brier Creek, and from that point the 71st Regiment restored its reputation.[14]

American officer Alexander Garden—an aide to General Nathanael Greene—said that "no act of inhumanity, or of oppression, was ever attached" to Lieutenant Colonel Archibald Campbell (who led the 71st Regiment in the capture of Savannah), or to Major Archibald McArthur (who led the regiment after the Siege of Charleston until he was taken prisoner at the Cowpens). Garden continued, "To the officers of the 63rd and 71st Regiment, with the exception of Weymess and Baird, the generous protection of property, and delicate attention to the sufferings of the afflicted, has been uniformly attributed."[15]

Colonel Stewart's War Stories

NINETEENTH-CENTURY SCOTTISH writer David Stewart gives a colorful but not wholly reliable account of the 71st Regiment in his two-volume work *Sketches of the Character, Manners, and Present State of the Highlanders of Scotland.*[1] An essay by Hugh Trevor-Roper in the book *The Invention of Tradition* contends that Stewart and Sir Walter Scott presented a view of Highland culture that was not grounded in historical fact. Trevor-Roper writes:

> Colonel David Stewart of Garth, who had joined the original 42nd Highlanders at the age of sixteen, had spent his entire adult life in the army, most of it abroad. As a half-pay officer after 1815, he devoted himself to the study first of the Highland regiments, then of Highland life and traditions: traditions which he had discovered more often, perhaps, in the officers' mess than in the straths and glens of Scotland. These traditions by now included the kilt and the clan tartans, both of which were accepted without question by the colonel.
>
> The notion that the kilt had been invented by an Englishman had indeed come to his ears, but he declined to entertain it for a minute: it was, he said, refuted by 'the universal belief of the people that the philibeg [short kilt] had been part of their garb as far back as tradition reaches.'
>
> He also declared with equal assurance that tartans had always been woven 'in distinctive patterns (or setts, as they were called) of the different clans, tribes, families and

districts.' For neither of these statements did he give any evidence.[2]

Stewart does not give any evidence for many of his statements about the 71st Regiment in the American Revolution. In a footnote about Lieutenant Colonel John Maitland, for example, Stewart states:

> During the skirmishing warfare of the Jerseys and Pennsylvania, in the years 1776 and 1777, he [Maitland] was particularly active. Ever on the alert, and having his Highlanders always ready, he attracted the particular notice of General Washington. Some communication having passed between them as old acquaintances, although then opposed as enemies, Colonel Maitland sent intimation to the American commander, that in future his men would be distinguished by a red feather in their bonnets, so that he could not mistake them, nor avoid doing justice to their exploits, in annoying his posts and obstructing his convoys and detachments; adding, that General Washington was too liberal not to acknowledge merit even in an enemy. Fraser's Highlanders wore the red feather after Colonel Maitland's death [immediately following the Siege of Savannah in 1779], and continued to do so till the conclusion of the war. Such was the origin of the red feather subsequently worn in the Highland bonnet, about which some idle tales have been repeated. In the year 1795, the red feather was assumed by the Royal Highland Regiment.[3]

The most glaring error of fact in the anecdote about the red feather is that Maitland could not have led Fraser's Highlanders in skirmishing warfare in 1776 and 1777 because he did not come to America until about 1777, and did not transfer to the 71st Regiment until late in 1778.[4] Also, it is unlikely that Maitland and Washington could have been old acquaintances—even though they both had served with British troops during the Seven Years' War—because Washington had served in North America and Maitland had served in Europe.

Another unsubstantiated claim in *Sketches* is that the Highlanders of the 42nd and 71st regiments were among the British troops under Cornwallis who came to the relief of the garrison at Princeton in January of 1777.[5]

Stewart's story of the Battle of Stono Ferry in June of 1779 varies from other, more official, accounts. Stewart writes:

> ...Colonel Maitland, with a battalion of Highlanders and some Hessians, was placed in a redoubt of hasty construction at Stono Ferry, an important pass, while the rest of the troops crossed over to John's Island. The communication had been kept up by a bridge of boats, but several of the boats having been removed by the Quartermaster-General, when he arrived with the fruits of his forage, the communication was interrupted. The separation of the British force was not to be neglected by the enemy, who had 5,000 men in the immediate neighbourhood. They, accordingly, pushed forward 2,000 men with the artillery. When their advance was reported, Captain Colin Campbell with 4 officers and 56 men, was sent out to reconnoiter, and to act according to circumstances. [A footnote says, "This gallant officer was son of Campbell of Glendaruel, in Argyle-shire."]
>
> A thick wood covered the approach of the enemy till they reached a clear field on which Captain Campbell's party stood. Disregarding this great inequality of numbers, and anxious to give time to those in the redoubt to prepare, he

instantly attacked with such vivacity, that the enemy were obliged to defend themselves. A desperate resistance ensued; all the officers and non-commissioned officers of the Highlanders fell, seven soldiers only remaining on their legs.

It was not intended that the resistance should be of this nature. But most of the party were men who had recently joined from prison [as prisoners of war], being some of those taken in Boston Harbour early in the war; and this being their first appearance before an enemy, they had not yet learned to retreat, nor had they forgotten what had been always inculcated in their native country, that to retreat was disgraceful. "When Captain Campbell fell, he desired such of his men as were able to make the best of their way to the redoubt; but they refused to obey, as it would bring lasting disgrace upon them all to leave their officers in the field, with none to carry them back." However, the enemy, either struck with this unexpected check from so insignificant a force, or waiting till the main body came up, ceased firing.

The seven men retired carrying their wounded officers along with them, and accompanied those of the soldiers who were able to walk. They were soon followed by the whole force of the enemy, determined to overpower those in the redoubts. In this they had in one part a partial success; the Hessians having got into confusion in the redoubt they occupied, the enemy forced an entrance, but the 71st having driven back those who had attacked their part of the redoubt, Colonel Maitland was enabled to detach two companies of the Highlanders to the support of the Hessians. The enemy were instantly driven out of the redoubt at the point of the bayonet, and while they were preparing for another attempt to storm, the 2d battalion of the Highlanders came up, when the Americans, despairing of success, retreated at all points, leaving many men killed and wounded.

The resistance offered by Captain Campbell, though not intended, and contrary, perhaps, to common practice in such cases, was, notwithstanding, highly honourable to those who made this determined stand, for no men need approach nearer to invincibility than those who fight against the most fearful odds, while life or the power of motion remains. This undaunted resistance also apparently saved the redoubt and those who defended it, for the time lost by the enemy in forcing their way through this little band of true soldiers, afforded time to their friends in the redoubt to prepare, and likewise to the 2d battalion in the island to march by the difficult and circuitous route left open for them.

[A footnote says, "The destruction of the bridge of boats by Lieutenant-Colonel Prevost was the cause of the delay in bringing to their support the 2d battalion from the island, and indeed, had nearly prevented their assistance entirely. Two temporary ferry-boats had been established, but the men who had charge of them being frightened by the firing, ran away and left the boats fixed on the wrong side. The enemy perceiving this from a height on the opposite side [the mainland] opened a galling fire from their great guns on the men as they stood on the banks of the river, without a cannon to return a shot. Lieutenant Robert Campbell, followed by a few soldiers, plunged into the water and swam across, returned with the boats, and thus enabled the battalion to cross over to the support of their friends. This brave and zealous officer was drowned some years afterwards in an attempt to save an old domestic who had fallen from a boat into the sea, in crossing from one of the islands of the Hebrides."]

> Nor was the firm resistance of those within the redoubt (if their embankments, hastily thrown up without guns or any other strength, could be so called) less honourable, seeing that 520 Highlanders and 200 Hessians successfully resisted all the efforts of an enemy 5,000 strong, (excepting the momentary impression on the Hessian part of the redoubt,) and this in comparison of the service performed with a trifling loss, which was only 3 officers and 32 soldiers killed and wounded, while that of the enemy exceeded the total strength of those attacked.[6]

Stewart notes that the commander of the Spring Hill Redoubt during the assault on Savannah in 1779 was a member of the 71st Regiment, Thomas Tawse. When Tawse was killed in action, Stewart writes, "Captain Archibald Campbell then assumed the command, and maintained his post till supported by the grenadiers of the 60th." As the Americans were driven back from the redoubt, Stewart writes, "a detachment of the 71st, ordered by Colonel Maitland to hasten to and assist those who were so hard pressed by superior numbers, could not overtake them."[7]

Stewart gives this account of the Battle of Camden in 1780:

> The British general moved from Cambden at 12 o'clock on the night of 15th August, with an intention of surprising and attacking the enemy. The American general moved from his ground at the same hour, and with a similar view of attacking the British. The hostile armies met half way, before 3 o'clock in the morning. The moon was full, and the night without a cloud. Some shots were exchanged by the advanced guards, but both generals, ignorant of each other's force, declined a general action, and lay on their arms till

morning. The ground on which they lay was a sandy plain with straggling trees, but a part of the ground on the left of the British was soft and boggy.

Each army formed the line of battle. The light infantry of the Highlanders, and the Welsh Fusiliers, were on the right; the 33rd regiment, and the Volunteers of Ireland, occupied the centre; the Provincials were on the left, with the marshy ground in their front. While the army was thus forming, Captain Charles Campbell, who commanded the Highland light companies on the right, placed himself on the stump of an old tree to reconnoiter, and observing the enemy moving as with an intention of turning his flank, he leaped down, saying to himself, "I'll see you damned first;" and calling to his men, "Remember you are light infantry; remember you are Highlanders: charge."

The attack was rapid and irresistible, and being made before the enemy had completed the movement by which they were to surround the right of the British, they were broken and driven from the field, before the battle commenced in the other parts of the line. When it did commence it was well supported on both sides, the centre of the enemy gaining ground.

There was a pause for some minutes, neither side firing or advancing, when Lord Cornwallis ordered the corps in the centre to open to their right and left, till a considerable space intervened; he then directed the Highlanders, "who began to be impatient at being left in the rear, while their friends were fighting in front," to move forward and occupy the vacant space. When this was done, his lordship cried out, "My brave Highlanders, now is your time." They instantly rushed forward; "the charge was like a torrent; the 33rd and Volunteers of Ireland accompanied the Highlanders, the enemy was penetrated and completely overthrown." [A footnote attributes the phrases in quotation marks to "Letter from Dr Chisholm of Bristol, an eye-witness."]

But the British charge did not strike on the whole of the American line. The thickness of the smoke prevented distinct vision, and such parts of the enemy's line, particularly on the right, as had not been acted upon by the charge, continuing to advance, gained the ground on which the Highlanders had been originally placed as a reserve. Here they gave three cheers for victory; but the smoke clearing up, they quickly saw their mistake; and a party of the Highlanders turning upon them, the greater part threw down their arms, while the remainder fled in all directions. The victory was complete, and decided by the bayonet, a very decisive instrument in a firm and steady hand.

The loss of the British was 1 captain, 1 subaltern, 2 serjeants, and 64 soldiers, killed; 2 field officers, 3 captains, 12 subalterns, 13 serjeants, and 213 soldiers, wounded. The Highlanders lost Lieutenant Archibald Campbell, and 8 soldiers, killed; and Captain Hugh Campbell, Lieutenant John Grant, 2 serjeants, and 30 privates, wounded.

[A footnote says, "In a letter from a respectable and intelligent eye-witness, Dr Chisholm of Bristol, the writer states, that there were many acts of individual prowess, the troops having several times closed on the enemy. 'One will suffice. A tough stump of a Sutherland Highlander, of the name of Mackay, afterwards my own bat-man, entered the battle with his bayonet perfectly straight, but brought it out twisted like a corkscrew, and with his own hand had put to death seven of the enemy.'"][8]

Stewart expresses mortification at the destruction of the 1st Battalion of the 71st Regiment at Cowpens in 1781:

> ...the Highlanders were ordered up; and rapidly advancing in charge, the enemy's front line moved off precipitately; and the second, which had as yet taken no share in the action, observing confusion and retrograding in their front, suddenly faced to the right, and inclined backwards; a manoeuvre by which a space was left for the front line to retreat, without interfering with the ranks of those who were now to oppose the advance of the Highlanders, "who ran in, with characteristic eagerness, desirous to take advantage of the confusion which appeared among the enemy." But the confusion was only in the front line; for Colonel Howard, commanding the reserve, threw in a fire upon the 71st when within forty yards of the hostile force.
>
> The fire was destructive; nearly one-half of their number fell; and those who remained were so scattered, having run over a space of five hundred yards at full speed, that they could not be united to form a charge with the bayonet, "the mode of attack in which their superiority lay." They were checked; but they did not fall back immediately, probably expecting that the first line and cavalry would push forward to their support. This did not happen; and after some irregular firing between them and Colonel Howard's reserve, the front line of the latter rallied, returned to the field, and pushed forward to the right flank of the Highlanders, who now saw no prospect of support, while their own numbers were diminishing, and the enemy increasing.
>
> They began to retire, and at length to run, the first instance of a Highland regiment running *from* an enemy!!! This retreat struck a panic into those whom they left in the

> rear, who fled in the greatest confusion; order and command were lost; the rout became general; few of the infantry escaped; and of the cavalry, who put their horses to full speed, not a man was taken.
>
> ...To the Highlanders it was particularly unfortunate, as being the first instance of defeat. But, as they were the most advanced in the attack, and the last in the retreat, and as their conduct before and afterwards was unexceptionable, it may be presumed, that, if they had been properly led on and supported, their conduct at Cowpens would have been worthy of the reputation they had acquired in all the other actions in which they had been engaged. The troops who fought at Stono Ferry ought to have died in the field at Cowpens.[9]

At Yorktown in the autumn of 1781, Stewart notes, "The enemy lost no time in commencing operations... A storm was attempted, the redoubts were carried, and the guns turned on the other parts of the entrenchments." He adds a footnote:

> One of these redoubts had been manned by some soldiers of the 71st. Although the defence of this redoubt was as well contested as that of the others, the regiment thought its honor so much implicated, that a petition was drawn up by the men, and carried by the commanding officer to Lord Cornwallis, to be permitted to retake it. There was no doubt of the success of the undertaking by men actuated by such a spirit, but as the retaking was not considered of importance in the existing state of the siege, the proposition was not acceded to.[10]

Stewart concludes his study of the 71st Regiment "by noticing the moral conduct of these men," which was "in every way equal to their military character." The men were "religious, brave, moral and humane," and their loyalty "proved to be genuine."[11]

Part 3: Biographical Sketches

Archibald Campbell (1739-1791)

Archibald Campbell compiled a distinguished record of service to his king and country. He was born August 24, 1739, at Inverary, Argyllshire. Before his nineteenth birthday he was appointed an ensign in the Corps of Engineers. He rapidly rose to the rank of captain-lieutenant and served in the West Indies.

By his twenty-ninth birthday he held the rank of lieutenant colonel and served as chief engineer in Bengal for more than four years. After a brief stint with the East India Company, he served as a lieutenant colonel in the East Indies.

He returned to Scotland, acquired the lands of Inverneill, and took a seat in Parliament in 1774 that he continued to hold while he served in the American war.[1]

In 1775 he helped raise the 2nd Battalion of the 71st Regiment. The regiment sailed from Scotland to reinforce the British forces in Boston. By the time the fleet reached America, Boston had been seized by the American rebels. Campbell was on one of the British transport ships that sailed into Boston Harbor and was captured by the Americans on June 16, 1776, and he became a prisoner of war.[2] If he was listed as commander of the 71st Regiment at Brandywine in September of 1777, as some sources indicate, it must have been as a bureaucratic matter only, because he would have still been a prisoner of war at that time.[3] Eventually, on May 6, 1778, Campbell was released in a prisoner exchange for Ethan Allen.[4]

Campbell commanded the British force that captured Savannah, Georgia, in December of 1778. He expected to be promoted from lieutenant colonel to brigadier general "to add weight and consequence to the trust reposed in me," but other officers objected on the basis of seniority. "Although I felt myself greatly disappointed in not obtaining the rank promised me," he wrote in a journal for publication, "yet the reflection of commanding three thousand men and of having an opportunity in exerting myself in the service of my king and country overbalanced every other consideration."[5]

In a letter not intended for publication, Campbell let his bitterness show. "I was obliged to march at the head of three thousand men as a lieutenant colonel in a country where lieutenant colonels and cobblers spring up like mushrooms, and are equally respected," Campbell complained to a friend. A colonel's name on a proclamation, Campbell wrote, "would have no other weight with the populace but what my arms enforced."[6]

After capturing Savannah, Campbell visited several small towns and settlements, urging Georgians to return to the fold as British subjects and to enroll in loyalist militia units. In the process, Campbell's simmering resentment over his rank came to a boil. He placed Commodore Hyde Parker's name ahead of his own name on a proclamation offering "the blessings of peace, freedom and protection most graciously tendered by His Majesty to his deluded subjects of America." Campbell wrote in his journal:

> As the name of Hyde Parker is placed in the first signature to this publication, and as it is certain from the instructions given me by His Majesty's Commissioners that neither this officer nor any other had authority to be joined with me in the reestablishment of civil government in Georgia, it is proper I should explain the motives which induced me to admit of his name being affixed to these publications and to precede my own in all such occasions.
>
> This officer had the title of commodore given him by Admiral Gambier, while it was my misfortune to have no

> distinction of that nature conferred upon me; being a lieutenant colonel only. Knowing well that such a title was become a mere drag among the rebels (cobblers and blacksmiths enjoying the rank in their army) I thought it more for the interest of government that I should sacrifice my own feelings on this occasion to the public good. Under the impression of such ideas, I entreated of Sir Hyde Parker to suffer me to use his name as the most effectual means of giving greater weight to these publications. Why the temporary rank of brigadier general was refused to a lieutenant colonel of four years standing, who had been selected as a fit officer to be entrusted with the command of eight battalions of infantry on a service of the first importance to the nation, especially as that extra rank could not interfere with or injure any superior officer in the line, is a question that can only be solved by those who had the power of granting it. If at a critical period of the war the punctilios of rank are to be considered of more essential consequence than the success of His Majesty's army, a superior officer however ill qualified might have been appointed to command the expedition to Georgia.[7]

Campbell's sensitivity to rank soon came up again when a higher-ranking British officer arrived in Savannah. General Augustine Prevost left East Florida and marched up the Georgia coast, capturing the fortified port of Sunbury. As Prevost approached Savannah, Campbell moved out of the best house in town to let Prevost move in. General Prevost arrived at Savannah in mid-January of 1779 and immediately took command of the army that Campbell had brought to Georgia. "In the midst of my successful career," Campbell wrote, "I felt this supercession severely, but he was my superior in rank and it was my duty to obey."[8]

Campbell told a friend that Prevost, at age fifty-nine, "seems a worthy man, but too old and inactive for this service. He will do in garrison, and I shall gallop with the light troop."[9]

While Prevost remained in Savannah, Campbell led an expedition up the Savannah River to Augusta and back down to the outposts established to protect Savannah. He sought permission to go home to marry his fiancée and to manage his personal affairs, which had fallen into disarray while he was a prisoner of war in America for two years before he was exchanged and assigned to conquer Georgia.[10]

Campbell embarked on a warship that sailed from Savannah on March 13 and reached Plymouth, England, on May 14. Two days later he met with Lord George Germain, the Secretary of State for the Colonies. Germain had written a letter to Campbell in March, but Campbell did not receive a copy of the letter until he reached England in May. British officials were encouraged, Germain wrote, "by knowing you were to command the troops appointed for the expedition to Georgia, to expect that every advantage would be derived from it which the exertion of great abilities, improved by a thorough knowledge of the military science, at the head of troops distinguished by their intrepid valour, would obtain."

Germain praised "the arrangements you had made for the security of the province and the establishment of good order and tranquility among the loyal inhabitants," calling them "equally judicious with the measure you had taken for its conquest."

On May 17 Campbell met with King George III, "kissed hands, and was most graciously received." Germain told Campbell that "His Majesty was most graciously pleased to declare that the rapidity of your success had exceeded his hopes" and that Campbell's achievements earned the king's "fullest approbation."[11]

Also, soon after arriving in London, Campbell received a letter from Sir Henry Clinton, the British commander in America. "Your establishment of civil government," Clinton said, was "highly proper." Clinton told Campbell "Your success has been completed."[12]

Writing from America, General Augustine Prevost gave Campbell credit for conceiving the strategy to impose military control over Georgia, although he gave his brother James Mark Prevost the credit for planning and executing the attack at Brier Creek. "I have before now expressed to your lordship how much I felt to be deprived of the assistance of an officer of Colonel Campbell's merit," Augustine Prevost told Germain. "Indeed it was not till after repeated solicitations and his mentioning his being unwell that I could possibly see him give up the execution of a plan formed by himself."

The American army's advance to Brier Creek, as Campbell predicted, "drew them into that snare," Augustine Prevost wrote, "which was so fatal to them, so glorious to His Majesty's troops, and honourable to Lieut-Colonel Prevost who planned and executed it so judiciously."[13]

The issue of rank continued to irritate Campbell. Germain told him "It gave me much concern to find that the jealousies of the senior officers should have interposed to prevent Sir Henry Clinton from giving you the extraordinary rank he had intended, and to which your merit so well entitles you." Germain continued, "I trust it will not be long before he will find an opportunity of gratifying your wishes and his own inclination."[14]

Campbell's wishes were gratified on December 8, 1779, ten months after the Battle of Brier Creek, when he was promoted to the rank of brigadier general in Jamaica.

He apparently was still in London in January of 1780, based a letter to a lieutenant in the 71st Regiment; some readers assume the lieutenant was Campbell's son, which is not plausible because Campbell did not have any children. The letter says:

LONDON, 15th January, 1780
My Dear Hugh:
In my last, I informed you that the Defence of Savannah gave great Satisfaction here; and it has had a very good Effect upon the Minds of the People, whose Spirits were down on Account of the Length of Time which elapsed without any Effort even, to do Good. And though this was in some Measure no more than a gallant Defence, yet it made an Impression almost equal to what a Victory would have done.

The Plan which is now understood to be determined upon here for carrying on the War, is to take a certain Number of Posts in America, in such a Way as to command the Trade of the Country, and to have no other Object in America than the maintaining of these Posts, and the ruling of the Trade by our Fleets.

The Posts said to be fixed upon, are Halifax, Penobscot, New York, Portsmouth in Virginia, Charlestown, Savannah and St. Augustine. To accomplish which, we imagine that you are now employed in taking Charlestown, and establishing a Post at Portsmouth.

These Objects being accomplished, we understand 12,000 Men are to be detached to the West Indies, which is to be the active Seat of War against the French and Spaniards.

It is evident that unless we can carry on an active and defensive War against them abroad, we can never succeed or do well. Last Campaign we were all defensive, and every

Thing went badly with us. I never wish to see such another Campaign.

We will be anxious, however, to know what our wise Heads in America will think of this plan for the American War. To be sure, the more Troops you can spare from thence to drub the common Enemies, the better. Yet I fear the Number mentioned is more than you can give, after putting the Posts mentioned in a proper Condition.

We have had Nothing new of any Moment going on since I wrote you. Indeed, Parliament has been adjourned all the Time, which prevents our furnishing so much as we otherwise do of the State Operations.

It is believed by many that there is an Alliance formed between us and Russia; and I am inclined to believe that that either is the Case, or that there is a Treaty in forwardness. They can very well spare us twenty Ships of the Line, which would enable us to detach a great Force to the West Indies. Indeed, it would completely restore us to the Superiority of the Seas. There is nothing settled yet between us and the Dutch, about our Right of searching their Ships. I expect our Court will persist in this Right, and I do not imagine the Dutch will chuse to go to War with us.

Farewell my dear Boy,
I ever am, unalterably yours,
A. Campbell.
Lieut., and Adjutant Hugh Campbell,
2nd Battalion, 71st Regiment, Georgia.[15]

Archibald Campbell was appointed lieutenant governor of Jamaica in 1781 and appointed governor in 1782. He retired from service in Jamaica in 1784, and the next year was created a Knight of the Bath.

He served as governor of Madras in India from 1786 to 1789 and also commanded the 74th Highlanders in 1787. In 1790 he was appointed Hereditary Usher of the White Rod. He died in 1791 and was buried in Westminster Abbey.[16]

Charles Campbell (c. 1755-1780)

Charles Campbell received a commission as a lieutenant in the 1st Battalion of the 71st Regiment in November 1775. He was promoted to fill a vacancy when a captain was killed in the capture of Savannah on December 29, 1778.[1]

Campbell wrote a letter describing the Siege of Charleston:

Charlestown
May 20th. 1780
Since my last to you, my dear Father, I have been an actor in two of the most obstinate and most successful contests that the British arms have experienced this war; the defense of Savannah and the reduction of Charlestown. As it must surprise the people of England, that a Rebel garrison should stand a six weeks siege, against Sir H.C. [Henry Clinton], and a British army, it would be unpardonable of me, not to give you some account of our operations before Charlestown. On the 26th of December last, Sir H. sailed from York, with an army of eight thousand men, and a number of men of war; hard and contrary winds scattered the fleet, and before the army landed in South Carolina, it was the middle of February. They took possession of Johns and James Islands to the southward of Charleston; got the transports and small craft up Stono river, that divides the two Islands, and was employed to near the end of March in landing stores and provisions, making every preparation for a siege, and waiting for a Corps of 1500 men that marched from Savannah across the country,

under the orders of General Paterson. About the 20th of March, the Light Infantry, and Grenadiers took position on the main, along Ashley river, stretching from Wapoo cut to Drayton's house, 12 miles above Charlestown. On the 28th, Paterson's corps joined, and early the next morning, the body of the army was thrown across Ashley river. On the 30th the town was invested.

Charlestown is a handsome and well built town situated on the extremity of a tongue of land formed by two large & navigable rivers, Cooper and Ashley, it lays open to the sea, and has the entrance of its harbor defended by a strong fort erected on Sullivan's Island. [An unsuccessful attack on the fort at Sullivan's Island in 1776] induced our Navy to hold the reduction of it exceeding difficult, and come to pass it hazardous. Our enemy deemed both impracticable. Charlestown is fortified to the Country by a very strong and well constructed entrenchment; covered with a wet and dry ditch, and a double abattis, and defended at every point by a numerous artillery. To the sea its covered by four Bastions mounting heavy cannon, and connected with curtains for musketry; its flanks to the rivers are protected with shipping and batteries.

The strength of Charlestown, its consequence to the country, the recent example shown them at Savannah, a belief that Fort Sullivan would effectually prevent our navy from getting up to the Town, and a persuasion that our army could not afford a Corps across Cooper river to cut off their retreat, induced them to throw their whole force into town and stand a siege.

Finding the town in this situation, and the enemy thus disposed, we opened our trenches on the evening of the 1st of April about eight hundred yards from their works. By the 10th, we finished our first parallel and completed our batteries. On this day we summoned the Town to surrender; their answer was short and spirited: a determination to hold out to the last extremity. A few days after this, we opened near 20 pieces of artillery, and a number of small mortars; their works being all of clay, our shot was of little effect, but our shells did some execution. A reinforcement arriving from York, Lord Cornwallis with a detachment of near 3000 men was thrown over Cooper river; his Lordship took a position along the banks of the river that prevented their receiving any supplies from the Country, and effectually cut off their retreat. To this movement the Admiral had passed fort Sullivan with little loss, and anchored within a mile of the Town. By the beginning of May we had drawn a parallel, and completed batteries within 150 yards of their works. On the eighth we summoned them again. but could not agree on the terms. Hostilities again commenced. and with more vigour than ever. On the 11th they sent a flag accepting of our terms, and on the 12th the garrison and town of Charlestown surrendered prisoners of war. By this conquest we have got near 300 pieces of artillery, 4 ships of war, and from five to six thousand prisoners...

My Mother has wrote that my Uncle intends purchasing me a Majority as soon as he can; if he has it immediately it will be of more service to me than two thousand pounds, ten years service. As I am but a young Captain I must give a great deal more than the

> regulation; if you can persuade Uncle to lodge £2000 in some Agents hands, and send me a letter of credit on him, I am almost certain of getting a Majority in a few months after the receipt of it. If you could procure me letters of recommendation to Sir H.C., Lord Cornwallis, and General, it would be of great service to me. When my Uncle, and you, consider that I am a Captain of near two years standing, without my Comm [commission] having cost me anything, and that I have been 6 years in the army, and during that period have not drawn much more than £200 and am now in a situation to trouble you more, accept for, I am persuaded you will not think my prompt request unreasonable if its granted I will soon be high in the army.
>
> Captain Charles Campbell[2]

Some accounts say Campbell took part in burning Thomas Sumter's house on May 28, 1780, but Banastre Tarleton—the commander of the British force involved—reported that the force did not include any element of the 71st Regiment.[3]

In the summer of 1780, Campbell was stationed at Ninety Six in command of the 71st Regiment's light companies, except for seventy men who had been detached to Tarleton's Legion. General Charles Cornwallis suggested that twenty of the light infantrymen should be selected for a cavalry troop in the 71st Regiment, and that Campbell should command the troop.[4] When the light companies were called in to assist Cornwallis against an advancing American army, they left Ninety Six on August 9 and arrived in Camden on August 13.[5]

At the Battle of Camden on August 16 the 71st Regiment was placed in reserve and supported other troops in a decisive British victory. Scottish writer David Stewart, who has been accused of not supporting his statements with evidence, gives the following statement about Campbell:[6]

> The light infantry of the Highlanders, and the Welsh Fusiliers, were on the right; the 33rd regiment, and the Volunteers of Ireland, occupied the centre; the Provincials were on the left, with the marshy ground in their front. While the army was thus forming, Captain Charles Campbell, who commanded the Highland light companies on the right, placed himself on the stump of an old tree to reconnoiter, and observing the enemy moving as with an intention of turning his flank, he leaped down, saying to himself, "I'll see you damned first;" and calling to his men, "Remember you are light infantry; remember you are Highlanders: charge." The attack was rapid and irresistible, and being made before the enemy had completed the movement by which they were to surround the right of the British, they were broken and driven from the field, before the battle commenced in the other parts of the line.[7]

Following the Battle of Camden, the light infantry "were exhausted by the fatigue of the preceding night's march, and by the action and pursuit of the day," according to Tarleton. Nevertheless, the light infantry and the British Legion set out the next morning to pursue American partisan commander Thomas Sumter. At dawn on August 18, Campbell led a detachment across the Wateree River "with instructions to hold out a white handkerchief on Rocky mount, if Colonel Sumpter continued his route up the Wateree," Tarleton said. "Captain Campbell, on his arrival at Rocky mount, took a prisoner, and displayed the appointed signal." Tarleton's infantry and artillery then crossed the river in boats while his cavalry "crossed the part that was not fordable by swimming."[8] Tarleton continued:

> In the mean time, Colonel Sumpter, with his detachment, consisting of one hundred continentals, seven hundred militia, and two pieces of cannon, directed his march towards the fords near the Catawba settlement, where he intended to pass the river, in order to take a position eligible for his own numbers, and well adapted to receive the fugitives of the American army. This officer, since the period that he received reinforcements from General Gates, had been fortunate in his operations: He had taken above one hundred British soldiers, he had secured one hundred and fifty loyal American militia, and he had captured near fifty wagons loaded with arms, stores, and ammunition. Information was obtained at Rocky mount, that these trophies of success were in Sumpter's possession, and under the escort of his advanced guard: The impossibility of reaching that part of his corps, without the knowledge of the main body, determined Lieutenant-colonel Tarleton to hang upon the rear, and watch an opportunity of attempting something in that quarter: He was sensible that no alarm had been given, and that no jealousy could yet be entertained of his having passed the Wateree. These incidents, which at first light appeared so favourable, were nearly counterbalanced by the diligence of Sumpter's march, by the exhausted condition of the British light troops, by the intense heat of the day, and by the ground yet to be gained before an attack could take place. When Tarleton arrived at Fishing creek at twelve o'clock, he found the greatest part of his command overpowered by fatigue; the corps could no longer be moved forwards in a compact and serviceable state: He therefore

determined to separate the cavalry and infantry most able to bear farther hardship, to follow the enemy, whilst the remainder, with the three-pounder, took post on an advantageous piece of ground, in order to refresh themselves, and cover the retreat in case of accident.

The number selected to continue the pursuit did not exceed one hundred legion dragoons and fifty foot soldiers. The light infantry furnished a great proportion of the latter. This detachment moved forwards with great circumspection: No intelligence, except the recent tracks upon the road, occurred for five miles. Two of the enemy's vedettes, who were concealed behind some bushes, fired upon the advanced guard as it entered a valley and killed a dragoon of the legion: A circumstance which irritated the foremost of his comrades to such a degree, that they dispatched the two Americans with their sabres before Lieutenant-colonel Tarleton could interpose, or any information be obtained respecting Colonel Sumpter. A serjeant and four men of the British legion soon afterwards approached the summit of the neighbouring eminence, where instantly halting, they crouched upon their horses, and made a signal to their commanding officer. Tarleton rode forwards to the advanced guard, and plainly discovered over the crest of the hill the front of the American camp, perfectly quiet, and not the least alarmed by the fire of the vedettes. The decision, and the preparation for the attack, were momentary. The cavalry and infantry were formed into one line, and, giving a general shout, advanced to the charge. The arms and artillery of the continentals were secured before the men could be assembled: Universal consternation immediately ensued throughout the camp; some opposition was, however, made from behind the wagons, in front of the militia. The numbers, and extensive encampment of the enemy, occasioned several conflicts before the action was decided. At length, the release of the regulars and loyal militia, who were confined in the rear of the Americans, enabled Lieutenant-colonel Tarleton to stop the slaughter, and place guards over the prisoners.

The pursuit could not with propriety be pushed very far, the quantity of prisoners upon the spot demanding the immediate attention of great part of the light troops. Lieutenant-colonel Tarleton lost no time in sending for the detachment left at Fishing creek, thinking this additional force necessary to repulse any attempt the enemy might make to rescue their friends. All the men he could assemble were likewise wanted to give assistance to the wounded, and to take charge of the prisoners; the troops who had gained this action having a just claim to some relaxation, in order to refresh themselves after their late vigorous exertions.

Captain Charles Campbell, who commanded the light infantry, was unfortunately killed near the end of the affair. His death cannot be mentioned without regret. He was a young officer, whose conduct and abilities afforded the most flattering prospect that he would be an honour to his country. The loss, otherwise, on the side of the British was inconsiderable; fifteen non-commissioned officers and men, and twenty horses, were killed and wounded.[9]

General Charles Cornwallis lamented the death of Campbell in his report on the Battle of Fishing Creek:

Lt Colonel Tarleton executed this service with his usual activity and military address. He procured good information of Sumpter's movements and by forced marches came up

> with and surprised him in the middle of the day on the 18th near the Catawba Fords. [Tarleton] totally destroyed or dispersed his detachment consisting then of 700 men, killing 150 on the spot and taking two pieces of brass cannon and 300 prisoners and 44 waggons. [Tarleton] likewise retook 100 of our men who had fallen into their hands, partly at the action at Hanging Rock and partly in escorting some wagons from Congarees to Camden, and he released 150 of our militia men or friendly country people who had been seized by the rebels. Captain Campbell, who commanded the light infantry, a very promising officer, was unfortunately killed in this affair. Our loss otherways was trifling.[10]

Scottish writer David Stewart gives a dramatic account of the Battle of Fishing Creek that contradicts some of the information provided by Tarleton and Cornwallis:

> ...General Sumpter, with a strong corps, occupied positions on the Catawba River, which commanded the road to Charlestown, and from which it was necessary to dislodge him. For this purpose, Colonel Tarleton was appointed to command the cavalry and a corps of light infantry, under Captain Charles Campbell of the 71st regiment. The heat was excessive; many of the horses had failed on the march, and not more than forty of the infantry were together in front, when, on the morning of the 18th, they came in sight of Fishing Creek, and saw a smoke at a short distance on their right. The serjeant of the advanced guard halted his party, and went forward with caution to ascertain the cause of the smoke. In a few minutes he saw an encampment, with arms piled, and with few sentinels, and no picquets. No persons were stirring except a few employed in cooking; the rest lay

in groups apparently asleep, as if harassed by a long march. The serjeant reported what he had seen to Captain Campbell, who commanded in front, and as not a moment was to be lost, as a discovery of their situation might have led to serious consequences, Captain Campbell, with his usual promptitude, formed as many of the cavalry as had come up, and with the forty of the Highland light infantry, rushed forward, and directing their route to the piled arms, and quickly secured them and surprised the camp. The success was complete; a few men were killed; nearly 500 prisoners surrendered, and the rest dispersed in all directions, General Sumpter fled without his coat. Thus the object of the expedition was in a few minutes accomplished, (before Colonel Tarleton came up,) and with trifling loss, had it not been for the death of Captain Campbell, who was killed by a random shot, which in a great measure counterbalanced the joy of so easy a victory. His death rendered his own men in a manner frantic, for he had secured the affection of those he commanded in a most singular degree.

[Footnote] Captain Campbell was son of Mr Campbell of Ardchattan. "He was a young man of promptitude and decision, and gave promise that he would be an honour to his profession and to his country."[11]

Major Archibald McArthur, who commanded both battalions of the 71st Regiment, informed Campbell's father that the spirited young officer had been killed in action:

Camp at Camden
August 20th 1780
Sir,

It gives one infinite concern to inform you that your son who escaped unhurt in the Action of the 16th instant, between our Army under Lord Cornwallis & the Rebel Army commanded by Genl. Gates, when the latter was totally defeated, but in the action of the 18th instant when Col. Tarleton with part of the Cavalry of the Legion not one hundred in number & Capt. Charles Campbell with nearly the same number of the Battn. of Light Infantry, which he commanded this campaign, surprised & defeated Col. Sumpter, who had not less than eight hundred men. Capt. Campbell advancing at the head of his men with his usual intrepidity received a musquet ball in his breast & instantly expired, much regretted not only by the 71st Regiment, but by the whole Army as a very spirited and intelligent officer. He was decently interred that evening on the field of Battle. His effects with the Regiment will be immediately disposed of, most of his baggage is at Savannah. When Ret. arrives it shall be disposed of, & so soon as his Campany's are & any debts he may be owing are paid, the ballance shall be remitted... for your behoof.

I have the honor to be Sir
Your most Able Son
Arch'd McArthur
Major 71st Regiment (Confederate)[12]

William Erskine (1728-1795)

William Erskine joined the Scots Greys in 1743 and obtained a commission as a cornet at Fontenoy in 1745. Scottish writer David Stewart says that Erskine's father commanded the regiment at the Battle of Fontenoy and William Erskine carried a standard. Stewart writes:

> In the morning of the battle Colonel Erskine tied the standard to his son's leg, and told him, "Go, and take good care of your charge; let me not see you separate; if you return alive from the field, you must produce the standard." After the battle the young Cornet rode up to his father, and showed him the standard as tight and fast as in the morning.[1]

William Erskine distinguished himself in service in Germany during the Seven Years' War (1756-1763), rising to the rank of major in the 15th Light Dragoons in March of 1759, and to the rank of lieutenant colonel in 1762. His regiment captured sixteen stands of colors at Emsdorf, and he presented them to King George III.

When the 71st Regiment was formed in anticipation of the War of the American Revolution, Erskine served as the lieutenant colonel of the 1st Battalion. He assumed command of the 71st Regiment when the regiment's other lieutenant colonel—Archibald Campbell of the 2nd Battalion—was captured as a prisoner of war in June of 1776. When the regiment was subdivided temporarily into three battalions in 1776, Erskine received an appointment as brigadier general in command of all three battalions. Under Erskine's command, the regiment fought in the Battle of Brooklyn in August of 1776 with Lieutenant Colonel

John Maitland in command of the 1st Battalion. In October of 1776, Erskine took responsibility as quartermaster of the army at New York. He received a promotion to colonel of the 80th Regiment in 1777. In addition to serving as quartermaster, he continued to lead troops into battle and participated in the Monmouth Campaign in the summer of 1778. Meanwhile, Campbell was released in a prisoner exchange in 1778 and was in command of the 71st Regiment in the summer of 1778. Erskine led five infantry battalions and a cavalry squadron in an expedition up the Hudson River in November of 1778, and commanded the eastern district of Long Island during the winter of 1778-79. He was promoted to major general in 1779. Erskine retired from the strenuous duties of quartermaster general in the summer of in 1779 and went to England.

After the American war, Erskine received a promotion to lieutenant general in 1787, and was awarded the title of baronet in 1791. He served as second in command to the Duke of York in the Flanders campaign of 1793-1795.[2]

Robert Jackson (1750-1827)

Robert Jackson was a surgeon's mate in the 71st Regiment. His biography "Life of Robert Jackson, M.D., Inspector-General of Army-Hospitals" is included as a preface to the third edition of his book *A View of the Formation, Discipline, and Economy of Armies*. He was the son of a poor farmer in Scotland near the falls of the River Clyde. He served three years as an apprentice to a surgeon in Lanarkshire and then studied in Edinburgh. To earn money while he was at the university, he spent two summers working on whaling ships in Greenland.[1]

Leaving the university without graduating, he went to Jamaica in 1774 and became an assistant to a general practitioner. He took medical responsibility for a detachment of the 60th Regiment, visiting the barracks several times a day and learning about tropical fevers. After three years, he decided to leave Jamaica partly because slavery offended him:

> ...his moral perceptions were shocked by the anomalies of the slave system, which he could not reconcile to equity or reason... The more he considered the matter of man's claiming man as property, and as goods and chattels, to be bought and sold at pleasure, the more revolting it seemed to his mind. Slavery too demoralizes in a variety of ways; and this must have been painfully perceptible to his pure and just spirit. He yearned to quit the place...[2]

Jackson decided to go the mainland and volunteer to help the British subdue the American Revolution. After he embarked, the ship's captain put him off because he did not have a pass to leave Jamaica. He walked 130 miles from the eastern end of Jamaica to the western end, falling ill from heat and poor nutrition, to catch a ship bound for New York. A fellow passenger offered to secure a commission in the New York Volunteers, but he could not afford to wait while the paperwork went through, so he investigated other opportunities:

> The first battalion of the 71st regiment (or Fraser's Highlanders) was encamped at the time [the summer of 1778] in MacGowan's Pass, about seven miles from New York. It was commanded by Lieutenant-colonel (afterward Sir Archibald) Campbell, an officer standing high in public opinion. Our adventurer... advanced to the colonel's marquee... [and] offered himself as a military volunteer to the 71st regiment. The colonel, on this, enquired if he was a native of Scotland? Being answered in the affirmative, the colonel next asked to whom he was known in New York? The answer was that he was known to no one in New York... Colonel Campbell proved himself on this occasion practically not only a judge of a gentleman but an illustration of the character by his frank and generous reply: "Sire, I require no testimony as to your being a gentleman. Your countenance and address satisfy me on that head. I will receive you into the regiment with pleasure—but then I have to inform you, Mr. Jackson, that there are seventeen on the list before you, who are of course entitled to prior promotion."
>
> Young Jackson was eminently one of nature's gentlemen, with the stamp of *her* aristocracy on his intellectual and open brow. Colonel Campbell recognized him intuitively for what he really was. The next question was, if the volunteer had been bred to a profession? "Yes, he had studied medicine, was now desirous to carry arms." This

question was followed by another, which came to the point, "When will you join?" "Tomorrow" was the prompt and characteristic reply... *"Tomorrow"* might be assumed as his motto in regard to any call of duty or trial.

Next morning, accordingly, he was in the camp at an early hour. As soon as he was ushered into the colonel's tent, an orderly was dispatched for the surgeon of the regiment, the colonel with considerable kindness observing that... one of the surgeon's mates was absent and probably would not return... The surgeon, Doctor Stewart, came in during the conference, and everything was speedily settled... Furnished with the not very luxurious outfit of a soldier's tent, blanket, and ration, he never in his life, perhaps, enjoyed a day of more unalloyed and hearty content, as he was often heard to declare, than when he joined the 71st. Though reclining on a bundle of straw, and after a dinner of which salt pork had formed the whole bill of fare, he felt comparatively as if he had been translated to Paradise. Rescued as he as from indigence and starvation, he had now the proud and blessed conviction that he was to earn his bread by the humble exertion of the talents God had bestowed upon him...

While the regiment remained at MacGowan's Pass, it continued healthy, but on moving to King's Bridge at the end of the month of July, it soon became very sickly. A division of labour now took place between himself and the other hospital mate of the corps; he undertaking the hospital duties, and his colleague those of the camp... Regimental hospitals in those days were... simply collections of sick men, huddled together, with little order or arrangement, how they could and as they could... No hospital clothing was provided by the state, and every sick man was expected to bring his own blanket. Fortunately a sick man does not require much food.

> In the days referred to his choice of esculents was limited to salt beef or pork, which he might wash down with his ration of rum. Our young hospital mate was not a man to shut his eyes where the well being of his fellow-creatures was in question. He had thought more on matters of hospital arrangement than the surgeon, who, like a sensible man, permitted him to make such alterations in internal economy as could be adopted without expense...[3]

Shortly after Jackson joined the 71st Regiment, Colonel Campbell led an expeditionary force that sailed southward, captured Savannah, and restored colonial rule in Georgia. Jackson continued to hone the expertise in treating tropical fevers that he had developed in Jamaica. Inevitably, the doctor became the patient:

> At Ebenezer in Georgia, at a season when the thermometer in the coolest part of the house often stood at ninety-six and even sometimes rose above it, I was seized with the ardent bilious fever, which at that time made dreadful ravage among the troops. For six or seven days I did not once shut my eyes; my thirst was great, yet every sort of liquid which I could procure was nauseous; the distinction of paroxysm and remission was no longer perceivable; the pulse at the wrist was neither uncommonly frequent nor strong; but the pulsation of the descending aorta was so great as to shake the whole frame; anxiety and restlessness were intolerable; in short, the torment was so excessive that human nature could scarcely suffer more. The situation was precarious; and without much reflection I indulged the desire of being carried to Savannah; though the distance was not less than twenty-five miles. An open carriage, the only conveyance

> which the country afforded, was provided for the purpose; and I was put into it, in a very feeble and distressed condition. Fortunately the day was cloudy, and cooler than ordinary. The roads were likewise soft and sandy. Though the carriage was very defective, the motion was no ways unpleasant; and I had not travelled two miles before I felt a wonderful increase of vigour. It rained heavily about half way, and before I reached Savannah, I was drenched to the skin. The effects which might have been expected, did not follow. Instead of being hurt, I was surprisingly benefited. I walked into the house with strength and firmness, ate something without dislike, and slept sound the following night; in short, obtained a perfect remission of the fever.[4]

At the Battle of Cowpens in 1781, American riflemen fired at Lieutenant Colonel Banastre Tarleton; he was not hit but his horse fell beneath him. Jackson offered his horse to Tarleton. Jackson was "an obscure individual," he told Tarleton, while Tarleton's "safety was of the highest importance to the army." Jackson's heroic self-sacrifice was described by a captain in Tarleton's Legion, but Tarleton himself did not acknowledge the "remarkable instance of duty and devotion" that perhaps saved his life and kept him from being taken prisoner. Jackson never mentioned the episode himself except to confirm that it was true.[5]

Riding Jackson's horse, Tarleton charged into the thick of the fighting. The American cavalry met the charge and drove off the British dragoons. The commander of the American cavalry—William Washington—took up pursuit of Tarleton. Washington was alone ahead of his men when Tarleton and a few of his horsemen turned to fight. In hand-to-hand combat, Washington broke his saber at the hilt. Tarleton himself charged in and swung his saber at Washington, who blocked it with his broken saber. Tarleton fired his pistol, missing Washington and wounding Washington's horse. As Washington's cavalry approached, Tarleton galloped away on Jackson's horse.[6]

Back at the battlefield, Jackson tied a white handkerchief to a stick as a flag of truce. "I am assistant-surgeon to the 71st Regiment; many of the men are wounded and in your hands," he told the Americans. "I therefore come to offer my services to attend them." The Americans took Jackson prisoner and allowed him to treat the wounded British soldiers. He took off his only shirt and tore it into bandages. Then the Americans asked him to treat their wounded men also. In gratitude, the Americans sent Jackson back to the British army without requiring a parole or a prisoner exchange.[7]

In another battle during the Southern Campaign, Jackson volunteered for a dangerous assignment:

> ...a building into which the sick and wounded had been carried was riddled by the shot of the enemy, and visiting it became so dangerous that the surgeons proposed casting lots to determine which of them should go and attend the wounded soldiers. Jackson, whose feelings were ever alive to the sufferings of his fellow-creatures, was present, and when the proposal was made to him, he said, "No, no, I will go and attend them."[8]

During the Siege of Yorktown, Jackson was attached to a brigade of grenadiers that was defending an advanced redoubt. General Thomas Saumarez later recalled Jackson's dedication and bravery:

> The enemy attempted to storm the fort three times, and was as often repulsed. I well remember at this period Dr. Jackson was taken very ill, so much so, that all the officers of the regiment were most anxious to obtain his assent to our making application for his removal to a place of greater safety and quiet, where he could have a greater chance of recovering his health and strength, being at the time exposed to the incessant cannonade of shot and shells from the enemy during the day and night; but my gallant friend declared he was fully determined to remain with us to the last, in order to render every assistance in his power.[9]

After the British surrendered at Yorktown, Jackson used a period of "enforced relaxation" as a prisoner of war to conduct "speculative contemplation" and to study various languages. After he was released on parole, he walked to British headquarters in New York in the midst of a very hard winter. Leaving America behind, he arrived in Ireland early in the summer of 1782. He stopped at Dublin and Edinburgh before walking to London, where he was offered lodging by Dr. Stewart, who had been the surgeon of the 71st Regiment when Jackson joined the regiment.

Early in 1783, Jackson began a seven-month walking tour of Europe, visiting France, Switzerland, Germany—where he was detained overnight as a vagabond—and Italy. After returning to London, he learned in January of 1784 that the 71st Regiment would soon be formally disbanded at Perth and decided to participate in the ceremony.[10]

> His feelings towards the regiment were warm and deep, and carried in them all that is felt of strong attachment in the symbolic words of "auld lang syne." Although the season

> was inclement, and snow deep on the ground, he desired to be with the regiment now about to be disbanded, and accordingly set out on foot. He accomplished the journey in three weeks, including some days of halt, where he fell in with friends. He had been from the year 1778 up to that time in a Highland regiment, and though very desirous to learn the Gaelic language, for the purpose of being able to read the poems of Ossian in the original, he was not, from the want of a grammatical guide, enabled to make much progress in it. At Perth, however, he found a grammar, and a person possessed of grammatical knowledge, and by this double aid, in the course of six weeks he made such progress as to be able to read, and tolerably understand the Gaelic bible, and such poems, fragments and songs as fell in his way; though of course it was not to be expected that he could speak it fluently.
>
> The regiment was at length disbanded, after which he made a pedestrian tour of the Highlands, proceeding to Inverness, and afterwards to the Isle of Skye. The country was new to him, and the mode of travelling congenial. He thus beheld the Highlander in his native mountains...[11]

After touring the Highlands, Jackson stayed in Edinburgh for a couple of months. He married the daughter of Dr. Stephenson of Edinburgh. "Being by this union placed in easy circumstances, he was enabled to pursue his studies in Paris." While in Europe he received a Doctor in Medicine degree. When he returned to England, he chose to practice medicine at Stockton-upon-Tees because his wartime friend Francis Skelly lived there. After seven years in private practice, he volunteered for the military when war broke out in 1793. He accompanied the Buffs to Flanders in 1794, and later received an appointment as inspector of hospitals on the Continent. When the infantry was withdrawn, he was ordered to England. In 1796, he was stationed in the West Indies and resumed his study of tropical diseases.[12]

In 1798, he and another military doctor who had been stationed in the West Indies took a tour of the United States. During the tour, Jackson came across Daniel Morgan, who had commanded the American troops at Cowpens, where Jackson had surrendered after giving his horse to Banastre Tarleton; the former victor and former prisoner embraced cordially.[13]

Jackson returned to England in 1798. In 1800 was appointed head of the army-depot hospital, and at the commencement of the Peninsular war he was appointed inspector-general of hospitals. He got into squabbles with bureaucrats and spent six months in prison for striking one of them on the shoulders with a cane. In 1811 he went once again to the West Indies, this time to serve as director of medical affairs. He returned to England in 1815, and continued publishing works on tropical fevers and military matters. In 1819, he went to Gibraltar to study an outbreak of fever, and then traveled around the Mediterranean. He died in 1827 at the age of seventy-seven.[14]

Roderick Mackenzie

Roderick Mackenzie provided an eye-witness account of the Battle of Cowpens and blamed the disaster on Banastre Tarleton, the British commander on the scene.

After the war, Mackenzie wrote *Strictures on Lt. Col. Tarleton's History of the Campaigns of 1780 and 1781.*[1] The book excoriates Tarleton for sacrificing the 1st Battalion of the 71st Regiment at Cowpens and for numerous other offenses throughout the war. Mackenzie blamed Britain's defeat in America on Tarleton, reasoning that if Tarleton had not lost a battalion of the 71st Regiment in addition to the light troops of the British army at Cowpens, then Cornwallis not only would have crushed the American army at Guilford Courthouse but also would have prevented the blockade at Yorktown.[2]

In critiquing Tarleton's History of the Campaigns, Mackenzie writes:

> From too great attention to his own exploits, Lieutenant Colonel Tarleton pays not that decent regard to those of others, which historical truth indispensably requires. He has not recorded the fall of several officers at the Siege of Augusta; and the whole of those who displayed such bravery in the defense of Ninety Six are, without exception, passed over in silence. Of the former of these sieges, he appears to know little indeed; and of the latter, though one of the most brilliant affairs which occurred during the war, he seems to the full as ignorant as he possibly may be of those of Candia or Rhodes.

> Exclusive of those already mentioned, the death of Captains Kelly and Hewlet, the wounds of Captains Nisbet and Robinson, of Lieutenants Toriano, Cowel, Mackay, Robinson, and others, certainly merited attention; and his neglect in not particularizing the officers who were sacrificed immediately under his own eye at Cowpens is still more unpardonable.[3]

Based on the text of his book, Mackenzie studied extensively. For instance, he refers to four historians who wrote about Mary, Queen of Scots. He mentions the Battle of Thermopylae in ancient Greece, the defense of Corsica by Chief Paoli, the military campaigns of Julius Caesar, and the exploits of eighteenth-century British General James Wolfe. Although Mackenzie was a British officer, he quotes an American opponent, David Ramsey, who wrote a book about the American Revolution in South Carolina. Other authors mentioned include Hume, Gibbons, Machiavelli, Boswell, and "a celebrated poet" named Ganganelli. In addition to "stricture," which means negative criticism or censure, his vocabulary includes "exordium," "vide," and "arcana imperii."[4]

Ed Brumby gives the following information in *71st Fraser Highland Regiment*:

> Ens. Roderick Mackenzie, 1st Battn.
> Volunteer Roderick Mackenzie to be Ens. 21st Sept 1779 vice William Mackintosh. He was at Cowpens Jan 1781. Promoted to Lt. in 2nd 71st 21st Oct 1781 vice Charles Barrington Mackenzie. He is not on the 1782 71st Army List. He was in London 5th April 1783 (TNA [The National Archives, Kew, London] WO12-1747 Capt. James Innes's Co.). He is on the 71st half pay list until 1792. He wrote a book

"Strictures on Lt. Col. Tarleton's History of the Campaigns of 1780 & 1781, in the Southern Provinces of North America". He died on or before 1789 (Warrand, Duncan, Some Mackenzie Pedigrees, p127). Son of Rev. Colin Mackenzie of Hilton (Burkes Landed Gentry).[5]

On the title page of *Strictures*, Mackenzie identifies himself as "Late Lieutenant in the 71st Regiment," leading readers to believe that he was the Lieutenant Mackenzie who was wounded at Cowpens. The records cited above, however, indicate that he was an ensign at the time of the Battle of Cowpens.

A lieutenant named Mackenzie in the 71st regiment played a role in a large prisoner exchange in the summer 1781. The commandant at Charleston wrote to General Charles Cornwallis: "Agreeable to the cartel established between Lt Colonel Carrington and Captain Cornwallis, I have the honor to inform your Lordship that Lieutenant McKenzie of the 71st Regiment proceeds with four American officers and one hundred and ninety eight privates in order to receive an equal number of our troops in exchange."[6] The commander also said, "Captain Duncanson is sent to receive the exchanged prisoners of the 71st Regiment, to which he belongs."[7] (Robertson Duncanson had been taken prisoner at Cowpens, and may have been exchanged by the summer). A month after the commandant at Charleston mentioned Mackenzie, the commander at Portsmouth, Virginia, wrote Cornwallis: "I send you a Lieutenant Mckensie, 71st, that went to York Town with the prisoners."[8] In a note to *The Cornwallis Papers*, editor Ian Saberton writes that "Lieutenant Mckensie" is "Perhaps Roderick MacKenzie."[9]

Aeneas Mackintosh (1751-1820)

Aeneas Mackintosh served as a captain in the 2nd Battalion of the 71st Regiment.[1]

Before the war, he had succeeded as the 23rd Chief of Clan Mackintosh when his uncle—known by the Gaelic name Angus and the classical name Aeneas—died in 1770. Angus had served as an army ranger in Colonial South Carolina and Georgia from about 1732 until 1740, when he inherited the Mackintosh estate at Moy and the title of chief. Angus retained his commission in the army and, therefore, served with government forces during the Jacobite Rising of 1745. His wife had raised troops from Clan Mackintosh for Bonnie Prince Charlie's doomed cause, earning her the nickname "Colonel Anne." Lady Anne Mackintosh moved to Edinburgh after the death of her husband so that her nephew could occupy the clan seat at Moy.[2]

After the 71st Regiment was authorized in 1775, Mackintosh recruited a company and was awarded the rank of captain in the regiment's 2nd Battalion. Nineteenth century Scottish writer David Stewart mentions Aeneas Mackintosh in an account of the voyage from Scotland to America in 1776:

> The transports with the 71st sailed in a large fleet, having the 42nd and other troops on board. A violent gale, however, scattered the fleet, and several of the single ships fell in with, and were attacked by, American privateers. A transport having Captain, now Sir Aeneas Mackintosh, and his company on board, with two six-pounders, made a resolute defense against a privateer with eight guns, till all the ammunition was expended, when they bore down with the intention of

boarding; the privateer, however, did not wait to receive the shock, and set sail, the transport being unable to follow.[3]

When Mackintosh attempted to return home at the end of the war, he encountered privateers once again. He and two lieutenants of the 71st—Lawrence Campbell and Archibald Campbell—were taken by an American privateer in October of 1782.[4]

These incidents at sea became part of clan folklore repeated two centuries later by 84-year-old storyteller Willie MacQueen:

> Now, when the American War of Independence was being fought around 1776, the chief of the Mackintoshes was first and foremost to help with the American War of Independence—to keep it for the British, of course. And you know, he mustered five hundred clansmen. They were made up of Mackintoshes and MacQueens and McPhersons and MacBains and, of course, there were Smiths among them because they were on his estate. They went across to America, and I think that they had a pretty hard time of it on their voyage: I think there were pirates and all.[5]

A legend arising from the Battle of Brier Creek in March of 1779 says Mackintosh rescued a Continental officer who was a distant relative. A Georgia history book published in 1900 gives this version of the legend:

> The only ray of light that shone through the darkness of this sad defeat was shed by the bravery of Col. Elbert and his command. He fought until he was struck down, and he was on the point of being killed by a soldier with uplifted bayonet when he made the masonic sign of distress. An officer

> noticed it, responded instantly, stayed the soldier's arm, and saved Col. Elbert's life...
>
> Col. McIntosh, the hero of Fort Morris, had stood his ground with Col. Elbert until nearly every man was killed, and then he was captured. As he was surrendering his sword, a British officer tried to kill him; and he was saved by the timely interference of his kinsman, Sir Aeneas McIntosh, of the British army.[6]

After the Siege of Savannah in 1779, *Rivington's Royal Gazette* announced the death of Eneas McIntosh, Paymaster of the 71st Regiment; a correction in a subsequent issue gave the Paymaster's name as Angus McIntosh and said another officer named Eneas McIntosh was reported to be still at Savannah.[7]

A dubious tale says that after the British captured Charleston in 1780, Roderick "Rory" McIntosh had an opportunity to meet his clan chief. Rory was among the Mackintosh clansmen who had emigrated to Georgia, and during the American Revolution he remained loyal to the British crown. John Couper tells the following tale in a letter written many years later:

> I recollect seeing, in St. Augustine, on some public day, Rory, Colonel McArthur, and Major Small, Scotch officers, parading the streets in full Highland costume, attended by their pipers.
>
> After Charleston fell, Rory went there from Savannah, by land, particularly to visit Major Small. On meeting, Rory said: "I have traversed, at the risk of my life, the rebellious Province of South Carolina to see my friend, the famous Major Small."

"Welcome! Welcome! The brave Roderick McIntosh! I have heard his Majesty speak with kindness and respect of Roderick McIntosh."

"Spare me – oh, spare me!" said Rory, "his Majesty is too good;" and the two hugged each other.

"I can offer you," said Major Small, "no greater mark of respect than by ordering my pipers to attend you whilst in Charleston."

The 71st Regiment was then in Charleston. Sir Æneas McIntosh, the chief of the border clan, was a captain in it. Sir Æneas was a slender delicate gentleman, educated in France. Rory, who could broke no chief that was not a powerful man, was sadly disconcerted. Sir Æneas politely asked him to dine with him the next day on calf's head.

"Calf's head!" said Rory. "I feed my negroes on calves' heads."

Rory never afterwards noticed his chief, but observed that he was of a spurious race.[8]

Rory's description of Aeneas Mackintosh, like most of Rory's tales, cannot be taken as actual fact. A delicate man could not have withstood the rigors of campaigning with an elite regiment like the 71st, which saw action in several of the major battles in the North before fighting at Savannah, Brier Creek, and Charleston. After Mackintosh returned to Scotland, he was a vigorous farmer who inspected his large estate by riding horseback through rugged terrain. His wife wrote that he had "the patriarchal character of a Highland Chief."[9]

The official Clan Mackintosh historian writes that Aeneas Mackintosh "went to America in 1776 and fought in the battle of Brooklyn, and in the campaigns from 1777 to 1781. When Lord Cornwallis capitulated, Aeneas and his men were taken prisoners, and were held until the war ended."[10] If Mackintosh was one of the three captains in the 71st Regiment at the Battle of Guilford Courthouse on March 15, 1781, he would have commanded a wing of the regiment.[11] Archival records, however, indicate that Mackintosh remained in Charleston at crucial periods during the campaign of 1781. Mackintosh was present at a court martial in Charleston on March 28, 1781, two weeks after the Battle of Guilford Courthouse. He was sick at Charleston on September 1, 1781, four weeks before the beginning of the Siege of Yorktown. In the period after Yorktown, he attended a court martial in New York on August 5, 1782.[12]

Mackintosh returned to Moy in the Highlands of Scotland in 1783, resuming his role as the 23rd Chief of Clan Mackintosh and managing the farms and forests on his estates. Not long after he returned to Scotland, Mackintosh mourned the death of his aunt Lady Anne Mackintosh—the renowned "Colonel Anne" of the Rising of 1745. "Much of what is known about Anne and the events around Moy," points out clan historian Robert McGillivray, "is contained in a manuscript written by Sir Aeneas Mackintosh, nephew of Anne's husband and subsequently 23rd Chief, who spent a good deal of time with her in later years."[13] The manuscript—with the title *Notes Descriptive and Historical Principally Relating to the Parish of Moy in Strathdearn and the Town and Neighbourhood of Inverness* by Sir Aeneas Mackintosh of Mackintosh—was printed for Alfred Donald Mackintosh of Mackintosh in 1892 at Inverness; Daniel McDonald Johnson donated one of the one hundred printed copies to the Ernest F. Hollings Special Collections Library at the University of South Carolina, where it is cataloged with the call number DA 890 .I6 M33 1892.

Mackintosh kept notes on a tour of his estates during seven weeks in September and October of 1784. His notes focus on his agricultural enterprises, and they also provide glimpses into the social and economic conditions in the area near Inverness. He was disturbed to discover that while he was fighting in America other landowners had infringed on his fishing rights:

> Salmon this far, till the Duke of Gordon shut up the mouth of the rivers at the Castle of Inverlochy by cruives (by what right to be enquired into) – fine meadow ground and corn field wants enclosing and a few belts of planting. No stones but out of the rivers, the moss close to the place – the Spean is the march betwixt the Duke of Gordon and me, and the Roy boundary twixt it and Achaderry. A fine bank of young oak fronting Keppoch extends for a mile and a half which can be easily enclosed – the Spean running the whole length... and the Roy the whole breadth, so that a straight line of a sunk fence faced with stone or a double turf dyke such as at Moy would do. Near the end of the oak there commences a birch and other wood tolerably high. The part of the oak wood near Spean can be cut in ten years.
>
> Achlochrich – A fine fall of water called a linn stops the salmon from getting further up the country. If people of the Duke had not stopped up the river would willingly be at the expense of blowing this linn. The farm a fine, flat, green hills but no wood – here is the burial place of the former family of Keppoch and Chapel built by one of the Lochiels, being one of seven built by him in order to pacify the Pope (by whom) for his great wickedness he had been ex-communicated.
>
> Murlagan – A bulwark necessary to be built in front of the house.
>
> Tullich and Dulderig – Fine flat corn country. The Charters relative to the Lochaber to be very pointedly examined

> with respect to the Proprietor's title and right of fishing, as for a few years past the same is totally monopolized by the Duke of Gordon's having quite shut up the mouth of the river with cruives and other engines wholly to prevent a single fish getting up the river.[14]

The notes describe the hazards of riding horseback through the rough terrain of the Scottish Highlands. "It rains very heavy in the afternoon," he observed on September 7, and when he resumes his journey, "Before we proceed two miles it turns dark and rains and blows." The next day, "Did not breakfast till ten, and it was twelve before I could get on horseback."[15]

> 8th (Sept.) Set off by seven, breakfast at Dalwhily, a farm possessed by Parson Robert Macpherson, and dine at Banchor. Proceeding from thence in the evening to Dunnaughtane, very near falling from my horse, but my servant prevents it. However, hurt my thigh very much. Was afraid I had dislocated my haunch bone; confined to bed several days. D. Stewart and Mr Grant attend me.
>
> On the 15th proceed in a Post Chaise to Moy.[16]

Mackintosh, who was in his early thirties and had recently returned from seven years of warfare and imprisonment, paid close attention to the pretty women he met during the tour. During the first part of the tour, he noted, "I and company retired early to a party of ladies assembled at Miss Mally McIntosh's, where we danced and supped."[17]

The next day he observed, "upon entering a neat house, found the Landlady a very agreeable young woman at the tea table to entertain us. She is Sister to Fassifearn."[18]

Two weeks later, although still recovering from a riding accident, he enjoyed the social life of Inverness:

> 17th (Sept.) Asked to dine at Provost Chisholm's, but Lord Hinderland asks us off to dine with some ladies. Accordingly attend him. There were present Lady Jannett Train, lately married to the Sheriff-Depute of Caithness, a very handsome, polite young lady; Mrs Forbes, Culloden, and Miss Grant, Dalvey. In evening all hands go to Mr Pierson's concert. Several young lassies sing and perform well on the Spinette. See some pretty girls... Miss Dallas, daughter to the late Professor of Cantrae, lately from Aberdeen, a showy girl, and has the appearance of a woman of fashion. Miss Campbell, daughter to the late Governor of Fort-George, promises to be pretty.
> ... 20th (Sept.) All the gentlemen who had been scholars to Mr Hector Fraser, late schoolmaster, dine together, and gave a ball to the ladies... The number of gentlemen was 50 and 100 ladies, well dressed, and a few well looked girls...[19]

The notes show that Mackintosh was an avid sportsman:

> 23rd (Sept.) The Colonel goes ashooting. Out of compliment I attend him on horseback through a rough moor to the west of the house covered with birch wood and shrubs. See from a dozen to 15 black game, of which he kills one, but by four, being tired and my leg very uneasy, return and obliged to wait dinner till seven in the evening.
>
> 24th (Sept.) The Colonel having applied for leave to shoot a roe buck, send my servant to attend him, and go myself to visit my farms in the neighborhood, which I frequently do. Return by four, when I understand that

> Thornton had killed a doe giving suck. I in consequence entertain him very coolly, and form in my mind that it was the first and last he should kill any time he should be at my house...
>
> 25th (Sept.) From irregular hours and my chagrin at Thornton's behavior, obliged to lie in bed longer than usual. Thornton goes to Inverness and carries the doe with him... The Colonel makes present of the deer at Inverness instead of leaving her with me.
>
> ... 8th (Oct.) Go afishing for the last time this year. The fish rise fast but don't fix firmly.[20]

Mackintosh constructed the fourth building known as Moy Hall in 1800 after fire destroyed the ancestral manor house.

King George created Mackintosh a baronet in 1812, and he became known as Sir Aeneas.

The fact that Mackintosh and his wife Margaret did not have any children became woven into a legend. Morrit of Rokeby wrote a poem titled "The Curse of Moy" that was published in *Minstrelcy of the Scottish Border* in 1802. According to the legend, a distraught woman put a curse on the Mackintosh chiefs that prevented them from having sons to succeed them. Sir Aeneas was the fourth chief who had no son to succeed him, and the next chief also was childless.[21]

When Mackintosh died, his widow honored his memory by having a tribute inscribed onto a seventy-foot granite obelisk:

> Sacred to the memory of Sir Aeneas Mackintosh
> Baronet Captain of Clan Chattan
> Who died at Moy Hall on 21st January 1820
> in the 69th year of his age
> Having in youth after the example of his forefathers

served his country in war
He retired to this ancient seat of his family
And married Margaret, youngest daughter of
Sir Ludovic Grant of Dalvey Baronet
And grand-daughter to Sir Patrick Grant of Dalvey Bart.
And Sir James Innes of Bahennie Bart.
Without relinquishing the Patriarchal character of a Highland Chief
He combined it with an exemplary observance
of all the duties of civilised society
And with the exercise of every domestic and social affection
His charities were extensive, unostentatious, and discriminating
His hospitality and Kindness were peculiarly felt
By all those whom the Remains of the Ancient Usages and feelings
of his country recommended to his Protection
His Paternal Regard to his Tenants displayed itself in a spontaneous remission of a third part of their Rents
During the general Distress which prevailed in the last years of his life
And it may be truly said of him
That it was his constant and earnest desire
To do Justice, to love Mercy, and to walk humbly with his God.

THIS MONUMENT IS ERECTED BY HIS WIDOW,
DAME MARGARET MACKINTOSH[22]

Duncan Macpherson of Cluny (1750-1817)

Duncan Macpherson's remarkable birth shortly after the Jacobite Rising of 1745 presaged a remarkable life. His father, Ewen Macpherson of Cluny, chief of Clan Macpherson, had enlisted in the British army and had sworn an oath of allegiance to the British crown on the eve of the Rising. After Bonnie Prince Charlie rallied Highlanders to support the Stewart dynasty's claim to the throne, Cluny broke his oath to the king and accepted a position as colonel in the Jacobite army, becoming known as Cluny of the '45. When the rising collapsed in April, 1746, Ewen fled for his life. In June, the British plundered and burned Cluny House, and Ewen's heartbroken father died shortly afterwards. The government declared Ewen to be a traitor, and confiscated the estate of Cluny. Ewen's son Duncan was born while Ewen remained a fugitive, often hiding in a cramped cave. Scottish writer David Stewart tells the story of Duncan's birth:

> During the chief's long confinement in the cave, his lady fitted up an old malt-kin as a kind of temporary residence. Here she was delivered of the son... As the Highlanders always marked any extraordinary circumstance, whether personal or otherwise, by some name or phrase characteristic of the fact, Colonel Macpherson was called *Duncan of the Kiln.*[1]

Duncan's parents fled to Europe in 1755, leaving their young son in Scotland under the guardianship of Duncan's uncle Major John Macpherson of the 78th Regiment of Foot. At the age of twenty-one, Duncan obtained the rank of captain in the 63rd Regiment of Foot, and later served in the 42nd Regiment.[2]

On the eve of the American Revolution, the Macphersons were among several families who took advantage of an opportunity to gain the favor of the British government after having lost their estates during the Jacobite Risings, as Stewart points out:

> ...in many cases, the tenants on the forfeited estates remitted to their attainted landlords, when in exile, the rents which they formerly paid them, while government received the full rents of the new leases. This generosity was exhibited on many other occasions, when the objects of their affection and respect required assistance. In the year 1757, Colonel Fraser, the son of Lord Lovat, without an acre of land, or a shilling to procure influence, found himself, in a few weeks, at the head of nearly 800 men [the Fraser's Highlanders who served in the French and Indian War in America] from his father's estate (then forfeited) and the estates of gentlemen of the clan. About the same period, and previously, numerous detachments of young men were sent to the Scotch Brigade in Holland, to procure commissions for the gentlemen who had lost their fortunes. In the year 1777, Lord Macleod, eldest son of the Earl of Cromarty, (attainted in 1746,) found his influence as effective as when his family were in full possession of their estate and honours. By the support of the Mackenzies, and other gentlemen of his clan, 900 Highlanders were embodied under his command... In the year 1776, the late Lochiel was a lieutenant in the 30th regiment, having returned from France after his father's death, and obtained a commission. This lieutenancy was his only fortune. The followers of his father's family raised 120 men for a company in the 71st regiment. Macpherson of Cluny, also, without a shilling, raised 140 men, for which he

was appointed major to the 71st, and thus secured an independency till his family estate was restored in 1783.[3]

Stewart received some of his information directly from Macpherson, who described the raising of the regiment in a letter written in 1817:

> With regard to the 71st Highlanders, they were raised in the year 1775, and in the short space (if I recollect right) of three months, and consisted of two battalions of 1000 rank and file each. The men were all from Scotland, and chiefly from the Highlands, and that is not surprising when I inform you that there were no less than seven chiefs in the regiment—viz., Lovat, Lochiel, Macleod, Mackintosh, Chisholm, Lamont of Lamont, and your humble servant, most of whom brought 100 men to the regiment. They got no drilling before they embarked, but they got a little while on the voyage to America, particularly in firing ball at a mark, at which they were very expert before they landed. They had only one fortnight's drilling on Staten Island before they were engaged with the enemy; and upon all occasions, whether battle, skirmish, or rencounter, from the day they were first engaged till the last—that is to say, whatever the general success or fate of the day was, that part of the enemy opposed to the 71st always gave way. The next year after they went abroad they had 200 recruits sent them, and out of the 2200 men, only 175 men came home alive, and I got the out-pension for most of them, being at that time a colonel in the 3d Regiment of Guards, and had, fortunately for them, every opportunity of attending the Chelsea Board. There is another circumstance worth mentioning, when the regiment was inspected on the Green of Glasgow they had 150

> supernumeraries that were obliged to be left behind, and, what is a little extraordinary, most of the companies had three or four men who stole on board ship unknown to their officers, and did not discover themselves until we were out of the sight of land for fear of being sent on shore again. These men followed the regiment merely out of attachment to their officers and comrades. Lochiel brought 100 fine Highlanders from Lochaber; and Mrs Macpherson tells me that the Clan Cameron remitted Lochiel's rents to him while in France, which is certainly much to their credit.[4]

At the Battle of Brier Creek in Georgia in March of 1779, Macpherson commanded the 1st Battalion as a detachment on one side of the creek while the rest of the British forces attacked the American camp on the other side of the creek. James Browne's nineteenth-century *History of the Highlands* gives this account:

> The front of this position [the American encampment] was protected by a deep swamp, and the only approach in that way was by a narrow causeway: on each flank were thick woods nearly impenetrable, except by the drier parts of the swamps which intersected them; but the position was more open in the rear. To dislodge the enemy from this stronghold, which caused considerable annoyance, Lieutenant-Colonel Duncan Macpherson [a major at the time], with the first battalion of the 71st, was directed to march upon the front of the position; whilst Colonel Prevost and Lieutenant-Colonels Maitland and Macdonald, with the 2d battalion, the light infantry, and a party of provincials, were ordered to attempt the rear by a circuitous route of many miles. These combined movements were executed with such

precision that, in ten minutes after Colonel Macpherson appeared at the head of the causeway in front, the fire of the body in the rear was heard. Sir James Baird, with the light infantry, rushing through the opening in the swamps, on the left flank, the enemy were overpowered after a short resistance.[5]

Macpherson transferred as a lieutenant colonel to the 73rd Regiment, which was serving in India. He set sail for Europe in the summer of 1779 to join his new regiment, but his ship was captured and he was held prisoner in Boston.[6] Macpherson and a fellow officer asked American commander in chief George Washington to expedite a prisoner exchange:

Cambridge 14th Septr 1779
Sir
Having been so unfortunate as to be taken Prisoners on our passage in the Sandwich packet to Europe by the Continental Frigate Dean commanded by Captain Nicolson, whose polite treatment to us has rendered our situation as agreable as circumstances could admit, Yet, as our anxiety to join our Regiment in the East Indies must naturally be very great, and that our private Affairs in Scotland must suffer considerably (not having been in that Country for these Six years past) by being detained long here, we beg your Excellency would be pleased to give directions to the Commissary General of Prisoners, to negociae an Exchange for us here, or permit us to go to New York by the way of Rhode Island on Parole, in order to effect one there, as we make no doubt Sr Henry Clinton will give such Officers as Your Excellency shall think proper (of equal Rank) in our room.

As we are convinced you have no other idea than making our Captivity as little dissagreable as possible we beg to have Your Excellency's answer when convenient. We have the honor to be with respect Sir Your Excellency's most obedient and very humble Servants
Duncan Macpherson
Lieut. Col: 73d Regt
David Ross
Capt. 73d Regt[7]

Macpherson was on parole by August of 1780 and was exchanged early in 1781. He returned to his old regiment—the 71st—with his new rank—lieutenant colonel—in June of 1781 while the regiment was in Portsmouth near Yorktown.[8] At Yorktown, Macpherson commanded British and Hessian troops in Redoubt 9 who engaged in vicious fighting when French troops assaulted the redoubt.[9] Macpherson once again became a prisoner of war when the British surrendered at Yorktown in October of 1781.

Macpherson returned to Scotland and in 1784 the estate of Cluny was restored to him. His military exploits became part of Highland folklore, as evidenced by a Gaelic poem about him that has been translated as:

In North America,
Frequently did he draw heavy swords,
The Frasers were of good conduct,
And under his control as was their custom,
Swift, well-equipped and fierce,
They would never tire of the pursuit.[10]

Macpherson retired from the army in 1798. At the age of forty-eight, he married Catherine, daughter of Sir Ewen Cameron of Fassifern, and they had four sons and four daughters. A few months before his death in 1817, he expressed various opinions in a letter to Stewart:

> I am clearly of your opinion, that much of the attachment of the people to their superiors is unnecessarily lost, though I cannot impute the whole blame to proprietors. In many instances the people themselves are entirely in the fault, and in other cases factors abuse the trust reposed in them, and of course the proprietor gets the whole blame of their oppressions. You have given two very striking and opposite instances, which may serve to illustrate the situation of landlord and tenant all over the nation. I mean Sir George Stewart and the Earl of Breadalbane. The one has well-paid rents and the offer of a large sum of money besides, for his accommodation, while the other with difficulty gets one-tenth of his. If a tenant has a fair bargain of his farm it is an absurdity to suppose that one bad year will distress him; but when the rent is so racked that he is only struggling in the best of times, a very little falling off in prices or seasons will totally ruin him, and I am sorry to say that much of the present distress is to be attributed to that cause. I am happy to have it in my power to tell you that my rents were all paid—that is, to a mere trifle, and even that trifle due by a few improvident individuals who would be equally in arrear in the best of times. The Duke of Gordon has not received more than one-half his rents either in Lochaber or Badenoch, and I have reason to believe his Grace's rents were better paid in the Low country. Belville has not exceeded one-tenth, and though I do not exactly know in what proportion the

Invereshie rent was paid, yet I know that it was a bad collection. The conduct of the family of Stafford is certainly unaccountable, for I am credibly informed that the old tenants offered a higher rent than those that came from England, consequently they are losers in every respect. I know it will be said by those who are advocates for depopulating the country that they could not stand to their offer, but neither could their successors; for a very large deduction has already been given them, and one man in particular has got five hundred pounds down. Upon the whole it is clear that the Marquis of Stafford was led into those arrangements (so disgraceful to the present age) by speculative men that wish to overturn the old system at once, without considering that their plans were at least only applicable to the present moment, and that such changes, even if necessary, should be done gradually and with great caution. I cannot dismiss this subject without making a few remarks on the conduct of Lady Stafford, and you will be astonished to learn that when her old and faithful adherents, who had given her such repeated proofs of their attachment, were cruelly oppressed by a factor, that she should refuse to listen to their complaints; and when that factor was tried for his life on charges of cruelty, oppression, and murder, it is most unaccountable that her Ladyship should exert all her influence to screen him from the punishment which he so richly deserved. I have only to add that as far as my own observations extend, much of the evil complained of arises from the absence of proprietors from their properties, by which they are in a great measure unacquainted with the real state of their tenants, and consequently open to every species of advice and misrepresentation.[11]

When Macpherson died on August 1, 1817, his oldest son Ewen inherited the estate of Cluny and the chiefship of Clan Macpherson; Ewen served in the 42nd Regiment as a young man, and commanded the Inverness-shire Highland Rifle Volunteers during the period when he became known as Old Cluny. Two other sons of Duncan and Catherine distinguished themselves in battle: Colonel John Cameron Macpherson fought in the Crimean War, and Colonel Archibald Fraser Macpherson served gallantly in India. A daughter of Duncan and Catherine married Robert Fitzroy, who served as captain of HMS *Beagle* during Charles Darwin's momentous voyage of discovery.[12]

Duncan Macpherson's service with the 71st Regiment is memorialized on a marble tablet at the Cluny burial place: "He served his country for upwards of thirty years, during six of which he commanded on active service in America, a battalion of the then 71st or Fraser Regiment."[13]

John Maitland (1732-1779)

John Maitland was the eighth son of the 6th Earl of Lauderdale. Maitland served as a captain of marines in 1757. He went on half pay in 1763 and returned to the active list in 1770. In 1774 he held a seat in the House of Commons for Haddington Burghs. He obtained the rank of major in 1775. He was on active service in America starting in about 1777. In May of 1778 he commanded a detachment of marines opposing American vessels in the Delaware. He received an appointment as the lieutenant colonel of the 1st Battalion of the 71st Regiment on October 14, 1778, not long after the battalion's previous lieutenant colonel, William Erskine, transferred to another regiment.[1] Georgia historian Alexander Lawrence paints this portrait of Maitland:

> It will be well to glance for a few moments at this forty-seven-year-old British soldier, for Lieutenant Colonel John Maitland of the Seventy-first Regiment of Scotch Foot is to play a large part in this drama of Revolutionary history. No family in Scotland was more illustrious than that of this youngest son of Charles, Sixth Earl of Lauderdale, a nobleman distinguished for "the sweetest disposition and finest accomplishments." [Citation: Sir Robert Douglas, *The Peerage of Scotland*, revised by John Philip Wood (Edinburgh, 1813, 2nd. ed.), II, 73.] From Thirlestane Castle, the magnificent seat of the Maitlands at Lauder, had come some of the great men of that country, among them the first Duke of Lauderdale, who was the "1" in the famous "Cabal" of the reign of Charles II. Within its massive walls, "Bonnie Prince Charlie" had found refuge after his defeat at Culloden, when

John Maitland was a boy. The lineage of Colonel Maitland was scarcely less distinguished on the side of his late mother, the former Elizabeth, Lady Ogilvy. Her father, who was Earl of Findlater and Seafield, had been Lord High Chancellor of Scotland.

Had he time for such musings, Colonel Maitland might well ponder the fate that had brought him from his seat in the House of Commons, where he represented the Borough of Haddington, to these climes. For the "easy fortune" and high station he enjoyed at home he had exchanged the hard life of a soldier in this rebellion-torn part of the world. An empty right sleeve attested the fact that he had already fulfilled his duty to King and country. A cannon ball had carried away that hand twenty years before during Admiral Boscawen's victorious action against the French in Lagos Bay, Spain, where Captain Maitland fought with the Marines, being "the only Commission Officer," he wrote, "wounded in that Ingagement." [Citation: The Memorial of Captain John Maitland of the Marines to His Grace the Duke of Newcastle (1761). Add. MS. 32930, fo. 406. The British Museum, London. Maitland requested that the rank of Major or Lieutenant Colonel be conferred upon him.]

With the coming of the American Revolution he had reentered the same branch of service with the rank of Major. In the fighting in the Jerseys in '78 he proved himself an alert, resourceful officer. Striking up the Delaware on one occasion, a British force commanded by Maitland and Captain John Henry of the navy had destroyed thirty-seven American vessels, including two frigates and eleven large merchantmen. During that year he was transferred at his request to the Seventy-first Regiment. He was "so beloved" among the Highland troops, it was said, that "they could have been put upon no service led on by him but what they would have gone with the greatest alacrity." Colonel Maitland was in fact universally popular—admired by friend, respected by foe. [Citation: From a letter dated November 8, 1779, written by a Scotch merchant who was posted in a redoubt at Savannah, *The Scots Magazine* (Edinburgh, December, 1779), 715].[2]

When the 71st Regiment participated in the expedition to Georgia led by Archibald Campbell in the winter of 1778-1779, Maitland served as the expedition's Deputy Adjutant General. The 1st Battalion, under his leadership, disembarked among the first troops and played a key role in securing the landing zone and then capturing Savannah. The 1st Battalion also accompanied Campbell on a march to Augusta in January and February of 1779.[3] When Campbell returned to England, Maitland assumed command of the 71st Regiment.[4]

In maneuvers preceding the Battle of Brier Creek in March of 1779, the 1st Battalion was detached under the command of Major Duncan Macpherson to keep the Americans from escaping across the creek, while Maitland led the 2nd Battalion of the 71st Regiment in the British force that attacked the Americans and earned a resounding victory.[5]

When the British launched an expedition to Charleston in April of 1779, Maitland led a division of two thousand men. The Highlanders crossed the Savannah River on boats and waded through cold swamp-water that rose to their waists and occasionally to their necks. When they emerged, they scattered the American defenders at Purrysburg.[6] A few days later, Maitland's division drove off five hundred Americans under John Laurens who attempted to make a stand on the banks of the Coosawhatchie River.[7]

The British withdrew from Charleston along the sea islands in June. The 71st Regiment under Maitland's command served as a rear guard and won a fierce battle at Stono Ferry.[8] The 2nd Battalion of the 71st returned to Savannah, while the 1st Battalion under Maitland formed the nucleus of a garrison at Beaufort. While at Beaufort, Maitland came down with a fever and never fully recovered.

With Savannah under siege in September of 1779, Maitland avoided American ships by leading the garrison from Beaufort to Savannah through small marshland creeks; sometimes the men had to drag their boats through the mud.[9] The British commander placed Maitland in command of all forces on the west side of Savannah.[10] On October 9, French and American forces launched an assault focusing on Maitland's position, and were driven back with horrendous losses.

Maitland died on October 25, 1779, of the fever that had afflicted him for months, and was buried in the Savannah cemetery. Noting that the "fatigues" of the siege damaged Maitland's health, Prevost described Maitland's death as "literally to have happened on Actual Service." Prevost said the loss of Maitland was "very much, and very justly regretted by all who knew him, both as a Gentleman, and as an Officer."[11] Maitland's eulogy was published in the *Royal Gazette*:

> The late Colonel Maitland was one of the most active officers at the commencement of and during the progress of the present war. His zeal and gallantry were sufficient incitements to lead him where danger dignified and rendered a post honourable. Though he possessed an early fortune, had a seat in the house of commons, and was of an advanced age, yet he never availed himself of such powerful pretensions, or expressed a desire of retiring from the field of honour.

> Unshaken loyalty, genuine patriotism, undaunted bravery, judicious conduct, steady coolness, and unremitting perseverance, constituted his character as an officer... his country will feel the loss of so accomplished a chief; his acquaintances long lament the loss of so valuable a friend; the indigent search in vain for another so eminently benevolent; and the soldiers, long accustomed to his pleasing command, lament his death, and revere his memory.[12]

Scottish writer David Stewart, who has been accused of not supporting his statements with evidence, gives the following statement about Maitland:[13]

> One of the first who died, after the cessation of hostilities [at the Siege of Savannah], was the Honourable Lieutenant-Colonel Maitland, son of the Earl of Lauderdale. He was originally in the Marines, but as this service did not afford a sufficient field for his active and enterprising mind, he was transferred to the line, and appointed major to Fraser's Highlanders. His arrival at Savannah, at a most critical moment, inspired confidence in his friends, while it struck the enemy with surprise, as they did not expect he would be able to penetrate by a circuitous route, after they had secured the fords and passes. Colonel Maitland lived in the trenches with the soldiers, and "by his courage, his kindness of heart, and affability with his men, secured their affection and fidelity. His dialect was Scotch:—proceeding from a tongue which never spoke in disguise, it carried conviction to all. Equally brave, generous, and unassuming, his memory will be respected while manly fortitude, unstained honour, and military talents, are held in estimation."[14]

In 1980, the vault in Savannah where Maitland had been interred was opened under supervision of medical and anthropological specialists. Maitland's remains were identified by his buttons, the absence of a right arm resulting from his wounds in the Seven Years' War, the body's position beneath a wooden floor in the vault, and a large "M" written on the wall. His remains were reinterred in the Maitland vault at the Lauderdale Aisle in Haddington, East Lothian.[15]

An exhibit at the Parris Island Museum on the U.S. Marine Corps Recruit Depot at Beaufort, S.C., near where Maitland commanded a garrison shortly before the Siege of Savannah, devotes about twenty feet of wall space and several dioramas to Maitland's exploits in honor of a fellow marine, even though he was on the enemy side in the American Revolution.[16]

The Georgia Historical Society holds a collection, identified as MS 0954, of photocopies of five original letters written from John Maitland to his brother, Alexander, between August 27, 1775, and July 8, 1776. In these letters, Maitland reports on his journey to America, discusses life in the army, and recounts the British capture of Staten Island, New York. Mildred Maitland Wiggins donated the letters in 1973; she acquired the material from the 17th Earl of Lauderdale, a descendant of one of John Maitland's five brothers.[17]

Archibald McArthur (1730-1805)

Archibald McArthur chose a military career at age seventeen and served in the Dutch Scots Brigade. Later, he joined the British army and served as a captain in the 54th Regiment in 1771. He was promoted to major in the 71st Highland Regiment in 1777. After an expedition including the 71st Regiment invaded Georgia, McArthur was appointed Commandant of the Town of Savannah on December 31, 1778.

McArthur distinguished himself at Stono Ferry in June of 1779, and led a daring sortie during the Siege of Savannah in September of 1779.[1]

McArthur assumed command of the 71st Regiment in the summer of 1780 following the departures of Archibald Campbell and Alexander MacDonald and the death of John Maitland. General Charles Cornwallis said, "I did not see any inconvenience in the command's devolving upon Major McArthur, who is an excellent officer."[2] Cornwallis detached the 71st Regiment to a post at Cheraw, showing confidence in McArthur's ability to operate at a distance from the main army. After the regiment withdrew from Cheraw, the Highlanders participated in the Battle of Camden in August of 1780 and the campaign toward Charlotte.

McArthur became a prisoner of war when the 1st Battalion of the 71st Regiment met its doom at Cowpens in January of 1781. The soldiers of the 71st absolved McArthur of any responsibility for the defeat and placed the blame entirely on Banastre Tarleton. Lieutenant Roderick Mackenzie, who was wounded and taken prisoner at Cowpens, observed that the Highlanders "had established their reputation in the several operations in that province, at Stono Ferry, at the sieges of Savannah and

Charlestown, and at the battle of Camden," and at Cowpens "they were led by an officer of great experience, who had come into the British service from the Scotch Dutch brigade."[3] McArthur surrendered to James Jackson, the Brigade Major of American militia, and Jackson introduced him to General Daniel Morgan, the American commander at Cowpens.[4]

AFTER HE WAS PAROLED and exchanged, McArthur commanded an assembly of recruits in Charleston. Lieutenant Colonel Nisbet Balfour—a fellow Scot who served as the British commandant of Charleston—dispatched McArthur to an unstable region near the Georgia border. Learning of "some parties of rebels having been within ten miles of Savannah," British officials expressed worry "for the safety of the plantations and inhabitants" in coastal Georgia. An official hoped "that Colonel Balfour may (by an exertion in South Carolina) give them a little relief, as I understand he has sent Major McArthur with a detachment to Pocotaligo, which is not very distant from the part of the river where they cross."[5] Balfour explained:

> The enemy in parties of two and three hundred have over run all the country to the southward, and I had detached McArthur with the debris of the British to Pocotaligo in order to cover that country and relieve [loyalist officer Edward] Fenwick, who with the militia were posted in a redoubt there. We came too late for the purpose of saving Fenwick, who was taken partly from his own imprudence and from the treachery of the militia, but McArthur, having forced the enemy to retire, must now be recalled to Dorchester, where a post must be established to prevent the enemy coming to our gates.

The situation of the posts at present will be, viz, at Monck's Corner 200 infantry and fifty mounted, at Dorchester 150 infantry and sixty mounted, at Nelson's 56 infantry, at Motte's House 54 infantry, at Congarees 76 infantry with militia, and at George Town 86 infantry with twenty mounted.

Lord Rawdon has at Camden the 63rd, Fanning's corps, Volunteers of Ireland and York Volunteers – the 64th and light infantry with Watson, who cannot now get to him. Cruger [at Ninety Six] has Innes's corps joined to him.[6]

Balfour gave orders on April 10, 1781, for McArthur to march to Dorchester:

"You will be pleased to proceed this evening with the British troops under your command from hence to Dorchester and, on your getting there, draw to you as soon as possible, if not already arrived, Colonel Fenwick's troop of dragoons, taking care by their field officers to embody the militia of that and the near districts. Should you find that no considerable numbers of the enemy are in those parts, you will then proceed to join Lt. Colonel Small at Monk's Corner and put yourself under his orders, sending me advice thereof.

But in case you find that the lt. colonel is moved onwards and likely to be opposed by an equal or superior force, you will with all possible dispatch endeavor with your corps to reinforce him, avoiding, in this endeavor, by all means any partial action, which would only weaken, without answering any essential ends or forwarding the chief objects of this march.[7]

By this time, American forces led by Henry Lee, Francis Marion and Thomas Sumter were threatening British outposts across the backcountry. The commander at Camden, Lieutenant Colonel Francis Rawdon, divided his forces and sent a detachment of nine hundred men under Lieutenant Colonel John Watson to protect posts near the Santee River. In a letter to Cornwallis, who was then in Virginia, Balfour said "I had mentioned your coming into this province by the way of George Town [a port on the northern coast of South Carolina] and that I had placed a vessel with provisions there for the use of the army, [and] also had provided boats and flats and stopped Watson's corps for a short time in order to support your passing the ferries. McArthur with his corps at the Eutaws was also ordered to join you when he heard of your approach."[8]

When the American army under General Nathanael Greene threatened Camden, Rawdon recalled Watson's detachment. "Lt. Colonel Watson had moved from George Town for many weeks up the Peedee and we were at a loss to know where he was," Balfour said. "However, having at length got at him, he was ordered instantly to Camden."[9]

Rawdon drove Greene away at the Battle of Hobkirk's Hill on April 25. Immediately after the battle, Rawdon reported that "Lee and Marion were so near I could not follow the success. Greene has rallied at Rugeley's, where Lee, Marion, Sumter and Pickens will join him tomorrow. McArthur, I hear, is at Thompson's with a reinforcement for me. What it is I know not, but I hope it will enable me to clear the country. Watson is not to be found."[10] Balfour reported to Cornwallis:

> Lt Colonel Watson cannot get to Camden, being at present just coming from George Town on this side the Santee in order to proceed up towards McCord's Ferry and there wait

> events, as his crossing would be very dangerous until we know more of Greene's movements.
>
> Lee and Marion have taken a post which Watson established at Wright's Bluff.
>
> McArthur with three hundred infantry and one hundred mounted and tolerably well appointed are towards Nelson's Ferry to cover the country, and another corps is at Dorchester.
>
> ...The movements of Lt Colonel Watson and the unfortunate idea of giving him the 64th Regiment has been of more prejudice than it is possible to describe, and it has not only lost us so very considerable a force but the troops have been let down and the enemy of course have gained much ground by it.[11]

A week after the battle, Rawdon reported "Greene is still at Rugely's, I suppose waiting for succour. Lee and Marion I believe have joined him. Sumter is collecting provisions for him in the fork. McArthur, I find, is not to cross Santee but I have now some hope of Watson. Be assured every exertion shall be made but nothing done rashly. I have provisions for a fortnight and horses plenty. Our action cost us two hundred and twenty men. Greene lost at the very least five hundred. Continental deserters come in fast."[12]

While Watson proceeded toward Camden in early May, Lee and Marion conducted a siege against a fortified house at a strategic location where the Congaree and Wateree rivers join to form the Santee. Balfour said "they invested Motte's House, where unluckily a reinforcement from McArthur with provisions for Camden had arrived but a few hours before. The garrison amounted to upwards of one hundred and twenty men commanded by McPherson [possibly Lieutenant Donald McPherson of the 2nd Battalion of the 71st Regiment]. They defended it until the enemy got near to the house by sap and with combustibles set fire to it, which obliged them to surrender at discretion."[13] Rawdon said the loss of Fort Motte "was heavy upon me as all the provisions had been forwarded from Nelson's to that post for the supply of Camden."[14]

Rawdon realized that the post at Camden was untenable and, at the urging of Balfour, decided to abandon it as soon as Watson returned. Rawdon reported:

> On the 7th of May Lt Colonel Watson joined me with his detachment, much reduced in number through casualties, sickness, and a reinforcement which he had left to strengthen the garrison at Georgetown. He had crossed the Santee near its mouth and re-crossed it a little below the entrance of the Congaree. By him I received the unwelcome intelligence that the whole interior country had revolted and that Marion and Lee (after reducing a small post where Lt Colonel Watson kept his baggage at Wright's Bluff) had crossed the Santee to support the insurgents upon the same night which he passed it to join me. Information reached me the same day that the post at Motte's house near the mouth of the Congaree was invested and batteries opened against it. I had long been sensible of the necessity for my retiring within the Santee, but whilst Lee and Marion were in a situation to retard my march in front at the same time that my rear was exposed to Greene, I conceived it impracticable without the disgrace of abandoning my stores and particularly my wounded at Camden. The measure even now could only be effected at Nelson's Ferry, which was sixty miles from me...On the 9th I published to the troops and to the militia my design of evacuating Camden, offering to such of

the latter as chose to accompany me every assistance that we could afford them. During the ensuing night I sent off all our baggage etc under a strong escort, and destroyed the works, remaining at Camden with the rest of the troops till ten o'clock the next day in order to cover the march. On the night of the 13th I began to pass the river at Nelson's Ferry, and by the evening of the 14th every thing was safely across... We brought off all the sick and wounded excepting about thirty who were too ill to be moved, and for them I left an equal number of Continental prisoners in exchange. We brought off all the stores of any kind of value, destroying the rest, and we brought off not only the militia who had been with us in Camden but also all the well affected neighbors on our route, together with the wives, children, Negroes and baggage of almost all of them.

...Lt Colonel Balfour was so good as to meet me at Nelson's. He took this measure that he might represent his circumstances to me... I agreed with him in the conclusion to be drawn from hence, that any misfortune happening to my corps might entail the loss of the province, but as Major McArthur had joined me with near three hundred foot and eight dragoons, I conceived I might, without hazarding too far, endeavor to check the enemy's operations on the Congaree.[15]

By late May, Rawdon established a camp at Moncks Corner to "cover those districts from which Charlestown draws its principal supplies." [16]

ABOUT 2,300 BRITISH TROOPS under Lieutenant Colonel Alexander Stewart fought about 2,100 Americans under General Nathanael Greene on September 8, 1781, at Eutaw Springs with horrendous casualties on both sides; the British suffered eighty-five killed, 350 wounded, and 257 missing.[17] "I stayed two days on the field of battle, burying my dead and taking care of my wounded," Stewart reported, "and then sent off as many of the wounded as I could get carriages to transport them on, and retired to Ferguson's Swamp without Greene's daring to fire a shot at me, where I was met by Colonel McArthur with near three hundred men, who had been posted at Monck's Corner for the preservation of the stores for the support of the army."[18]

The Americans trailed the British toward Charleston, but McArthur's reinforcements thwarted any opportunity to strike. "M'Arthur was called up from Fairlawn to cover Gen. Stewart's retreat," said American officer Otho Holland Williams. "It was Gen. Greene's intention to have renewed the action the next day; and in hopes to prevent a junction with M'Arthur, Lee and Marion had been detached to watch the line of communication between the Eutaws and Fairlawn. By the simultaneous movements of the two corps, so as to meet at mid-distance and outnumber Marion, their junction and retreat was effectually secured... Gen. Greene pressed the pursuit on the road to Charleston during the whole of one day; but finding that Col. Stewart still retired before him, and being now left at liberty to watch the movements of Lord Cornwallis, and his wounded and prisoners requiring attention, he resolved to retire again to the High Hills of Santee."[19]

Greene reported with satisfaction that "the enemy burnt their provisions at Dorchester, and quitted their post at Fair Lawn."[20]

Although he took part in some of the most bitterly-contested campaigns in South Carolina, McArthur gained the respect of the state's residents. American officer Alexander Garden of

Charleston said that "no act of inhumanity, or of oppression, was ever attached" to McArthur.[21]

McARTHUR RECEIVED a promotion dated April 24, 1781, to lieutenant colonel in command of the 3rd Battalion of the 60th Regiment, known as the Royal Americans.[22] Three of the four battalions of the 60th Regiment had been stationed in East Florida at the beginning of the war, and detachments had come north to participate in the conquest of Georgia, the defense of Savannah, and the conquest of South Carolina.

When the British evacuated Charleston, McArthur sailed to St. Augustine in October of 1782 with loyalist refugees from South Carolina and Georgia, along with provisions for the refugees. Unable to enter the St. Augustine harbor because of what McArthur called "this horrid bar," the supply vessels entered the St. Johns River north of St. Augustine to be unloaded. The elements of the 60th Regiment stationed in St. Augustine received orders for reassignment and departed on the ship that McArthur arrived on. Although an officer of the 60th Regiment, McArthur commanded a hodge-podge of loyalist units from Florida, North Carolina and South Carolina, totaling four hundred men, supported by a small detachment of Royal Artillery.[23]

McArthur faced the task of distributing the supplies fairly among the refugees, and finding locations for the refugees to settle in Florida. He deemed Florida suitable "for a company or two of old fogies, they might smoke their pipes and tell their lies in great tranquility without fear of flux or ague." In December of 1781, McArthur estimated that 2,428 white refugees accompanied by 3,609 black people had found their way to Florida, and expressed concern over feeding the multitudes.[24]

Because Charleston had ceased to be the regional British headquarters, McArthur was promoted in January of 1783 to brigadier general in command of the Southern District. In September of 1783, Britain and Spain signed a peace treaty providing for the cession of East Florida to Spain, giving the British eighteen months to remove residents, government property, and military equipment. More than half of the provincial troops in Florida were discharged at St. Augustine, and the rest were transported to the Bahamas or Nova Scotia. In November, three companies, totaling 150 men, of the 37th Regiment evacuated from New York and joined McArthur's command at St. Augustine.[25]

In July of 1784, the British governor of East Florida transferred rule to a Spanish governor. Spanish military officers treated McArthur with professional courtesy, and the transition proceeded peacefully. McArthur brought off the three companies of the 37th Regiment and the detachment of Royal Artillery in August and sailed for the Bahamas.[26]

LATER IN HIS CAREER, McArthur received assignments to Canada, the Caribbean, and Europe. After getting married in Germany, he retired in 1790 at the age of sixty. He died in Bayreuth, Germany, on July 11, 1805.[27]

Francis Skelly (died 1793)

Francis Skelly was "apparently a son of the Reverend John Skelly and his wife Elizabeth, daughter of Alexander, 10th Duke of Gordon," says an annotated edition of the journal of Lieutenant Colonel Archibald Campbell.[1]

Skelly began his military career as an ensign in the 25th Regiment in 1767 and served at Minorca; he was promoted to lieutenant in 1770. He transferred to the 1st Battalion of the 71st Regiment as a captain in 1775.[2] He was a friend of Captain John Peebles of the grenadier company of the 42nd Regiment; Peebles's diary mentions Skelly on six occasions in locations ranging from New Jersey to Savannah.[3] In November of 1778, when organizing the expedition to conquer Georgia, Archibald Campbell assigned Captain Skelly the duties of Major of Brigade.[4]

Skelly kept a journal from April 28 through September 12, 1779, that gives details of General Augustine Prevost's incursion into South Carolina and the fighting at Stono Ferry; the journal is available online at:
"Journal of Brigade Major F Skelly," ed. John A. Robertson, *Southern Campaigns of the American Revolution* 3:12.1 (Dec, 2006), 24-27, http://southerncampaign.org/newsletter/v3n12.pdf.

Skelly served as an aide to General Alexander Leslie from 1781 to the end of the war, and was promoted to major in 1783.

In 1788 Skelly served as a major in the 74th Regiment under Colonel Archibald Campbell. In 1791 Skelly was promoted to lieutenant colonel. He died in India in 1793.[5]

Notes

New York and New Jersey

[1] George Germain to William Howe, March 28, 1776, Whitehall, in K.G. Davies, ed., *Documents of the American Revolution* (Dublin: Irish University Press, 1976), 12: 94.

[2] Archibald Campbell to William Howe, June 19, 1776, Boston, in J.P. MacLean, *An Historical Account of the Settlements of Scotch Highlanders in America Prior to the Peace of 1783: Together with Notices of Highland Regiments and Biographical Sketches* (Cleveland: Helman-Taylor, 1900, available online through HathiTrust), 344-46.

[3] Campbell to Howe, June 19, 1776, in MacLean, *Historical Account*, 346-47.

[4] William Howe to George Germain, August 6, 1776, Staten Island, in Davies, *Documents of the American Revolution*, 12: 179.

[5] David Stewart, *Sketches of the Character, Manners, and Present State of the Highlanders of Scotland*, 1822 (Edinburgh: John Donald Publishers, 1977), 2: 46, 49-51.

[6] John J. Gallagher, *The Battle of Brooklyn 1776* (Edison, N.J.: Castle Books, 2002), 91.

[7] Barnet Schecter, *The Battle for New York* (New York: Penguin, 2003), 129.

[8] Schecter, *Battle for New York*, 131-32.

[9] Gallagher, *Battle of Brooklyn*, 103; Christopher Ward, *The War of the Revolution* (New York: McMillan, 1952) 1: 216.

[10] Ernest R. Dupuy and Trevor N. Dupuy, *The Compact History of the Revolutionary War* (New York: Hawthorn Books, 1963), 122-31; Ward, *War of the Revolution*, 1: 216.

[11] Dupuy, *Compact History,* 133.

[12] William Howe to George Germain, Sept. 3, 1776, Newtown, Long Island, in Davies, *Documents of the American Revolution*, 12: 217-18.

[13] David Smith, *New York 1776* (Oxford, U.K.: Osprey, 2008), 51; Mark M. Boatner III, *Encyclopedia of the American Revolution* (New York: David McKay Company, 1976) 653; Ward, *War of the Revolution*, 225; Dupuy, *Compact History,* 133-34; David Stewart, *Sketches of the Character, Manners, and Present State of the Highlanders of Scotland*, 1822 (Edinburgh: John Donald Publishers, 1977), 1: 359, 2: 51-52.

[14] Dupuy, *Compact History,* 136-38.

[15] Dupuy, *Compact History,* 139-146.

[16] Dupuy, *Compact History,* 148-50.

[17] Dupuy, *Compact History,* 139-146. 150-52.

[18] Smith, *New York 1776,* 80-85; Dupuy, *Compact History,* 153-57.

[19] Dupuy, *Compact History,* 158-60.

[20] Ron Chernow, *Washington: A life* (New York: Penguin Press, 2010), 285-86; Elswyth Thane, *The Fighting Quaker: Nathanael Greene* (New York: Hawthorne Books, 1972), 102.

[21] Dupuy, *Compact History,* 166-74.

[22] Dupuy, *Compact History*, 176.

[23] Boatner, *Encyclopedia*, 890-94; Dupuy *Compact History*, 180-83; Scottish writer David Stewart says in *Sketches* 1: 365 that the Highlanders of the 42nd and 71st regiments were among the British troops under Cornwallis; *Battle of Princeton Mapping Project* shows in Appendix III: 3 that Captain George Munro of the light company of the 2nd Battalion of the 71st Regiment was present at Princeton.

Brandywine

[1] David Stewart, *Sketches of the Character, Manners, and Present State of the Highlanders of Scotland*, 1822 (Edinburgh: John Donald Publishers, 1977), 2: 52; Michael C. Harris, *Brandywine: A Military History of the Battle that Lost Philadelphia but Saved America, September 11, 1777* (El Dorado Hills, Calif.: Savas Beatie, 2017), 33, 51.

[2] Harris, *Brandywine*, 57-58, 67, 68, 75, 187.

[3] Harris, *Brandywine*, 71-72, 78, 81.

[4] *Journal of Ambrose Serle* qtd. in Harris, *Brandywine*, 89.

[5] Harris, *Brandywine*, 99.

[6] Qtd. in Harris, *Brandywine*, 101-02.

[7] "Montresor Journals" qtd. in Harris, *Brandywine*, 96.

[8] "Montresor Journals" qtd. in Harris, *Brandywine*, 101.

[9] Qtd. in Harris, *Brandywine*, 101.

[10] Harris, *Brandywine*, 101-10.

[11] Harris, *Brandywine*, 111, 113, 115.

[12] Qtd. in Harris, *Brandywine*, 116, 125.

[13] Harris, *Brandywine*, 116, 121.

[14] Harris, *Brandywine*, 111, 124; *John Peebles' American War: Diary of a Scottish Engineer, 1776-1782*, ed. Ira D. Gruber (Mechanicsburg, Pa.: Stackpole Books, 1998), 129.

[15] Harris, *Brandywine*, xxxi, xxxv, 14, 143-44, 153; *John Peebles' American War*, 131.

[16] Harris, *Brandywine*, 146, 162, 202-03.

[17] Harris, *Brandywine*, 193, 220-22, 409.

[18] Harris, *Brandywine*, 223-24.

[19] Harris, *Brandywine*, 225-29.

[20] Harris, *Brandywine*, 232-34.

[21] Harris, *Brandywine*, 234-36.

[22] Harris, *Brandywine*, 236-37, 239, 244, 245.

[23] Harris, *Brandywine*, 255-57.

[24] Harris, *Brandywine*, 191-92.

[25] Harris, *Brandywine*, 248-51, 260, 273, 279.

[26] Harris, *Brandywine*, 281-320.

[27] Harris, *Brandywine*, 325.

[28] Harris, *Brandywine*, 326-27.

[29] Harris, *Brandywine*, 330.

[30] Harris, *Brandywine*, 334, 340, 365.

[31] Harris, *Brandywine*, 368, 341.

[32] Harris, *Brandywine*, 379.

[33] Harris, *Brandywine*, 85-86; *John Peebles' American War*, 134.

[34] Harris, *Brandywine*, 375.

[35] Harris, *Brandywine*, 389.

[36] Thomas J. McGuire, *Battle of Paoli* (Mechanicsburg, Pa.: Stackpole Books, 2000), 29, 30; Christopher Ward, *The War of the Revolution*, ed. John Richard Alden (New York: Macmillan, 1952), 355.

[37] McGuire, *Battle of Paoli*, 35.

[38] McGuire, *Battle of Paoli*, 37.

[39] McGuire, *Battle of Paoli*, 37-44.

[40] Ward, *War of the Revolution*, 373.

[41] Harris, *Brandywine*, 392, 404.

[42] David Stewart, *Sketches of the Character, Manners, and Present State of the Highlanders of Scotland*, 1822 (Edinburgh: John Donald Publishers, 1977), 2: 52.

[43] "The Life of Robert Jackson, M.D." in Robert Jackson, *A View of the Formation, Discipline, and Economy of Armies*, 3rd ed. (London: Parker, Furnivall and Parker, 1845), xxvii; Mark Boatner, *Encyclopedia of the American Revolution* (New York: David McKay, 1976), 691.

[44] Robert Jackson, *A Treatise on the Fevers of Jamaica, with Some Observation on the Intermitting Fevers of America*, 1795, (retrieved online through Sabin Americana), 55.

[45] Jackson, *Treatise on the Fevers*, 63-64.

Georgia

[1] Archibald Campbell, *Journal of an Expedition against the Rebels of Georgia in North America under the Orders of*

Archibald Campbell Esquire Lieut. Colol. of His Majesty's 71st Regimt. 1778, ed. Colin Campbell (Augusta, Georgia: Richmond County Historical Society, 1981), 21.

[2] Alexander A. Lawrence, "General Robert Howe and the British Capture of Savannah in 1778," *Georgia Historical Quarterly* 36.4 (1952), 307.

[3] Robert Jackson, *A Treatise on the Fevers of Jamaica, with Some Observation on the Intermitting Fevers of America*, 1795, (retrieved online through Sabin Americana), 192.

[4] Campbell, *Journal of an Expedition*, 21.

[5] Campbell, *Journal of an Expedition*, 23-26.

[6] Lawrence, "General Robert Howe and the British Capture of Savannah," 316, 320-21.

[7] Campbell, *Journal of an Expedition*, 28.

[8] Lawrence, "General Robert Howe and the British Capture of Savannah," 324-25; Campbell, *Journal of an Expedition*, 43-44.

[9] Campbell, *Journal of an Expedition*, 42.

[10] Jackson, *Treatise on the Fevers*, 201.

[11] Campbell, *Journal of an Expedition*, 40.

[12] Campbell, *Journal of an Expedition*, 46.

[13] Campbell, *Journal of an Expedition*, 48-49.

[14] Campbell, *Journal of an Expedition*, 49-50, 108 n. 45.

[15] Campbell, *Journal of an Expedition*, 50-52.

[16] Campbell, *Journal of an Expedition*, 53.

[17] Campbell, *Journal of an Expedition*, 54.

[18] Campbell, *Journal of an Expedition*, 54, 120 n. 136.

[19] Campbell, *Journal of an Expedition*, 57-58.

[20] Campbell, *Journal of an Expedition*, 62-68.

[21] Campbell, *Journal of an Expedition*, 68.

[22] Campbell, *Journal of an Expedition*, 70.

[23] Campbell, *Journal of an Expedition*, 74-75.

[24] David S. Heidler, "The American Defeat at Briar Creek, 3 March 1779," *Georgia Historical Quarterly* 66.3 (Fall 1982), 322; Joshua B. Howard, "'Things here wear a melancholy appearance:' The American Defeat at Briar Creek," *Georgia Historical Quarterly* 88.4 (Winter 2004), 486, 490.

[25] John C. Dann, *The Revolution Remembered: Eyewitness accounts of the War for Independence* (Chicago: University of Chicago Press, 1980), 177.

[26] Heidler, "The American Defeat at Briar Creek," 325; William Moultrie, *Memoirs of the American Revolution*, (New York: The New York Times & Arno Press, 1968), 1: 341; David K. Wilson, *The Southern Strategy: Britain's Conquest of South Carolina and Georgia, 1775-1780* (Columbia: University of South Carolina Press, 2005), 94; David Stewart, *Sketches of the Character, Manners, and Present State of the Highlanders of Scotland*, 1822 (Edinburgh: John Donald Publishers, 1977), 2: 56.

[27] Heidler, "The American Defeat at Briar Creek," 325; Wilson, *The Southern Strategy*, 94.

[28] Heidler, "The American Defeat at Briar Creek," 328; Wilson, *The Southern Strategy*, 98-99; Moultrie, *Memoirs*, 1: 340-42.

[29] Dann, *The Revolution Remembered*, 179.

[30] Heidler, "The American Defeat at Briar Creek," 328-29; Wilson, *The Southern Strategy,* 96; Dann, *The Revolution Remembered,* 179.

[31] Archibald Campbell, *Journal of an Expedition*, 77.

[32] Wilson, *The Southern Strategy,* 96.

[33] Dann, *The Revolution Remembered,* 181.

[34] Heidler, "The American Defeat at Briar Creek," 330; Wilson, *The Southern Strategy,* 96; Howard, "'Things here wear a melancholy appearance,'" 494; David Stewart, *Sketches of the Character, Manners, and Present State of the Highlanders of Scotland,* 1822 (Edinburgh: John Donald Publishers, 1977), 2: 56.

[35] Moultrie, *Memoirs,* 1: 324-25.

[36] K.G. Davies, *Documents of the American Revolution, 1770-178* (Shannon: Irish University Press, 1972), 17: 78.

Stono Ferry

[1] William Moultrie, *Memoirs of the American Revolution,* 1802 (New York: The New York Times & Arno Press, 1968), 2:374.

[2] Arlin C. Migliazzo, *To Make This Land Our Own: Community, Identity, and Cultural Adaptation in Purrysburg Township, South Carolina, 1732—1865* (Columbia: University of South Carolina Press, 2007), 273; Warren Ripley, *Battleground: South Carolina in the Revolution* (Charleston: Post-Courier, 1983), 25.

---

3 Augustine Prevost to Henry Clinton, May 21, 1779, James Island Near Charleston, in K.G. Davies, *Documents of the American Revolution* (Shannon: Irish University Press, 1972), 17: 127-29.

4 Charles Shaw to Lord George Germain, Aug. 7, 1779, Savannah, in Davies, *Documents*, 17:180. Shaw gives location of the Creek nation as "upward of 300 miles" from Savannah and notes "the prodigious distance they had to march." Shaw writes that "one hundred and twenty Indians crossed over to Carolina with the army, about forty returned from Purrysburgh and the rest acted with the troops in their progress through South Carolina." See also David Tait to Lord George Germain, Aug. 6, 1779, Savannah, in Davies, *Documents*, 17:180. "About the middle of April Mr. McIntosh arrived with fifty Indians and about the same time fifty more of his party came to this town [Savannah] and were employed by Lieut.-Colonel Prevost on a small excursion into South Carolina," Tait writes. "After their return most of them joined the other Indians at Ebenezer and with them crossed into Carolina with the army, with whom most part have been all the campaign and have behaved very well."

5 "Journal of Brigade Major F Skelly," ed. John A. Robertson, *Southern Campaigns of the American Revolution* 3:12.1 (Dec, 2006), 24-27, http://southerncampaign.org/newsletter/v3n12.pdf.

6 David Stewart, *Sketches of the Character, Manners, and Present State of the Highlanders of Scotland*, 1822 (Edinburgh: John Donald Publishers, 1977), 2:101-02.

7 Robert Jackson, *A Treatise on the Fevers of Jamaica, with Some Observation on the Intermitting Fevers of America*, 1795, (retrieved online through Sabin Americana), 57.

[8] Prevost to Clinton, May 21, 1779, in Davies, *Documents of the American Revolution* 17: 127.

[9] *Journal of Major General von Knoblauch's Hessian Garrison Regiment,* qtd. in Daniel T. Elliott, *The Revolutionary War Battlefield at Purysburg, South Carolina: Search and Discovery*, LAMAR Institute Publication Series, Report Number 209 (Savannah: The Lamar Institute, 2016) 58.

[10] Prevost to Clinton, May 21, 1779, in Davies, *Documents of the American Revolution* 17: 127.

[11] Patrick O'Kelley, *Nothing But Blood and Slaughter* (Barbecue, N.C.: Patrick O'Kelly, 2004), 1: 272-73.

[12] "Journal of Brigade Major F Skelly," 25.

[13] Prevost to Clinton, May 21, 1779, in Davies, *Documents of the American Revolution* 17: 127.

[14] O'Kelley, *Nothing But Blood and Slaughter,* 1: 274-75.

[15] William Moultrie, *Memoirs of the American Revolution,* 1802 (New York: The New York Times and Arno Press, 1968), 1:397-98.

[16] Moultrie, *Memoirs,* 1:407.

[17] Moultrie, *Memoirs,* 1:399.

[18] Moultrie, *Memoirs,* 1:430.

[19] Moultrie, *Memoirs,* 1:432.

[20] "Journal of Brigade Major F Skelly," 25.

[21] "Journal of Brigade Major F Skelly," 25.

[22] Moultrie, *Memoirs,* 1:427-35.

[23] Augustine Prevost to Lord George Germain, June 10, 1779, St. John's Island 12 miles from Charleston, in Davies, *Documents of the American Revolution* 17: 142.

[24] "Journal of Brigade Major F Skelly," 25.

[25] "Journal of Brigade Major F Skelly," 25.

[26] "Journal of Brigade Major F Skelly," 25.

[27] Col. Grimke to J. Kean, Camp at Sommers, S.C., June 21, 1779, in Moultrie, *Memoirs,* 1:495-99.

[28] Charles Stedman, *History of the Origin, Progress and Termination of the American War*, 1794 (New York: New York Times and Arno Press, 1969), 2: 117.

[29] Robert Jackson, *A View of the Formation, Discipline, and Economy of Armies*, 3rd ed. (London: Parker, Furnivall and Parker, 1845), 290-91.

[30] Moultrie, *Memoirs,* 2:29.

[31] William Moultrie to John Maitland, Sheldon, S.C., July 20, 1779, in Moultrie, *Memoirs,* 2:31-32.

[32] Benjamin Lincoln to William Moultrie, near Stono, S.C., June 20, 1779, in Moultrie, *Memoirs,* 1:493.

[33] Ward, *The War of the Revolution*, 686.

[34] "Journal of Brigade Major F Skelly," 25.

[35] Charles Stedman, *History of the Origin, Progress and Termination of the American War*, 1794 (New York: New York Times and Arno Press, 1969), 2: 118.

[36] Augustine Prevost to Lord George Germain, Aug. 4, 1779, Savannah, in Davies, *Documents of the American Revolution* 17: 175.

[37] Augustine Prevost to William Moultrie, Johns Island, S.C., June 17, 1779, in Moultrie, *Memoirs,* 1:481.

[38] John Maitland to William Moultrie, Beaufort, S.C., July 10, 1779, in Moultrie, *Memoirs,* 2:30.

[39] Augustine Prevost to Henry Clinton, May 21, 1779, James Island near Charleston, in Davies, *Documents of the American Revolution* 17: 129.

[40] Robert Jackson, *A Treatise on the Fevers of Jamaica, with Some Observation on the Intermitting Fevers of America,* 1795, (retrieved online through Sabin Americana), 194.

[41] Augustine Prevost to Lord George Germain, June 10, 1779, St. John's Island 12 miles from Charleston, in Davies, *Documents of the American Revolution* 17: 142.

[42] "Journal of Brigade Major F Skelly," 26.

Siege of Savannah

[1] Benjamin Kennedy, ed., *Muskets, Cannon Balls & Bombs: Nine narratives of the Siege of Savannah in 1779* (Savannah: The Beehive Press, 1974), 122-23; Alexander A. Lawrence, *Storm over Savannah: The story of Count d'Estaing and the Siege of the Town in 1779* (Athens: University of Georgia Press, 1951), 157.

[2] Kennedy, *Muskets,* 104.

[3] Robert Jackson, *A Treatise on the Fevers of Jamaica, with Some Observation on the Intermitting Fevers of America,* 1795, (retrieved online through Sabin Americana), 194.

[4] Lawrence, *Storm,* 49-51.

---

[5] Kennedy, *Muskets,* 51.

[6] Kennedy, *Muskets,* 73.

[7] Qtd. in Franklin B, Hough, ed,, *The Siege of Savannah by the Combined American and French Forces under the command of Gen. Lincoln and the Count d'Estaing in the Autumn of 1779,* 1866 (Spartanburg, S.C.: The Reprint Company, 1975), 63-64.

[8] David Stewart, *Sketches of the Character, Manners, and Present State of the Highlanders of Scotland,* 1822 (Edinburgh: John Donald Publishers, 1977), 2: 62.

[9] Hough, *Savannah,* 66.

[10] Kennedy, *Muskets,* 15-16.

[11] Kennedy, *Muskets,* 97.

[12] Stewart, *Sketches,* 2: 62.

[13] Kennedy, *Muskets,* 131-32.

[14] Kennedy, *Muskets,* 99.

[15] Kennedy, *Muskets,* 109-114.

[16] William Harden, *A History of Savannah and South Georgia,* (Atlanta: Cherokee Publishing Company, 1969), 1: 218.

[17] Kennedy, *Muskets,* 100.

[18] Harden, *History of Savannah,* 219.

[19] Elizabeth Lichtenstein Johnston, *Recollections of a Georgia Loyalist,* 1836 (Spartanburg: The Reprint Company, 1974), 57-59.

[20] Hough, *Savannah* 71-73.

[21] Hough, *Savannah* 84-85.

[22] Rupert Furneaux, *The Pictorial History of the American Revolution as told by Witnesses and Participants,* (Chicago: JG. Ferguson, 1973), 299; Ian Saberton, *The Cornwallis Papers* (Uckfield, England: Naval & Military Press, 2010), 1: 178, n. 6.

[23] Kennedy, *Muskets,* 73.

[24] Kennedy, *Muskets,* 102.

[25] Stewart, *Sketches,* 2:63.

[26] Alexander Garden, *Anecdotes of the Revolutionary War,* 1822, (Spartanburg, S.C.: Reprint Company, 1972), 12-13.

[27] Kennedy, *Muskets,* 101.

[28] Furneaux, *Pictorial History,* 306.

[29] Hough, *Savannah,* 167-68.

[30] Johnston, *Recollections of a Georgia Loyalist,* 61-63.

[31] Hough, *Savannah* 147-48.

[32] Hough, *Savannah,* 168.

[33] Lawrence, *Storm,* 141.

[34] Ian Saberton, *The Cornwallis Papers* (Uckfield, England: Naval & Military Press, 2010), 1: 178, n. 36.

Siege of Charleston

[1] For a detailed account, see Carl P. Borick, *A Gallant Defense: The Siege of Charleston, 1780* (Columbia: University of South Carolina Press, 2003).

[2] Bernard A. Uhlendorf, trans. and ed., *The Siege of Charleston with an account of the province of South Carolina: Diaries and letters of Hessian officers from the von Jungkenn Papers in the William L. Clements Library* (Ann Arbor: University of Michigan Press, 1938), 375.

[3] Uhlendorf, *Siege of Charleston,* 209.

[4] Diary of Lieut. Anthony Allaire, online at https://www.tngenweb.org/revwar/kingsmountain/al-laire.html

[5] Diary of Lieut. Anthony Allaire.

[6] Diary of Lieut. Anthony Allaire.

[7] Diary of Lieut. Anthony Allaire.

[8] Diary of Lieut. Anthony Allaire.

[9] Diary of Lieut. Anthony Allaire.

[10] Charles Baxley, "Fratricide at McPherson's Plantation," *Southern Campaigns of the American Revolution* vol. 13, no. 3, unpublished draft, Jan.23, 2017.

[11] Ed Southern, ed., *Voices of the American Revolution in the Carolinas* (Winston-Salem, N.C.: John F. Blair, 2009), 59-60.

[12] Banastre Tarleton, *A History of the Campaigns of 1780 and 1781 in the Southern Provinces of North America*, 1787 (Spartanburg, S.C.: Reprint Company, 1967), 15-17.

[13] Lachlan McIntosh, "Journal of the Siege of Charlestown, 1780," in *Lachlan McIntosh Papers in the University of Georgia Libraries University of Georgia Libraries: Miscellanea Publications, No. 7,* ed. Lilla Mills Hawes (Athens: University of Georgia Press, 1968), 106.

[14] McIntosh, "Journal of the Siege," 106.

[15] McIntosh, "Journal of the Siege," 107-08.

[16] Uhlendorf, *Siege of Charleston,* 265.

[17] Uhlendorf, *Siege of Charleston,* 263.

[18] McIntosh, "Journal of the Siege," 109.

[19] McIntosh, "Journal of the Siege," 110.

[20] McIntosh, "Journal of the Siege," 112.

[21] Franklin B. Hough, ed., *The Siege of Charleston by the British Fleet and Army under the command of Admiral Arbuthnot and Sir Henry Clinton which terminated with the surrender of that place on the 12th of May, 1780* (Spartanburg, S.C.: The Reprint Company, 1975), 120-21.

[22] Carl P. Borick, *A Gallant Defense: The Siege of Charleston, 1780* (Columbia: University of South Carolina Press, 2003) 223; Carl P. Borick, *Relieve us of this Burthen: American Prisoners of War in The Revolutionary South, 1780-1782* (Columbia: The University of South Carolina Press, 2012) 4-26.

[23] Brian Hicks, "Doomed British infantry officer describes siege of Charleston," *The Post and Courier*, 16 Nov. 2008, https://www.postandcourier.com/news/doomed-british-infantry-officer-describes-siege-of-charleston/article_089f98b7-b60e-52e7-8b08-0588229cef27.html

Cheraw and Camden

[1] Charles Cornwallis to Henry Clinton, Aug. 6, 1780, Charlestown, in Ian Saberton, *The Cornwallis Papers* (Uckfield, England: Naval & Military Press, 2010), 1: 178.

---

[2] Ian Saberton, *The Cornwallis Papers* (Uckfield, England: Naval & Military Press, 2010), 1: 35.

[3] Charles Cornwallis to Nisbet Balfour, June 13, 1780, Camden, S.C., in Ian Saberton, *The Cornwallis Papers* (Uckfield, England: Naval & Military Press, 2010), 1: 87.

[4] Charles Cornwallis to George Germain, Aug. 20, 1780, Camden, S.C., in in K.G. Davies, *Documents of the American Revolution* (Shannon: Irish University Press, 1972), 18: 145.

[5] Banastre Tarleton, *A History of the Campaigns of 1780 and 1781 in the Southern Provinces of North America*, 1787 (Spartanburg, S.C.: Reprint Company, 1967), 87.

[6] Robert Jackson, *A Treatise on the Fevers of Jamaica, with Some Observation on the Intermitting Fevers of America*, 1795, (retrieved online through Sabin Americana), 195.

[7] Archibald McArthur to Charles Cornwallis, June 13, 1780, Camp at Cheraw Hill, S.C., in Ian Saberton, *The Cornwallis Papers*, 1: 133.

[8] McArthur to Cornwallis, June 13, 1780, in Saberton, *The Cornwallis Papers*, 1: 133.

[9] McArthur to Cornwallis, June 13, 1780, in Saberton, *The Cornwallis Papers*, 1: 132-33.

[10] Archibald McArthur to Charles Cornwallis, June 14, 1780, Camp at Cheraw Hill, S.C., in Saberton, *The Cornwallis Papers*, 1: 133-34.

[11] Charles Cornwallis to Archibald McArthur, June 18, 1780, Camden, S.C., in Saberton, *The Cornwallis Papers*, 1: 134.

[12] Archibald McArthur to Charles Cornwallis, June 14, 1780, Camp at Cheraw Hill, S.C., in Saberton, *The Cornwallis Papers*, 1: 133-34.

[13] Archibald McArthur to Charles Cornwallis, June 18, 1780, Camp at Cheraw Hill, S.C., in Saberton, *The Cornwallis Papers,* 1: 137.

[14] Edward McCrady, *The History of South Carolina in the Revolution*, 1901 (New York: Russell & Russell, 1969), 642-43.

[15] "The 71st Regiment of Foot," *Historical Marker Database*, https://www.hmdb.org/m.asp?m=54803. The Civic League of Cheraw in 2011 erected a memorial headstone at the site believed to be the grave of an officer, and placed smaller markers at the supposed grave of another officer and at a depression in the ground where several soldiers may have been buried together. In *The History of South Carolina in the Revolution,* published in 1901, Edward McCrady writes "Not many years ago quite a perceptible sink in the earth was pointed out as the spot where many of them were buried in one common grave," 645. See also Carl Julien and Chapman J. Milling, *Beneath So Kind a Sky: The Scenic and Architectural Beauty of South Carolina* (Columbia: University of South Carolina Press, 1947), notes to plate XLI.

[16] McCrady, *The History of South Carolina in the Revolution,* 643-44.

[17] McCrady, *The History of South Carolina in the Revolution,* 644-45.

[18] McCrady, *The History of South Carolina in the Revolution,* 645. McCrady gives his source as Gregg, *History of the Old Cheraws,* 309, 312.

[19] Charles Cornwallis to George Germain, Aug. 20, 1780, Camden, S.C., in in K.G. Davies, *Documents of the American Revolution* (Shannon: Irish University Press, 1972), 18: 146.

[20] Cornwallis to Germain, Aug. 20, 1780, in Davies, *Documents of the American Revolution* 18: 147.

[21] Archibald McArthur to Charles Cornwallis, July 29, 1780, Camden, S.C., in Saberton, *The Cornwallis Papers,* 1: 364.

[22] William Mills to Archibald McArthur, July 3, 1780, in Saberton, *The Cornwallis Papers*, 1: 196.

[23] Robert Jackson, *A Treatise on the Fevers of Jamaica, with Some Observation on the Intermitting Fevers of America,* 1795, (retrieved online through Sabin Americana), 53-54.

[24] Jackson, *A Treatise on the Fevers of Jamaica*, 227.

[25] Cornwallis to Germain, Aug. 20, 1780, in Davies, *Documents of the American Revolution* 18: 147.

[26] Jackson, *A Treatise on the Fevers of Jamaica*, 196.

[27] Jackson, *A Treatise on the Fevers of Jamaica*, 227; Banastre Tarleton, *A History of the Campaigns of 1780 and 1781 in the Southern Provinces of North America*, 1787 (Spartanburg, S.C.: Reprint Company, 1967), 98.

[28] Francis Rawdon to Charles Cornwallis, July 27, 1780, Camden, in Saberton, *The Cornwallis Papers*, 1: 218.

[29] McCrady, *The History of South Carolina in the Revolution*, 645-47. Regarding "Lord" Nairne, Saberton says the lieutenant could have been either John Nairne or William Nairne, who served in the 1st Battalion of the 71st Regiment (*Cornwallis* Papers 1:320 n. 17). O'Kelly calls him "Captain-Lieutenant John Nairne" (*Nothing but Blood and Slaughter* 2:208).

[30] Tarleton, *History of the Campaigns*, 98.

[31] James Wemyss to Charles Cornwallis, July 28, 1780, George Town, in Saberton, *The Cornwallis Papers*, 1: 319-20.

[32] Charles Cornwallis to James Wemyss, July 30 and 31, 1780, Charlestown, in Saberton, *The Cornwallis Papers,* 1: 320.

[33] Charles Cornwallis to Francis Rawdon, Aug. 1, 1780, Charlestown, in Saberton, *The Cornwallis Papers,* 1: 221; Charles Cornwallis to Francis Rawdon, July 30, 1780, Charlestown, in Saberton, *The Cornwallis Papers,* 1: 216.

[34] Charles Cornwallis to Henry Clinton, Aug. 6, 1780, Charlestown, in Saberton, *The Cornwallis Papers,* 1: 177.

[35] Jackson, *A Treatise on the Fevers of Jamaica,* 227-228, 196.

[36] Francis Rawdon, Jan. 19, 1801, quoted in Jim Piecuch, *The Battle of Camden: A Documentary History* (Charleston, History Press, 2006), 58-59.

[37] Charles Cornwallis to Henry Clinton, Aug. 10, 1780, Charlestown, in Saberton, *The Cornwallis Papers,* 1: 179.

[38] Jackson, *A Treatise on the Fevers of Jamaica,* 196.

[39] Charles Cornwallis to George Germain, Aug. 20, 1780, Camden, in Saberton, *The Cornwallis Papers,* 2: 10.

[40] Archibald McArthur to Charles Cornwallis, July 29, 1780, Camden, in Saberton, *The Cornwallis Papers,* 1: 364-65.

[41] Banastre Tarleton, *A History of the Campaigns of 1780 and 1781 in the Southern Provinces of North America,* 1787 (Spartanburg, S.C.: Reprint Company, 1967), 103-04.

[42] Peter McCandless, "Revolutionary Fever: Disease and War in the Lower South, 1776-1783" (*Transactions of the American Clinical and Climatological Association,* vol. 118, 2007), 235; Tarleton, *History of the Campaigns,* 136; Aeneas Mackintosh served as a captain in the 2nd Battalion throughout the war, according to Margaret Mackintosh, *The History of Clan*

Mackintosh and Clan Chattan (Edinburgh: The Pentland Press Limited, 1997), 65-66.

[43] Tarleton, *History of the Campaigns,* 105-06.

[44] Charles Cornwallis to George Germain, Aug. 21, 1780, Camden, in Saberton, *The Cornwallis Papers*, 2: 11-15, and in Davies, *Documents of the American Revolution*, 18:148-52.

[45] H.L. Landers, *The Battle of Camden, South Carolina, August 16, 1780* (Washington: United States Government Printing Office, 1929), 45; Mark Urban, *Fusiliers: The Saga of a British Redcoat Regiment in the American Revolution* (New York: Walker and Company, 2007), 210.

[46] Tarleton, *History of the Campaigns,* 137-38.

[47] Charles Cornwallis to Francis Rawdon, Aug. 4, 1780, Charlestown, in Saberton, *The Cornwallis Papers,* 1: 227.

[48] Cornwallis to Germain, Aug. 21, 1780, in Saberton, *The Cornwallis Papers*, 2: 14.

[49] Brian Hicks, "Doomed British infantry officer describes siege of Charleston," *The Post and Courier*, 16 Nov. 2008, https://www.postandcourier.com/news/doomed-british-infantry-officer-describes-siege-of-charleston/article_089f98b7-b60e-52e7-8b08-0588229cef27.html

Charlotte and Winnsboro

[1] Charles Cornwallis to Henry Clinton, Aug. 23, 1780, Camden, in Ian Saberton, *The Cornwallis Papers* (Uckfield, England: Naval & Military Press, 2010), 2: 16.

[2] Charles Cornwallis to Nisbet Balfour, Sept. 3 and 6, 1780, Camden, in Saberton, *The Cornwallis Papers*, 2: 73.

[3] Charles Cornwallis to Henry Clinton, Sept. 22, 1780, Camp at Waxhaw, in Saberton, *The Cornwallis Papers*, 2: 44-45.

[4] Charles Cornwallis to Lieutenant Archibald Campbell, Sept. 20, 1780, Waxhaw, in Saberton, *The Cornwallis Papers*, 2: 284.

[5] Charles Cornwallis to George Germain, Sept. 19, 1780, Waxhaws, in Davies, *Documents of the American Revolution*, 18: 170.

[6] Journal of Lieutenant John Money, Sept. 21, 1780, Crawford's on Waxhaw Creek, in Saberton, *The Cornwallis Papers*, 2: 88.

[7] Robert Jackson, *A Treatise on the Fevers of Jamaica, with Some Observation on the Intermitting Fevers of America*, 1795, (retrieved online through Sabin Americana), 197-98.

[8] William R. Davie, *Revolutionary War Sketches of William R. Davie,* Blackwell P. Robinson, ed. (Raleigh: North Carolina Department of Cultural Resources, 1976), 21-25; John Buchanan, *The Road to Guilford Courthouse: The American Revolution in the South* (New York: John Wiley & Sons, 1997), 186-88; Charles Cornwallis to Nisbet Balfour, Sept. 21, 1780, Waxhaw, in Saberton, *The Cornwallis Papers*, 2: 88.

[9] John Buchanan, *The Road to Guilford Courthouse: The American Revolution in the South* (New York: John Wiley & Sons, 1997), 188-90; Charles Cornwallis to Nisbet Balfour, Sept. 27, 1780, Charlottetown, in Saberton, *The Cornwallis Papers*, 2: 99.

---

[10] Charles Cornwallis to Archibald McArthur, Sept. 29, 1780, Charlottetown, in Saberton, *The Cornwallis Papers*, 2: 280.

[11] William Kitty to Charles Cornwallis, Oct. 13, 1780, Camden, in Saberton, *The Cornwallis Papers*, 2: 291.

[12] Patrick Ferguson to Charles Cornwallis, Sept. 30, 1780, Between Green River and Pacolet, in Saberton, *The Cornwallis Papers*, 2: 161; Charles Cornwallis to Patrick Ferguson, Oct. 8, 1780, Charlottetown, in Saberton, *The Cornwallis Papers*, 2: 166.

[13] Charles Cornwallis to Nisbet Balfour, Aug. 29, 1780, Camden, in Saberton, *The Cornwallis Papers*, 2: 64-65.

[14] Patrick Ferguson to Charles Cornwallis, Oct. 5, 1780, Bufflow Creek, in Saberton, *The Cornwallis Papers*, 2: 165.

[15] Charles Cornwallis to Archibald McArthur, Oct. 5, 1780, Charlottetown, in Saberton, *The Cornwallis Papers*, 2: 64-65.

[16] Cornwallis to Ferguson, Oct. 5, 1780 Charlottetown, in *Cornwallis Papers*, 2: 161.

[17] Cornwallis to Ferguson, Oct. 5, 1780 Charlottetown, in *Cornwallis Papers*, 2: 164.

[18] Ferguson to Cornwallis, Oct. 5, 1780, Bufflow Creek, in *Cornwallis Papers* 2: 164.

[19] Ferguson to Cornwallis, Oct. 6, 1780, King Mountain, in *Cornwallis Papers* 2: 164.

[20] Cornwallis to Ferguson, Oct. 8, 1780 Charlottetown, in *Cornwallis Papers*, 2: 166.

[21] Abraham DePeyster to Charles Cornwallis, Oct. 11, 1780, Camp near Gilbert Town, in *Cornwallis Papers,* 2: 166-67.

[22] Charles Cornwallis to Nisbet Balfour, Oct. 3, 1780, Charlottetown, in Saberton, *The Cornwallis Papers*, 2: 106.

[23] Saberton, *The Cornwallis Papers*, 2: 31.

[24] Charles Stedman, *History of the Origin, Progress and Termination of the American War*, 1794 (New York: New York Times and Arno Press, 1969), 2: 224-25.

[25] Francis Rawdon to Banastre Tarleton, Oct. 23, [1780], Smith's Plantation, in Tarleton, *History of the Campaigns*, 197.

[26] Francis Rawdon to George Turnbull, Oct. 27, 1780, McClarkin's near Lee's Mill, in Saberton, *The Cornwallis Papers*, 2: 262.

[27] Tarleton, *History of the Campaigns*, 168-69.

[28] Charles Cornwallis to Henry Clinton, Dec. 3, 1780, Winnsboro, in Davies, *Documents of the American Revolution*, 18: 244; Stedman, *History of the American War*, 2: 226.

[29] Jackson, *A Treatise on the Fevers of Jamaica,* 197.

[30] McArthur to Cornwallis, Dec. 2, 1780, Camp at Byerley's Ferry, in Saberton, *The Cornwallis Papers*, 3: 322.

[31] Cornwallis to McArthur, Dec. 3, 1780, Wynnesborough, in Saberton, *The Cornwallis Papers*, 3: 322; Cornwallis to Rawdon, Dec. 4, 1780, Wynnesborough, in Saberton, *The Cornwallis Papers*, 3: 193.

[32] Cornwallis to McArthur, Nov. 16, 1780, Winsborough, in Saberton, *The Cornwallis Papers*, 3: 193.

[33] Rawdon to Cornwallis, Nov. 24, 1780, Camden, in Saberton, *The Cornwallis Papers*, 3: 169.

[34] Cornwallis to Rawdon, Nov. 25, 1780, Wynnesborough, in Saberton, *The Cornwallis Papers*, 3: 171.

[35] Cornwallis to Rawdon, Nov. 26, 1780, Wynnesborough, in Saberton, *The Cornwallis Papers*, 3: 172.

[36] Rawdon to Cornwallis, Nov. 26, 1780, Camden, in Saberton, *The Cornwallis Papers*, 3: 175.

[37] Cornwallis to McArthur, Nov. 30, 1780, Wynnesborough, in Saberton, *The Cornwallis Papers*, 3: 321.

[38] McArthur to Cornwallis, Dec. 2, 1780, Camp at Byerley's Ferry, in Saberton, *The Cornwallis Papers*, 3: 322.

[39] Cornwallis to McArthur, Dec. 3, 1780, Wynnesborough, in Saberton, *The Cornwallis Papers*, 3: 322.

[40] Cornwallis to Rawdon, Dec. 3, 1780, Wynnesborough, in Saberton, *The Cornwallis Papers*, 3: 191.

[41] Cornwallis to McArthur, Dec. 3, 1780, Wynnesborough, in Saberton, *The Cornwallis Papers*, 3: 322.

[42] Cornwallis to Rawdon, Dec. 4, 1780, Wynnesborough, in Saberton, *The Cornwallis Papers*, 3: 193.

[43] Cornwallis to Rawdon, Dec. 11, 1780, Wynnesborough, in Saberton, *The Cornwallis Papers*, 3: 204.

[44] Cornwallis to John Harris Cruger, Nov. 11, 1780, Wynnesborough, in Saberton, *The Cornwallis Papers*, 3: 268.

[45] Cornwallis to Clinton, Dec. 3, 1780, in Davies, *Documents of the American Revolution*, 18: 246.

[46] John Harris Cruger to Cornwallis, Nov. 14, 1780, Ninety Six, in Saberton, *The Cornwallis Papers*, 3: 270.

[47] McArthur to Cornwallis, Nov. 13, 1780, Camp at Byerly's Ferry (formerly Shirar's), in Saberton, *The Cornwallis Papers,* 3: 270.

[48] Cornwallis to Rawdon, Nov. 14, 1780, Winsborough, in Saberton, *The Cornwallis Papers,* 3: 145.

[49] McArthur to Cornwallis, Nov. 18, 1780, Camp at Bryerly's Ferry, in Saberton, *The Cornwallis Papers,* 3: 270.

[50] Tarleton, *History of the Campaigns,* 174-75.

[51] Cornwallis to McArthur, Nov. 22, 1780, Wynnesborough, in Saberton, *The Cornwallis Papers,* 3: 322.

[52] Cornwallis to Tarleton, Nov. 23, 1780, Wynnesborough, in Saberton, *The Cornwallis Papers,* 3: 342.

[53] Tarleton to Cornwallis, Nov. 22, 1780, Near the Head of Tiger, and Nov. 24, 1780, On Tiger, in Saberton, *The Cornwallis Papers,* 3: 341, 343.

[54] Saberton, *The Cornwallis Papers,* 3: 6.

[55] Cornwallis to Rawdon, Nov. 24, 1780, Winsborough, in Saberton, *The Cornwallis Papers,* 3: 168.

[56] Cornwallis to Tarleton, Nov. 25, 1780, Wynnesborough, in Saberton, *The Cornwallis Papers,* 3: 344.

[57] Tarleton to Cornwallis, Nov. 28, 1780, in Saberton, *The Cornwallis Papers,* 3: 346.

[58] Cornwallis to Clinton, Dec. 3, 1780, in Davies, *Documents of the American Revolution,* 18: 246-47; Tarleton, *History of the Campaigns,* 174-80; Christopher Ward, *The War of the Revolution,* ed. John Richard Alden (New York: Macmillan, 1952), 2: 746-47; Mark M. Boatner III, *Encyclopedia of the American Revolution* (New York: David McKay Company, 1976), 78-80.

---

[59] Tarleton, *History of the Campaigns*, 184.

[60] Henry Haldane to McArthur, Dec. 22, 1780, Wynnesborough, in Saberton, *The Cornwallis Papers*, 3: 327.

[61] McArthur to Haldane, Dec. 24, 1780, Camp at Owens's Plantation, in Saberton, *The Cornwallis Papers*, 3: 270.

[62] McArthur to Haldane, Dec. 25, 1780, Camp at Owens's Plantation, in Saberton, *The Cornwallis Papers*, 3: 329.

[63] McArthur to Tarleton, Dec. 26, 1780, Owens's Plantation, and McArthur to Cornwallis, Dec. 26, 1780, Camp at Owens's Plantation, in Saberton, *The Cornwallis Papers*, 3: 330, 356.

[64] McArthur to Cornwallis, Dec. 26, 1780, Camp at Owens's Plantation, in Saberton, *The Cornwallis Papers*, 3: 330.

Cowpens and Guilford Courthouse

[1] Charles Cornwallis to Francis Rawdon, Jan. 3, 1781, Wynnesboro, in Ian Saberton, *The Cornwallis Papers* (Uckfield, England: Naval & Military Press, 2010), 3: 239.

[2] Henry Haldane to Archibald McArthur, Jan. 2, 1781, in *Cornwallis Papers* 3: 331.

[3] Banastre Tarleton, *A History of the Campaigns of 1780 and 1781 in the Southern Provinces of North America*, 1787 (Spartanburg, S.C.: Reprint Company, 1967), 210-11.

[4] Cornwallis to Rawdon, Jan. 3, 1781, in *Cornwallis Papers*, 3: 239; Cornwallis to Banastre Tarleton, Jan. 5, 1781, Wynnesborough, in *Cornwallis Papers* 3: 359-60.

[5] Tarleton, *Campaigns*, 212.

[6] Saberton, *Cornwallis Papers* 3: 11; Lawrence E. Babits, *A Devil of a Whipping: The Battle of Cowpens* (Chapel Hill: University of North Carolina Press, 1998), 45.

[7] Cornwallis to Tarleton, Jan. 5, 1781, in *Cornwallis Papers* 3: 359-60.

[8] Tarleton, *Campaigns*, 214.

[9] Roderick Mackenzie, *Strictures on Lt. Col. Tarleton's History of the Campaigns of 1780 and 1781* (London: Printed for the Author, 1787, available online through Sabin Americana), 96.

[10] Information for this account of the Battle of Cowpens is derived from numerous sources including Lawrence E. Babits, *A Devil of a Whipping: The Battle of Cowpens* (Chapel Hill: University of North Carolina Press, 1998), throughout; John Buchanan, *The Road to Guilford Courthouse: The American Revolution in the South* (New York: John Wiley & Sons, 1997), 296-333; Burke Davis, *The Cowpens-Guilford Courthouse Campaign* (New York: J.B. Lippincott, 1962), 18-48; M.F. Treacy, *Prelude to Yorktown: The Southern Campaigns of Nathanael Greene* (Chapel Hill: University of North Carolina Press, 1963), 88-128; Don Higginbotham, *Daniel Morgan: Revolutionary Rifleman* (Chapel Hill: University of North Carolina Press, 1961), 135-55.

[11] Joseph Johnson, *Traditions and Reminiscences Chiefly of the American Revolution,* 1851, (Spartanburg, S.C.: Reprint Company, 1972), 449-50; "From the Memoir of Major Thomas Young" in *Voices of the American Revolution in the Carolinas,* ed. Ed Southern (Winston-Salem, N.C.: John F. Blair, 2009), 181-82.

[12] M.F. Treacy, *Prelude to Yorktown: The Southern Campaigns of Nathanael Greene* (Chapel Hill: University of North Carolina Press, 1963), 98.

[13] Mackenzie, *Strictures*, 96-97.

[14] Treacy, *Prelude to Yorktown*, 97.

[15] Don Higginbotham, *Daniel Morgan: Revolutionary Rifleman* (Chapel Hill: University of North Carolina Press, 1961), 136.

[16] Mackenzie, *Strictures*, 97.

[17] Johnson, *Traditions*, 450; Higginbotham, *Daniel Morgan,* 137.

[18] *The Spirit of 'Seventy-Six: The Story of the American Revolution as Told by Participants,* ed. Henry Steele Commager and Richard B. Morris (New York: Bobbs-Merrill, 1958), 2: 1153.

[19] James P. Collins, *Autobiography of a Revolutionary Soldier*, 1859 (available online through HathiTrust), 57; John Buchanan, *The Road to Guilford Courthouse: The American Revolution in the South* (New York: John Wiley & Sons, 1997), 323.

[20] Mackenzie, *Strictures*, 98.

[21] Mackenzie, *Strictures*, 99.

[22] Buchanan, *Road to Guilford,* 324; Treacy, *Prelude to Yorktown*, 106.

[23] Mackenzie, *Strictures*, 99-100.

[24] Mackenzie, *Strictures*, 111; Robert D. Bass, *The Green Dragoon: The Lives of Banastre Tarleton and Mary Robinson* (New York: Henry Holt, 1957), 158.

[25] *Spirit of 'Seventy-Six* 2: 1157.

[26] Babits, *Devil of a Whipping*, 197 n. 99, citing *the Pennsylvania Packet* 17 Feb. 1781.

[27] James Jackson to Daniel Morgan, Jan. 20, 1795, U.S. Senate Chambers, Philadelphia, and Jackson to Morgan, Feb. 9, 1795, Philadelphia, in Theodorus Bailey Myers, *Cowpens Papers* (Charleston: News and Courier Book Press, 1881), 46, 47.

[28] Henry Lee, *The Campaign of 1781 in the Carolinas*, 1824 (Spartanburg, S.C.: Reprint Company, 1975), 98.

[29] Buchanan, *Road to Guilford,* 326; Robert D. Bass, *The Green Dragoon: The Lives of Banastre Tarleton and Mary Robinson* (New York: Henry Holt, 1957), 159.

[30] Cornwallis to Henry Clinton, Jan. 18, 1781, Camp on Turkey Creek, Broad River, in *Cornwallis Papers* 3: 36.

[31] Mackenzie, *Strictures*, 101-02.

[32] Lawrence E. Babits, *A Devil of a Whipping: The Battle of Cowpens* (Chapel Hill: University of North Carolina Press, 1998), 132-33.

[33] *Spirit of 'Seventy-Six* 2: 1159.

[34] Mackenzie, *Strictures*, 107-10.

[35] Tarleton, *Campaigns*, 217, 251.

[36] Mackenzie, *Strictures*, 111-12, 118.

[37] Cornwallis to Rawdon, Jan. 21, 1781, Buffalo Creek, in *Cornwallis Papers* 3: 359-60.

[38] Lawrence E. Babits and Joshua B. Howard, *Long, Obstinate and Bloody: The Battle of Guilford Courthouse* (Chapel Hill: University of North Carolina Press, 2009), 67-68.

---

[39] Babits and Howard, *Long, Obstinate and Bloody,* 59-60.

[40] Cornwallis to James Henry Craig, March 8, 1781, Camp on Reedy Fork, in *Cornwallis Papers* 4: 26.

[41] Tarleton, *Campaigns*, 238.

[42] Returns of troops in *Cornwallis Papers* 4: 61, 63.

[43] Babits and Howard, *Long, Obstinate and Bloody,* 79.

[44] Babits and Howard, *Long, Obstinate and Bloody,* 86-88, 219.

[45] Babits and Howard, *Long, Obstinate and Bloody,* 96, 99.

[46] Babits and Howard, *Long, Obstinate and Bloody,* 104, quoting the pension application of James Martin.

[47] Babits and Howard, *Long, Obstinate and Bloody,* 108, quoting Caruthers, *Revolutionary Sketches*, 140.

[48] Babits and Howard, *Long, Obstinate and Bloody,* 124.

[49] Babits and Howard, *Long, Obstinate and Bloody,* 112.

[50] Babits and Howard, *Long, Obstinate and Bloody,* 125-26.

[51] Babits and Howard, *Long, Obstinate and Bloody,* 128.

[52] Cornwallis to George Germain, March 17, 1781, Guildford, in *Cornwallis Papers* 4: 18.

[53] Babits and Howard, *Long, Obstinate and Bloody,* 166.

[54] Babits and Howard, *Long, Obstinate and Bloody,* 218.

[55] Cornwallis to Clinton, April 10, 1781, Camp near Wilmington, in *Cornwallis Papers* 4: 109.

[56] Cornwallis to Germain, March 17, 1781, in *Cornwallis Papers* 4: 19.

[57] Cornwallis to Germain, March 17, 1781, in *Cornwallis Papers* 4: 17.

[58] *Cornwallis Papers* 4: 8, 64.

[59] Babits and Howard, *Long, Obstinate and Bloody,* 224.

[60] *Spirit of 'Seventy-Six,* ed. Commager and Morris, 2: 1166, quoting Lee, *Memoirs* 1:343-359.

[61] Charles O'Hara to the Duke of Grafton, April 20, 1781, Camp near Wilmington Cape Fear River, in "Letters of Charles O'Hara to the Duke of Grafton," ed. George C. Rogers, Jr., *South Carolina Historical Magazine* 65:3 (July 1964), 177.

[62] Cornwallis to Clinton, April 10, 1781, Guildford, in *Cornwallis Papers* 4: 109.

[63] Cornwallis to Germain, March 17, 1781, in *Cornwallis Papers* 4: 19.

[64] Return of the wounded left at New Garden Meeting House, in *Cornwallis Papers* 4: 68, 70.

Yorktown

[1] Charles Cornwallis to George Germain, March 17, 1781, Guildford, in Ian Saberton, *The Cornwallis Papers* (Uckfield, England: Naval & Military Press, 2010), 4: 20; Cornwallis to Henry Clinton, April 10, 1781, Camp near Wilmington, in *Cornwallis Papers* 4: 110.

[2] Banastre Tarleton, *A History of the Campaigns of 1780 and 1781 in the Southern Provinces of North America*, 1787 (Spartanburg, S.C.: Reprint Company, 1967), 281.

---

[3] Charles O'Hara to the Duke of Grafton, April 20, 1781, Camp near Wilmington Cape Fear River, in "Letters of Charles O'Hara to the Duke of Grafton," ed. George C. Rogers, Jr., *South Carolina Historical Magazine* 65:3 (July 1964), 178.

[4] Cornwallis to Clinton, April 10, 1781, in *Cornwallis Papers* 4: 110.

[5] Cornwallis to Clinton, April 10, 1781, in *Cornwallis Papers* 4: 110.

[6] State of the troops at Wilmington, 15th April 1781, in *Cornwallis Papers* 4: 142-44; State of the troops marching to Virginia, 1st May 1781, in *Cornwallis Papers* 4: 184.

[7] Hutcheson to Cornwallis, April 9, 1781, in in *Cornwallis Papers* 4: 136.

[8] O'Hara to the Duke of Grafton, in *South Carolina Historical Magazine* 65:3 (July 1964), 177.

[9] William Phillips to Henry Clinton, April 19, 1781, Hampton Road on board the Maria, in *Cornwallis Papers* 5: 49.

[10] Ian Saberton, *The Cornwallis Papers* (Uckfield, England: Naval & Military Press, 2010), 5: 3.

[11] Jon Meacham, *Thomas Jefferson: The Art of Power* (New York: Random House, 2012), 140.

[12] Charles Stedman, *History of the Origin, Progress and Termination of the American War*, 1794 (New York: New York Times and Arno Press, 1969), 2: 387.

[13] Matthew H. Spring, *With Zeal and Bayonets Only: The British Army on Campaign in North America, 1775-1783* (Norman: University of Oklahoma Press, 2008), 318 n. 93.

[14] Saberton, *Cornwallis Papers*, 5: 124-25, n. 81; Leslie to Cornwallis, July 12, 1781, Portsmouth, *Cornwallis Papers*, 5: 180.

[15] Cornwallis to Clinton, April 10, 1781, Camp near Wilmington, in *Cornwallis Papers* 4: 112.

[16] Cornwallis to O'Hara, August 2, 1781, York Town, in *Cornwallis Papers* 6: 43; Cornwallis to O'Hara, August 4, 1781, York Town, in *Cornwallis Papers* 6: 44.

[17] O'Hara to Cornwallis, August 5, 1781, Portsmouth, in *Cornwallis Papers* 6: 44-45.

[18] Cornwallis to O'Hara, August 6, 1781, York, in *Cornwallis Papers* 6: 45.

[19] Cornwallis to O'Hara, August 7, 1781, York, in *Cornwallis Papers* 6: 46.

[20] Cornwallis to Clinton, August 12, 1781, York in Virginia, in *Cornwallis Papers* 6: 19.

[21] Cornwallis to Clinton, Oct. 20, 1781, York Town, Virginia, in *Cornwallis Papers* 6: 128.

[22] Henry Lumpkin, *From Savannah to Yorktown: The American Revolution in the South* (Columbia: University of South Carolina Press, 1981), 241.

[23] Lumpkin, *From Savannah to Yorktown*, 311.

[24] Jerome Greene, *The Guns of Independence: The Siege of Yorktown* (New York: Savas Beatie, 2011), 65, 67.

[25] Lawrence E. Babits, *A Devil of a Whipping: The Battle of Cowpens* (Chapel Hill: University of North Carolina Press, 1998), 144.

[26] Greene, *Guns of Independence*, 236, 240-45.

[27] Greene, *Guns of Independence*, 236, 247-53.

[28] Roderick Mackenzie, *Strictures on Lt. Col. Tarleton's History "of the campaigns of 1780 and 1781* (London: Printed for the Author, 1787), 102; Lawrence E. Babits and Joshua B. Howard, *Long, Obstinate and Bloody: The Battle of Guilford Courthouse* (Chapel Hill: University of North Carolina Press, 2009), 188.

[29] Return of the killed, wounded and missing in the army under Lord Cornwallis from the 28th of September to the 19th of October, 1781, in Henry P. Johnston, *The Yorktown Campaign and the Surrender of Cornwallis*, 1881 (Alexandria, Va.: Eastern National Park and Monument Association, 1958), 193-94; J.P. MacLean, *Scottish Highland Regiments in the American Revolution* (Auburn, Alabama: Scotpress, 2005), 35.

[30] Lumpkin, *From Savannah to Yorktown* 234-45; Ernest Dupuy and Trevor Dupuy, *The Compact History of the Revolutionary War* (New York: Hawthorne, 1963), 438-453; Donald Barr Chidsey, *Victory at Yorktown* (New York: Crown, 1962), 154-57.

[31] General return of officers and privates surrendered prisoners of war the 19th of October, 1781, in Johnston, *Yorktown Campaign*, 164-65; Margaret Mackintosh, *The History of Clan Mackintosh and Clan Chattan* (Edinburgh: The Pentland Press Limited, 1997), 65.

[32] David Stewart, *Sketches of the Character, Manners, and Present State of the Highlanders of Scotland*, 1822 (Edinburgh: John Donald Publishers, 1977), 2:80.

About the 71st Regiment

[1] Edward E. Curtis, *The Organization of the British Army in the American Revolution* (New Haven: Yale University Press, 1926), 51, 72.

[2] Curtis, *Organization,* 3-4; *John Peebles' American War: Diary of a Scottish Engineer, 1776-1782*, ed. Ira D. Gruber (Mechanicsburg, Pa.: Stackpole Books, 1998), 526, 529.

[3] David Stewart, *Sketches of the Character, Manners, and Present State of the Highlanders of Scotland*, 1822 (Edinburgh: John Donald Publishers, 1977), 2: 43-44.

[4] Matthew P. Dziennik, *The Fatal Land: War Empire and the Highland Soldier in British America (*New Haven: Yale University Press, 2015), 161.

[5] Curtis, *Organization*, 69-70.

[6] Stewart, *Sketches*, 2:44-46.

[7] Archibald Campbell to William Howe, June 19, 1776, Boston, in J.P. MacLean, *An Historical Account of the Settlements of Scotch Highlanders in America Prior to the Peace of 1783: Together with Notices of Highland Regiments and Biographical Sketches* (Cleveland: Helman-Taylor, 1900, available online through HathiTrust), 347.

[8] John J. Gallagher, T*he Battle of Brooklyn 1776* (Edison, N.J.: Castle Books, 2002), 183; Stewart, *Sketches*, 2: 44, 50-52.

[9] *John Peebles' American War: Diary of a Scottish Engineer, 1776-1782*, ed. Ira D. Gruber (Mechanicsburg, Pa.: Stackpole Books, 1998), 516.

[10] Mark M. Boatner III, *Encyclopedia of the American Revolution* (New York: David McKay Company, 1976), 170; "Life of Robert Jackson, M.D., Inspector-General of Army-Hospitals" in *A View of the Formation, Discipline, and Economy of Armies*, 3rd ed., by Robert Jackson (London: Parker, Furnivall and Parker, 1845), xvii.

[11] Archibald Campbell, *Journal of an Expedition against the Rebels of Georgia in North America under the Orders of Archibald Campbell Esquire Lieut. Colol. of His Majesty's 71st Regimt. 1778*, ed. Colin Campbell (Augusta, Georgia: Richmond County Historical Society, 1981), 9.

[12] Campbell, *Journal* 79-80.

[13] Charles Cornwallis to Henry Clinton, Aug. 6, 1780, Charlestown, in Ian Saberton, *The Cornwallis Papers* (Uckfield, England: Naval & Military Press, 2010), 1: 178.

[14] Lawrence E. Babits and Joshua B. Howard, *Long, Obstinate and Bloody: The Battle of Guilford Courthouse* (Chapel Hill: University of North Carolina Press, 2009), 86-88, 219.

[15] Saberton, *Cornwallis Papers*, 5: 124-25, n. 81; Leslie to Cornwallis, July 12, 1781, Portsmouth, in Saberton, *Cornwallis Papers*, 5: 180.

[16] Campbell, *Journal*, 109 n. 54.

[17] Cornwallis to Clinton, April 10, 1781, Camp near Wilmington, in Saberton, *Cornwallis Papers* 4: 112.

[18] General return of officers and privates surrendered prisoners of war the 19th of October, 1781, in Henry P. Johnston, *The Yorktown Campaign and the Surrender of Cornwallis, 1781* (Alexandria, Va.: Eastern National Park and Monument Association, 1958, available online through HathiTrust), 164-65;

Margaret Mackintosh, *The History of Clan Mackintosh and Clan Chattan* (Edinburgh: The Pentland Press Limited, 1997), 65.

[19] Dziennik, *The Fatal Land*, 232.

[20] Stewart, *Sketches*, 1: 385.

[21] Stewart, 2:80; Dziennik, *The Fatal Land*, 141.

[22] Campbell, *Journal of an Expedition*, 107 n. 7.

[23] Curtis, *Organization of the British Army,* 11 n. 24; Michael. Brander, *The Scottish Highlanders and Their Regiments* (New York: Barnes and Noble, 1996), 129.

[24] Campbell, *Journal of an Expedition,* 18.

[25] Stephanie A. Briggs, "The 71st Fraser's Highlanders Encamped at Cheraw, South Carolina, in the Summer of 1780 during the American Revolutionary War," https://fraser-clan.net/wp-content/uploads/2014/11/71stFrasersHighlanders_booklet_2014_v2.pdf.

[26] Charles Mackubin Lefferts, *Uniforms of the American, British, French, and German Armies in the War of the American Revolution 1775-1783*, 1926 (Old Greenwich, Conn.: WE Inc., 1971), 193.

[27] Robin May, *The British Army in North America 1775-1783* (London: Osprey, 1974), 40; "71st Fraser's Highlanders Encamped at Cheraw."

[28] Qtd. in May, *British Army in North America*, 40.

[29] Charles Cornwallis to Nisbet Balfour, Sept. 3 and 6, 1780, Camden, in Saberton, *The Cornwallis Papers*, 2: 73.

[30] "71st Fraser's Highlanders Encamped at Cheraw;" "Uniforms of the Fraser Highlanders," *Military Wiki*, https://military-

history.fandom.com/wiki/71st_Regiment_of_Foot,_Fraser%27s_Highlanders; Don Troiani, *Don Troiani's Soldiers of the American Revolution* (Mechanicsburg, PA: Stackpole Books, 2007), 44.

31 Troiani, *Soldiers of the American Revolution*, 44.

32 Carl P. Borick, " 'Whatever is to be Performed or Endured:' The Charleston Museum's 71st Regiment Cartridge Box Badge," *The Charleston Museum*, https://www.charlestonmuseum.org/news-events/whatever-is-to-be-performed-or-endured/

33 Franklin B, Hough, ed., *The Siege of Savannah by the Combined American and French Forces under the command of Gen. Lincoln and the Count d'Estaing in the Autumn of 1779*, 1866 (Spartanburg, S.C.: The Reprint Company, 1975), 55.

34 James Legg, "The Camden Burial Project, Part I; Background and Preliminary Results," *Legacy* 27:1 (Spring 2023), 4-8.

35 "Camden Burials in South Carolina," *The Royal Regiment of Scotland*, https://www.theroyalregimentofscotland.org/latest-news/camden-burials-in-south-carolina ; "British Embassy Attendance and Involvement at the Camden Burial Funer and Burial," *South Carolina Battleground Preservation Trust*, https://www.scbattlegroundtrust.org/british-embassy-attendance-and-involvement-at-the-camden-burial-funeral-and-burial; "Schedule of Events for the Camden Burials," *South Carolina Battleground Preservation Trust*, https://www.scbattlegroundtrust.org/schedule .

Accusations of Atrocities

[1] British officer's letter from the Periodical Room (Microfilm 3284), courtesy of the Library of Congress in *Behind the Lines: Powerful and Revealing American and Foreign War Letters—and One Man's Search to Find Them*, ed. Andrew Carroll (New York: Scribner, 2005), 108-09. See also an excerpt titled "From an Officer in Gen. Frazer's Bat., 71st Regt." in Henry Onderdonk, *Revolutionary Incidents of Suffolk and Kings Counties: with an account of the Battle of Long Island and the British prisons and prison-ships at New York* (New York: Leavitt, 1849), 138.

[2] Onderdonk, *Revolutionary Incidents*, 138.

[3] David Smith, *New York 1776* (Oxford, U.K.: Osprey, 2008), 51.

[4] William E. Cox, "Brigadier-General John Ashe's Defeat in the Battle of Brier Creek," *Georgia Historical Quarterly* 57.2 (Summer 1973), 302.

[5] Alexander A. Lawrence, "General Robert Howe and the British Capture of Savannah in 1778," *Georgia Historical Quarterly* 36.4 (1952): 307.

[6] Colin Campbell, ed., *Journal of an Expedition against the Rebels of Georgia in North America under the Orders of Archibald Campbell Esquire Lieut. Colol. of His Majesty's 71st Regimt. 1778* (Augusta, Georgia: Richmond County Historical Society, 1981), 105.

[7] "Narrative of Mordecai Sheftall," *Setting Out to Begin a New World: Colonial Georgia, A Documentary History,* ed. Edward J. Cashin (Savannah: Beehive Press, 1995), 182-183.

[8] Elizabeth Lichtenstein Johnston, *Recollections of a Georgia Loyalist,* (Spartanburg: The Reprint Company, 1974), 48-49.

[9] Lawrence, "General Robert Howe," 323-24.

[10] Campbell, *Journal of an Expedition,* 110.

[11] Lawrence, "General Robert Howe," 323.

[12] Campbell, *Journal of an Expedition,* 77; K.G. Davies, *Documents of the American Revolution, 1770-178* (Shannon: Irish University Press, 1972), 17: 78.

[13] Quoted in Cox, "Brigadier-General John Ashe's Defeat," 299-300. Historians who have used the manuscript as a source have given two slightly different citations: Draper microfilm, volume 13DD33, on file at Kings Mountain National Military Park; Draper Microfilm Collection, 3 DD 89-91, State Historical Society of Wisconsin, Madison.

[14] Campbell, *Journal of an Expedition,* 105; Howard, 498.

[15] Alexander Garden, *Anecdotes of the Revolutionary War,* 1822 (Spartanburg, S.C.: Reprint Company, 1972), 264.

Colonel Stewart's War Stories

[1] David Stewart, *Sketches of the Character, Manners, and Present State of the Highlanders of Scotland,* 1822 (Edinburgh: John Donald Publishers, 1977.

[2] Hugh Trevor-Roper, "The Highland Tradition of Scotland" in *The Invention of Tradition*, eds. Eric Hobsbawm and Terence Ranger (Cambridge: Cambridge University Press, 1992), 29.

[3] Stewart, *Sketches,* 2: 65.

[4] "Maitland, Hon. John (1732-79)," *The History of Parliament Online,* https://www.historyofparliamentonline.org/volume/1754-1790/member/maitland-hon-john-1732-79.

[5] Stewart, *Sketches,* 1: 365.

[6] Stewart, *Sketches,* 2: 58-60.

[7] Stewart, *Sketches,* 2: 63.

[8] Stewart, *Sketches,* 2: 67-69.

[9] Stewart, *Sketches,* 2: 71-73.

[10] Stewart, *Sketches,* 2: 78.

[11] Stewart, *Sketches,* 2: 79.

Archibald Campbell

[1] Archibald Campbell, *Journal of an Expedition against the Rebels of Georgia in North America under the Orders of Archibald Campbell Esquire Lieut. Colol. of His Majesty's 71st Regimt. 1778*, ed. Colin Campbell (Augusta, Georgia: Richmond County Historical Society, 1981), ix.

[2] Campbell, *Journal of an Expedition,* ix.

[3] Michael C. Harris, *Brandywine: A Military History of the Battle that Lost Philadelphia but Saved America, September 11, 1777* (El Dorado Hills, Calif.: Savas Beatie, 2017), 409.

[4] Campbell, *Journal of an Expedition,* ix-x.

[5] Campbell, *Journal of an Expedition,* 7.

[6] Campbell, *Journal of an Expedition,* 103, n. 12

[7] Campbell, *Journal of an Expedition,* 36-37.

[8] Campbell, *Journal of an Expedition,* 40.

[9] Campbell, *Journal of an Expedition,*102, n. 5.

[10] Joshua B. Howard, "'Things here wear a melancholy appearance:' The American Defeat at Briar Creek," *Georgia Historical Quarterly* 88.4 (Winter 2004), 498; David K. Wilson, *The Southern Strategy: Britain's Conquest of South Carolina and Georgia, 1775-1780* (Columbia: University of South Carolina Press, 2005), 90.

[11] Campbell, *Journal of an Expedition,* 79-80.

[12] Campbell, *Journal of an Expedition,* 79.

[13] K.G. Davies, *Documents of the American Revolution, 1770-178* (Shannon: Irish University Press, 1972), 17:143.

[14] Campbell, *Journal of an Expedition,* 81.

[15] Royal Gazette, June 17, 1780, qtd. in Franklin B. Hough, ed., *The Siege of Charleston* (Spartanburg, S.C.: The Reprint Company, 1975), 143-46.

[16] Campbell, *Journal of an Expedition,* x.

Charles Campbell

[1] Ian Saberton, *The Cornwallis Papers* (Uckfield, England: Naval & Military Press, 2010), 1: 227 n. 57; Archibald Campbell,

Journal of an Expedition against the Rebels of Georgia in North America under the Orders of Archibald Campbell Esquire Lieut. Colol. of His Majesty's 71st Regimt. 1778, ed. Colin Campbell (Augusta, Georgia: Richmond County Historical Society, 1981), 82.

[2] Qtd. in Don Corbly, ed., *Letters, Journals, and Diaries of Ye Colonial America* (Lulu Enterprises Incorporated, 2009), 392-94.

[3] Saberton, *Cornwallis Papers*, 1: 227 n. 57.

[4] Charles Cornwallis to Francis Rawdon, Aug. 4, 1780, Charlestown, in Saberton, *The Cornwallis Papers*, 1: 227.

[5] Saberton, *Cornwallis Papers*, 1: 227 n. 57.

[6] Hugh Trevor-Roper, "The Highland Tradition of Scotland" in *The Invention of Tradition*, eds. Eric Hobsbawm and Terence Ranger (Cambridge: Cambridge University Press, 1992), 29.

[7] David Stewart, *Sketches of the Character, Manners, and Present State of the Highlanders of Scotland*, 1822 (Edinburgh: John Donald Publishers, 1977), 2: 67-68.

[8] Banastre Tarleton, *A History of the Campaigns of 1780 and 1781 in the Southern Provinces of North America*, 1787 (Spartanburg, S.C.: Reprint Company, 1967), 111-12.

[9] Tarleton, *History of the Campaigns*, 112-15.

[10] Cornwallis to Germain, Aug. 21, 1780, in Saberton, *The Cornwallis Papers*, 2: 14.

[11] Stewart, *Sketches*, 2: 69-70.

[12] Qtd. in Corbly, *Letters, Journals, and Diaries*, 394.

William Erskine

[1] David Stewart, *Sketches of the Character, Manners, and Present State of the Highlanders of Scotland,* 1822 (Edinburgh: John Donald Publishers, 1977), 2: 46.

[2] Mark M. Boatner III, *Encyclopedia of the American Revolution* (New York: David McKay Company, 1976), 170, 349; *John Peebles' American War: Diary of a Scottish Engineer, 1776-1782,* ed. Ira D. Gruber (Mechanicsburg, Pa.: Stackpole Books, 1998), 516; John J. Gallagher, T*he Battle of Brooklyn 1776* (Edison, N.J.: Castle Books, 2002), 183; David Stewart, *Sketches of the Character, Manners, and Present State of the Highlanders of Scotland,* 1822 (Edinburgh: John Donald Publishers, 1977), 2: 44, 50-52.

Robert Jackson

[1] "Life of Robert Jackson, M.D., Inspector-General of Army-Hospitals" in *A View of the Formation, Discipline, and Economy of Armies,* 3rd ed., by Robert Jackson (London: Parker, Furnivall and Parker, 1845), xvii-xxi.

[2] "Life of Robert Jackson," xxii.

[3] "Life of Robert Jackson," xxvii-xxxi.

[4] Robert Jackson, *A Treatise on the Fevers of Jamaica, with Some Observation on the Intermitting Fevers of America,* 1795, (retrieved online through Sabin Americana), 226-27.

[5] "Life of Robert Jackson," xxxiv- xxxv.

[6] Buchanan, *Road to Guilford,* 326; Robert D. Bass, *The Green Dragoon: The Lives of Banastre Tarleton and Mary Robinson* (New York: Henry Holt, 1957), 159.

[7] "Life of Robert Jackson," xxiv-xxxv.

[8] "Life of Robert Jackson," xxxvi.

[9] Jackson, *View of the Formation of Armies*, xxxiii n.

[10] "Life of Robert Jackson," xxxvi, xxxviii, xl, xli-lvi.

[11] "Life of Robert Jackson," lvi-lvii.

[12] "Life of Robert Jackson," lviii-lxix.

[13] "Life of Robert Jackson," lxxi-lxxii.

[14] "Life of Robert Jackson," lxxii, lxxx, lxxxvii, lxxxix, xc, xcvii, cvii.

Roderick Mackenzie

[1] Roderick Mackenzie, *Strictures on Lt. Col. Tarleton's History of the Campaigns of 1780 and 1781* (London: Printed for the Author, 1787, available online through Sabin Americana), ii, 119.

[2] Mackenzie, *Strictures*, 88-89.

[3] Mackenzie, *Strictures*, 26-27.

[4] Mackenzie, *Strictures*, 4, 7, 10, 11, 13, 16, 21, 37-38, 106.

[5] Ed Brumby, *71st Fraser Highland Regiment in the American War of Independence* (Anchorprint, 2012), 212.

[6] Balfour to Cornwallis, June 22, 1781, Charles Town, in Ian Saberton, *The Cornwallis Papers* (Uckfield, England: Naval & Military Press, 2010), 5: 283.

---

[7] Balfour to Cornwallis, June 22, 1781, Charles Town, in Saberton, *Cornwallis Papers*, 5: 283.

[8] Leslie to Cornwallis, July 17, 1781, Portsmouth, in Saberton, *Cornwallis Papers*, 5: 189.

[9] Saberton, *Cornwallis Papers*, 5: 189, n. 60.

Aeneas Mackintosh

[1] Margaret Mackintosh of Mackintosh, *The History of Clan Mackintosh and Clan Chattan* (Edinburgh: The Pentland Press Limited, 1997), 65.

[2] Angus MacKintosh, "Lady MacKintosh of the '45," *The Celtic Monthly* Dec. 1902, 49.

[3] David Stewart, *Sketches of the Character, Manners and Present State of the Highlanders of Scotland,* 1822 (Edinburgh: John Donald Publishers, 1977), 2:48.

[4] Ed Brumby, *71st Fraser Highland Regiment in the American War of Indepence* (Anchorprint, 2012), 212.

[5] Charlie Fraser Larimer, ed., *Tales of Dunlichity: The Stories of Willie MacQueen* (Chicago: Sigourney Press, 2001), 61.

[6] Frances Letcher Mitchell, *Georgia Land and People* (Spartanburg, S.C.: The Reprint Company, 1974), 75.

[7] Franklin B. Hough, *The Siege of Savannah by the Combined American and French Forces under the command of Gen. Lincoln and the Count d'Estaing in the Autumn of 1779,* 1866 (Spartanburg, S.C.: The Reprint Company, 1975), 55.

[8] George White, *Historical Collections of Georgia*, 1855 (Baltimore: Genealogical Publishing Company, 1969), 473.

[9] Margaret Mackintosh, *History of Clan Mackintosh,* 66.

[10] Margaret Mackintosh, *History of Clan Mackintosh,, 65.*

[11] Lawrence E. Babits and Joshua B. Howard, *Long, Obstinate and Bloody: The Battle of Guilford Courthouse* (Chapel Hill: University of North Carolina Press, 2009), 86-88, 219.

[12] Ed Brumby, *71st Fraser Highland Regiment in the American War of Indenpence* (Anchorprint, 2012), 212.

[13] Robert McGillivray, "Colonel Anne of the '45," *Clan Chattan: The Journal of Clan Chattan* XI.2 (2002), 73.

[14] *Notes by a Highland Chief in 1784: Notes by Sir Aeneas Mackintosh of Mackintosh* (Bruceton Mills, W.Va.: Scotpress/ Unicorn Limited, 1997), 2.

[15] *Notes by a Highland Chief,* 6.

[16] *Notes by a Highland Chief,* 7.

[17] *Notes by a Highland Chief,* 5.

[18] *Notes by a Highland Chief,* 5.

[19] *Notes by a Highland Chief,* 7.

[20] *Notes by a Highland Chief,* 8.

[21] Margaret Mackintosh, *History of Clan Mackintosh,* 66-68.

[22] Margaret Mackintosh, *History of Clan Mackintosh,* 65-66.

Duncan Macpherson of Cluny

[1] David Stewart, *Sketches of the Character, Manners, and Present State of the Highlanders of Scotland,* 1822 (Edinburgh: John Donald Publishers, 1977), 2: 56.

[2] "MacPherson," *Electric Scotland*, https://www.electricscotland.com/webclans/m/macpher2.html; Ian Saberton, *The Cornwallis Papers* (Uckfield, England: Naval & Military Press, 2010), 5: 124 n. 81.

[3] Stewart, *Sketches*, 1: 119 (1st ed.), 1: 125-26 (2nd ed.).

[4] Alexander Macpherson, *Glimpses of the Church and Social Life in the Highlands in Olden Times* (Edinburgh: William Blackwood and Sons, 1893), 341.

[5] Qtd. in Macpherson, *Glimpses*, 342-43.

[6] Archibald Campbell, *Journal of an Expedition against the Rebels of Georgia in North America under the Orders of Archibald Campbell Esquire Lieut. Colol. of His Majesty's 71st Regimt. 1778*, ed. Colin Campbell (Augusta, Georgia: Richmond County Historical Society, 1981), 109 n. 54.

[7] "To George Washington from Lieutenant Colonel Duncan Macpherson and Captain David Ross, 14 September 1779," *National Archives Founders Online*, https://founders.archives.gov/?q=duncan%20macpherson&s=1111311111&sa=&r=1&sr=

[8] "To Washington from Macpherson," *National Archives Founders Online*; Campbell, *Journal of an Expedition*, 109 n. 54.

[9] Jerome Greene, *The Guns of Independence: The Siege of Yorktown* (New York: Savas Beatie, 2011), 236, 247-53.

[10] Matthew P. Dziennik, "Through an Imperial Prism: Land, Liberty, and Highland Loyalism in the War of American Independence," *Journal of British Studies* 50: 2 (April 2011), 340-41, 241 n. 33.

[11] Macpherson, *Glimpses*, 342.

[12] Saberton, *Cornwallis Papers* 5: 124-25 n. 81; Macpherson, *Glimpses,* 287, 344.

[13] Macpherson, *Glimpses,* 344.

John Maitland

[1] Mark M. Boatner III, *Encyclopedia of the American Revolution* (New York: David McKay Company, 1976), 670; "Maitland, Hon. John (1732-79)," *The History of Parliament Online,* https://www.historyofparliamentonline.org/volume/1754-1790/member/maitland-hon-john-1732-79.

[2] Alexander A. Lawrence, *Storm over Savannah: The story of Count d'Estaing and the Siege of the Town in 1779* (Athens: University of Georgia Press, 1951), 26-28.

[3] Archibald Campbell, *Journal of an Expedition against the Rebels of Georgia in North America under the Orders of Archibald Campbell Esquire Lieut. Colol. of His Majesty's 71st Regimt. 1778,* ed. Colin Campbell (Augusta, Georgia: Richmond County Historical Society, 1981), 19, 46, 82.

[4] Campbell, *Journal* 79-80.

[5] David S. Heidler, "The American Defeat at Briar Creek, 3 March 1779," *Georgia Historical Quarterly* 66.3 (Fall 1982), 325; Joshua B. Howard, "'Things here wear a melancholy appearance:' The American Defeat at Briar Creek," *Georgia Historical Quarterly* 88.4 (Winter 2004), 486, 490.

[6] Robert Jackson, *A Treatise on the Fevers of Jamaica, with Some Observation on the Intermitting Fevers of America,* 1795, (retrieved online through Sabin Americana), 57.

[7] Patrick O'Kelley, *Nothing But Blood and Slaughter* (Barbecue, N.C.: Patrick O'Kelly, 2004), 1: 272-73.

[8] Augustine Prevost to Lord George Germain, Aug. 4, 1779, Savannah, in Davies, *Documents of the American Revolution* 17: 175.

[9] Alexander A. Lawrence, *Storm over Savannah: The story of Count d'Estaing and the Siege of the Town in 1779* (Athens: University of Georgia Press, 1951), 49-51.

[10] Rupert Furneaux, *The Pictorial History of the American Revolution as told by Witnesses and Participants,* (Chicago: JG. Ferguson, 1973), 299.

[11] Lawrence, *Storm,* 141.

[12] Qtd. in Franklin B, Hough, ed., *The Siege of Savannah by the Combined American and French Forces under the command of Gen. Lincoln and the Count d'Estaing in the Autumn of 1779*, 1866 (Spartanburg, S.C.: The Reprint Company, 1975), 110-12.

[13] Hugh Trevor-Roper, "The Highland Tradition of Scotland" in *The Invention of Tradition*, eds. Eric Hobsbawm and Terence Ranger (Cambridge: Cambridge University Press, 1992), 29.

[14] David Stewart, *Sketches of the Character, Manners, and Present State of the Highlanders of Scotland*, 1822 (Edinburgh: John Donald Publishers, 1977), 64-65.

[15] "Colonel John Maitland and the Siege of Savannah 1779 - Part 2," *Clan Maitland*, https://clanmaitland.uk/history/century-18th/16-john-maitland/61-colonel-john-maitland-and-the-siege-of-savannah-1779-part-2.

[16] "Colonel John Maitland and the Siege of Savannah 1779 - Part 2;" "The Parris Island Museum," *Beaufort.com,* https://www.beaufort.com/the-parris-island-museum/ .

[17] "John Maitland letters," *Georgia Historical Society,* http://ghs.galileo.usg.edu/ghs/view?docId=ead/MS%200954-ead.xml.

Archibald McArthur

[1] Stephanie A. Briggs, "The 71st Fraser's Highlanders Encamped at Cheraw, South Carolina, in the Summer of 1780 during the American Revolutionary War," https://fraserclan.net/wp-content/uploads/2014/11/71stFrasersHighlanders_booklet_2014_v2.pdf; Ian Saberton, *The Cornwallis Papers* (Uckfield, England: Naval & Military Press, 2010), 1: 87 n. 30; Mark M. Boatner III, *Encyclopedia of the American Revolution* (New York: David McKay Company, 1976), 688.

[2] Charles Cornwallis to Henry Clinton, Aug. 6, 1780, Charlestown, in Ian Saberton, *The Cornwallis Papers* (Uckfield, England: Naval & Military Press, 2010), 1: 178.

[3] Roderick Mackenzie, *Strictures on Lt. Col. Tarleton's History of the Campaigns of 1780 and 1781* (London: Printed for the Author, 1787, available online through Sabin Americana), 111.

[4] Lawrence E. Babits, *A Devil of a Whipping: The Battle of Cowpens* (Chapel Hill: University of North Carolina Press, 1998), 197 n. 101.

[5] Alured Clarke to Charles Cornwallis, May 3, 1781, St. Augustine, in Saberton, *Cornwallis Papers,* 5: 335-36.

[6] Nisbet Balfour to Charles Cornwallis, April 20, 1781, Charles Town, in Saberton, *Cornwallis Papers,* 4: 171-72.

[7] Nisbet Balfour to Archibald McArthur, April 10, 1781, Charles Town, in Saberton, *Cornwallis Papers,* 6: 264-65.

[8] Nisbet Balfour to Charles Cornwallis, May 21, 1781, Charles Town, in Saberton, *Cornwallis Papers,* 5: 275.

[9] Nisbet Balfour to Charles Cornwallis, May 21, 1781, Charles Town, in Saberton, *Cornwallis Papers,* 5: 275.

[10] Francis Rawdon to J.H. Craig, April 27, 1781, copied in J.H. Craig to Charles Cornwallis, May 13, 1781, Wilmington, in Saberton, *Cornwallis Papers,* 4: 170.

[11] Nisbet Balfour to Charles Cornwallis, April 26, 1781, Charles Town, in Saberton, *Cornwallis Papers,* 4: 177.

[12] Francis Rawdon to Charles Cornwallis, May 2, 1781, Camden, in Saberton, *Cornwallis Papers,* 5: 287; Theodore P. Savas and J. David Dameron, *A Guide to the Battles of the American Revolution* (El Dorado Hills, Calif.: Savas Beatie, 2006), 292-97.

[13] Nisbet Balfour to Charles Cornwallis, May 21, 1781, Charles Town, in Saberton, *Cornwallis Papers,* 6: 276.

[14] Francis Rawdon to Charles Cornwallis, May 24, 1781, Camp at Monk's Corner, in Saberton, *Cornwallis Papers,* 5: 289.

[15] Francis Rawdon to Charles Cornwallis, May 24, 1781, Camp at Monk's Corner, in Saberton, *Cornwallis Papers,* 5: 288-89.

[16] Francis Rawdon to Charles Cornwallis, May 24, 1781, Camp at Monk's Corner, in Saberton, *Cornwallis Papers,* 5: 290.

[17] Theodore P. Savas and J. David Dameron, *A Guide to the Battles of the American Revolution* (El Dorado Hills, Calif.: Savas Beatie, 2006), 324-29.

[18] Alexander Stewart to Charles Cornwallis, September 26, 1781, St. Clair's Plantation, in Saberton, *Cornwallis Papers,* 6: 169.

[19] "Otho Holland Williams: Narrative of the Battle of Eutaw Springs" in *The American Revolution: Writings from the War of Independence,* ed. John H. Rhodehamel (New York: Library of America, 2001), 719-20.

[20] Nathanael Greene to the President of Congress, September 11, 1781, Near Ferguson's Swamp, in *Voices of the American Revolution in the Carolinas*, ed. Ed Southern (Winston-Salem, N.C.: John F. Blair, 2009), 241.

[21] Alexander Garden, *Anecdotes of the Revolutionary War*, 1822 (Spartanburg, S.C.: Reprint Company, 1972), 264.

[22] Boatner, *Encyclopedia*, 688; Saberton, *Cornwallis Papers,* 1: 87 n. 30.

[23] Edward J. Cashin, *The King's Ranger: Thomas Brown and the American Revolution on the Southern Frontier* (New York: Fordham University Press, 1999), 156-57; "Military Establishment in St. Augustine 1763 – 1784" in the Miscellaneous Documents Collection of the *University of Florida Digital Collections,* https://ufdc.ufl.edu/UF00047638/00001/pdf/0, 6; Patrick Tonyn to Earl of Shelburne, November 14, 1782, St. Augustine, in K.G. Davies, ed., *Documents of the American Revolution* (Dublin: Irish University Press, 1976), 21: 136-37.

[24] Cashin, *The King's Ranger*, 157.

[25] "Military Establishment in St. Augustine 1763–1784," 6, 7; Charles Loch Mowat, *East Florida as a British Province 1763-1784* (Gainesville: University of Florida Press, 1964), 109.

[26] "Military Establishment in St. Augustine 1763–1784," 7; J. Leitch Wright, Jr., *Florida in the American Revolution* (Gainesville: University Presses of Florida, 1975), 135, 138.

[27] Briggs, "The 71st Fraser's Highlanders," https://fraser-clan.net/wp-content/uploads/2014/11/71stFrasersHighlanders_booklet_2014_v2.pdf.

Francis Skelly

[1] Archibald Campbell, *Journal of an Expedition against the Rebels of Georgia in North America under the Orders of Archibald Campbell Esquire Lieut. Colol. of His Majesty's 71st Regimt. 1778*, ed. Colin Campbell (Augusta, Georgia: Richmond County Historical Society, 1981), 104 n. 17.

[2] Ian Saberton, *The Cornwallis Papers* (Uckfield, England: Naval & Military Press, 2010), 5: 180 n. 44.

[3] *John Peebles' American War: Diary of a Scottish Engineer, 1776-1782*, ed. Ira D. Gruber (Mechanicsburg, Pa.: Stackpole Books, 1998), 93, 95, 331, 345, 348, 478.

[4] Campbell, *Journal of an Expedition*, 9.

[5] Campbell, *Journal of an Expedition*, 104 n. 17.

Bibliography

Babits, Lawrence E. *A Devil of a Whipping: The Battle of Cowpens*. Chapel Hill: University of North Carolina Press, 1998.

--- and Joshua B. Howard. *Long, Obstinate and Bloody: The Battle of Guilford Courthouse*. Chapel Hill: University of North Carolina Press, 2009.

Bass, Robert D. *The Green Dragoon: The Lives of Banastre Tarleton and Mary Robinson*. New York: Henry Holt, 1957.

Battle of Princeton Mapping Project: Report of Military Terrain Analysis and Battle Narrative. Robert A. Selig, Matthew Harris, Wade P. Catts, ed. Princeton, N.J.: Princeton Battlefield Society, 2010.

Baxley, Charles. "Fratricide at McPherson's Plantation." *Southern Campaigns of the American Revolution* 13: 3, unpublished draft, Jan. 23, 2017.

Bingham, Caroline. *Beyond the Highland Line: Highland History and Culture*. London: Constable, 1991.

Boatner III, Mark M. *Encyclopedia of the American Revolution*. New York: David McKay Company, 1976.

Bodle, Wayne. *The Valley Forge Winter: Civilians and soldiers in war*. University Park: The Pennsylvania State University Press, 2004.

Borick, Carl P. *A Gallant Defense: The Siege of Charleston, 1780*. Columbia: University of South Carolina Press, 2003.

---. *Relieve us of this burthen: American Prisoners of War in The Revolutionary South, 1780-1782*. Columbia: The University of South Carolina Press, 2012.

---. "'Whatever is to be Performed or Endured:' The Charleston Museum's 71st Regiment Cartridge Box Badge," *The Charleston Museum*, https://www.charlestonmuseum.org/news-events/whatever-is-to-be-performed-or-endured/

Brander, Michael. *The Scottish Highlanders and Their Regiments*. New York: Barnes and Noble, 1996.

Briggs, Stephanie A. "The 71st Fraser's Highlanders Encamped at Cheraw, South Carolina, in the Summer of 1780 during the American Revolutionary War." https://fraserclan.net/wp-content/uploads/2014/11/71stFrasersHighlanders_booklet_2014_v2.pdf.

Brumby, Ed. *71st Fraser Highland Regiment in the American War of Independence*. Anchorprint, 2012.

Buchanan, John. *The Road to Guilford Courthouse: The American Revolution in the South*. New York: John Wiley & Sons, 1997.

Campbell, Colin, ed. *Journal of an expedition against the rebels of Georgia in North America under the orders of Archibald Campbell Esquire Lieut. Colol. of His Majesty's 71st Regimt.*

1778. Augusta, Ga.: Richmond County Historical Society, 1981.

Carroll, Andrew. *Behind the Lines: Powerful and Revealing American and Foreign War Letters—and One Man's Search to Find Them*. New York: Scribner, 2005.

Cashin, Edward J. and Heard Robertson. *Augusta and the American Revolution: Events in the Georgia Back Country, 1773-1783*. Augusta, Ga.: Richmond County Historical Society, 1975.

---. *The King's Ranger: Thomas Brown and the American Revolution on the Southern Frontier*. New York: Fordham University Press, 1999.

Chernow, Ron. *Washington: A life*. New York: Penguin Press, 2010.

Coleman, Kenneth. *The American Revolution in Georgia*. Athens: University of Georgia Press, 1958.

"Colonel John Maitland and the Siege of Savannah 1779 - Part 2," *Clan Maitland*, https://clanmaitland.uk/history/century-18th/16-john-maitland/61-colonel-john-maitland-and-the-siege-of-savannah-1779-part-2

Commager, Henry Steele and Richard B. Morris, eds. *The Spirit of 'Seventy-Six: The Story of the American Revolution as Told by Participants*. 2 vols. New York: Bobbs-Merrill, 1958. (The pagination is continuous from v. 1 through v. 2, and a one-volume edition published by Harper & Row in 1967 apparently has the same information on the page with the same number.)

Corbly, Don, ed. *Letters, Journals and Diaries of Ye Colonial America*. Lulu Enterprises Incorporated, 2009.

Coulter, E. Merton. *Georgia: A short history*. Third Edition. Chapel Hill: University of North Carolina Press, 1960.

Curtis, Edward E. *The Organization of the British Army in the American Revolution*. New Haven: Yale University Press, 1926.

Dann, John C. *The Revolution Remembered: Eyewitness accounts of the War for Independence*. Chicago: University of Chicago Press, 1980.

Davis, Burke. *The Cowpens-Guilford Courthouse Campaign*. New York: J.B. Lippincott, 1962.

---. *George Washington and the American Revolution*. New York: Random House, 1975.

Davis Jr., Robert Scott. *Encounters on a March Through Georgia in 1779: The Maps and Memorandums of John Wilson, Engineer, 71st Highland Regiment*. Sylvania, Ga.: Partridge Pond Press, 1986.

---. *Georgians in the Revolution: At Kettle Creek (Wilkes County) and Burke County*. Easley, S.C.: Southern Historical Press, 1996.

Davies, K.G. *Documents of the American Revolution*. 21 vols. Shannon: Irish University Press, 1972.

"Diary of Lieut. Anthony Allaire, of Ferguson's Corps: Memorandum of Occurrences during the Campaign of 1780, Part 1: 5 Mar 1780-30 Jun 1780," first published in Lyman C. Draper's *Heroes of Kings Mountain* in 1881 on pages 484-515, available online as "The 1780 Diary of Loyalist Lieutenant Anthony Allaire of Kings Mountain" in *Tennesseans in the Revolutionary War* at https://www.tngenweb.org/revwar/kingsmountain/allaire.html

Dziennik, Matthew P. *The Fatal Land: War Empire and the Highland Soldier in British America*. New Haven: Yale University Press, 2015.

---. "Through an Imperial Prism: Land, Liberty, and Highland Loyalism in the War of American Independence." *Journal of British Studies* 50: 2 (April 2011). 332-358.

Dobson, David. *Directory of Scots in the Carolinas, 1680-1830*. Baltimore: Genealogical Publishing, 1986.

---. *Scottish Emigration to Colonial America, 1607-1785*. Athens: University of Georgia Press, 1994.

Dupuy, R. Ernest and Trevor N. Dupuy. *The Compact History of the Revolutionary War*. New York: Hawthorn Books, 1963.

Edgar, Walter. *South Carolina: A History*. Columbia: University of South Carolina Press, 1998.

Elliott, Daniel T. *The Revolutionary War Battlefield at Purysburg, South Carolina: Search and Discovery*. LAMAR Institute Publication Series, Report Number 209. Savannah: The Lamar Institute, 2016.

Fitzpatrick, John C. *The Writings of George Washington from the Original Manuscript Sources 1745-1799*. 39 vols. Washington: United States Government Printing Office, 1931-44.

Furneaux, Rupert. *The Pictorial History of the American Revolution as told by Witnesses and Participants*. Chicago: JG. Ferguson (distributed by Doubleday), 1973.

Garden, Alexander. *Anecdotes of the Revolutionary War in America with Sketches of Characters.* 1822. Spartanburg, S.C.: Reprint Company, 1972.

Greene, Jerome. *The Guns of Independence: The Siege of Yorktown.* El Dorado Hills, Calif.: Savas Beatie, 2011.

Gruber, Ira D., ed. *John Peebles' American War: Diary of a Scottish Engineer, 1776-1782.* Mechanicsburg, Pa.: Stackpole Books, 1998.

Harden, William. *A History of Savannah and South Georgia.* Vol. 1. Atlanta: Cherokee Publishing Company, 1969.

Hawes, Lilla M., ed. *Collections of the Georgia Historical Society Vol. XII: The Papers of Lachlan McIntosh, 1774-1779.* Savannah: Georgia Historical Society, 1957.

---, ed. "The Papers of James Jackson 1781-1798." *Collections of the Georgia Historical Society Vol. XI.* Savannah: Georgia Historical Society, 1935.

---, ed. *University of Georgia Libraries Miscellanea Publications, No. 7: Lachlan McIntosh Papers in the University of Georgia Libraries.* Athens: University of Georgia Press, 1968.

Hicks, Brian. "Doomed British infantry officer describes siege of Charleston." *The Post and Courier,* 16 Nov. 2008. https://www.postandcourier.com/news/doomed-british-infantry-officer-describes-siege-of-charleston/article_089f98b7-b60e-52e7-8b08-0588229cef27.html

Howard, Joshua B. "'Things here wear a melancholy appearance:' The American defeat at Briar Creek." *Georgia Historical Quarterly* 88.4 (Winter 2004): 477-98.

Hough, Franklin B., ed. *The Siege of Charleston by the British Fleet and Army under the command of Admiral Arbuthnot and Sir Henry Clinton which terminated with the surrender of that place on the 12th of May, 1780*. 1867. Spartanburg, S.C.: The Reprint Company, 1975.

---, ed. *The Siege of Savannah by the Combined American and French Forces under the command of Gen. Lincoln and the Count d'Estaing in the Autumn of 1779*. 1866. Spartanburg, S.C.: The Reprint Company, 1975.

Hunter, James. *A Dance Called America: The Scottish Highlands in the United States and Canada*. Edinburgh: Mainstream Publishing, 1994.

Jackson III, Harvey Hardaway. *Lachlan McIntosh and the politics of revolutionary Georgia*. 1979. Athens: University of Georgia Press, 2003.

Jackson, Robert. *A Treatise on the Fevers of Jamaica, with Some Observation on the Intermitting Fevers of America*. 1795. Retrieved online through Sabin Americana.

---. *A View of the Formation, Discipline, and Economy of Armies*, 3rd ed. London: Parker, Furnivall and Parker, 1845. Available online through HathiTrust.

James, William Dobein. *A sketch of the life of Brig. Gen. Francis Marion and a history of his brigade from its rise in June 1780 until disbanded in December, 1782, with descriptions of characters and scenes not heretofore published. Containing also an appendix with copies of letters which passed between several of the leading characters of that day, principally from Gen. Greene to Gen. Marion*. Marietta, Ga.: Continental Book Co., 1948.

Johnson, Dan. "Battle site rarely gets recognition," *The Sylvania Telephone,* 9 Aug. 1996, 1-2.

Johnson, Joseph. *Traditions and Reminiscences Chiefly of the American Revolution.* 1851. Spartanburg, S.C.: Reprint Company, 1972.

Johnson, Samuel. *A Journey to the Western Islands of Scotland.* 1775. Boston: Houghton Mifflin, 1965.

Johnston, Elizabeth Lichtenstein. *Recollections of a Georgia Loyalist.* 1836. Spartanburg: The Reprint Company, 1974.

Johnston, Henry P. *The Yorktown Campaign and the Surrender of Cornwallis, 1781.* 1881. Alexandria, Va.: Eastern National Park and Monument Association, 1958. Available online through HathiTrust.

Jolly, William. *Flora Macdonald in Uist: a Study of the Heroine in her Native Surroundings.* Appended to *The Life of Flora Macdonald* by Alexander Macgregor. Stirling: Eneas Mackay, 1932.

Jones Jr., Charles C., ed. *The Siege of Savannah by the Fleet of Count D'Estaing in 1779.* 1874. New York: The New York Times & Arno Press, 1968.

"Journal of Brigade Major F Skelly." Ed. John A. Robertson, *Southern Campaigns of the American Revolution* 3:12.1, Dec, 2006, 24-27. http://southerncampaign.org/newsletter/v3n12.pdf.

Julien, Carl and Chapman J. Milling. *Beneath So Kind a Sky.* 1947. Columbia: University of South Carolina Press, 1969.

Kennedy, Benjamin, ed. *Muskets, Cannon Balls & Bombs: Nine narratives of the Siege of Savannah in 1779.* Savannah: The Beehive Press, 1974.

Landers, H.L. *The Battle of Camden, South Carolina, August 16, 1780*. Washington: United States Government Printing Office, 1929.

Larimer, Charlie Fraser, ed. *Tales of Dunlichity: The Stories of Willie MacQueen*. Chicago: Sigourney Press, 2001.

Lawrence, Alexander A. "General Robert Howe and the British Capture of Savannah in 1778." *Georgia Historical Quarterly* 36.4 (1952): 303-327.

---. *Storm over Savannah: The story of Count d'Estaing and the Siege of the Town in 1779*. Athens: University of Georgia Press, 1951.

Lefferts, Charles Mackubin. *Uniforms of the American, British, French, and German Armies in the War of the American Revolution 1775-1783*. Ed. Alexander J. Wall. Published by the New York Historical Society, 1926. Old Greenwich, Conn.: WE Inc., 1971.

"Life of Robert Jackson, M.D., Inspector-General of Army-Hospitals." In *A View of the Formation, Discipline, and Economy of Armies*, 3rd ed., by Robert Jackson, xvii-cxxi. London: Parker, Furnivall and Parker, 1845. Available online through HathiTrust.

Lumpkin, Henry. *From Savannah to Yorktown: The American Revolution in the South*. Columbia: University of South Carolina Press, 1981.

Mackenzie, Roderick. *Strictures on Lt. Col. Tarleton's History of the Campaigns of 1780 and 1781, in the Southern Provinces of North America: wherein military characters and corps are vindicated from injurious aspersions, and several important transactions placed in their proper point of view: in a series of letters to a friend*. London: Printed for the Author, 1787. Available online through Sabin Americana.

Mackintosh, Aeneas. *Notes by a Highland Chief in 1784: Notes by Sir Aeneas Mackintosh of Mackintosh.* Bruceton Mills, W.Va.: Scotpress/ Unicorn Limited, 1997.

---. *Notes Descriptive and Historical Principally Relating to the Parish of Moy in Strathdearn and the Town and Neighbourhood of Inverness.* Inverness: Printed for Alfred Donald Mackintosh of Mackintosh, 1892. (Available at Ernest F. Hollings Special Collections Library at the University of South Carolina, where it is cataloged with the call number DA 890 .I6 M33 1892).

Mackintosh, Margaret, revised by Lachlan Mackintosh of Mackintosh, 30th Chief of Mackintosh. *The History of Clan Mackintosh and Clan Chattan.* Edinburgh: The Pentland Press Limited, 1997.

Maclean, Fitzroy. *Highlanders: A History of the Scottish Clans.* New York: Penguin, 1995.

MacLean, J.P. *An Historical Account of the Settlements of the Scotch Highlanders in America prior to the Peace of 1783, together with notices of Highland Regiments and Biographical Sketches.* 1900. Baltimore: Genealogical Publishing Company, 1968.

---. *Scottish Highland Regiments in the American Revolution.* 1900. (Extracted, with additional notes, from *An Historical Account of the Settlements of the Scotch Highlanders in America prior to the Peace of 1783, together with notices of Highland Regiments and Biographical Sketches*). Auburn, Alabama: Scotpress, 2005.

---. *Flora MacDonald in America.* Lumberton, N.C.: A.W. McLean, 1909.

MacLean, John. *Historical and Traditional Sketches of Highland Families and of the Highlands.* 1848. 24 June 2013. http://www.electricscotland.com/books/ highlands8.htm.

Macpherson, Alexander. *Glimpses of the Church and Social Life in the Highlands in Olden Times.* Edinburgh: William Blackwood and Sons, 1893.

"Maitland, Hon. John (1732-79)," *The History of Parliament Online,* https://www.historyofparliamentonline.org/volume/1754-1790/member/maitland-hon-john-1732-79. Published in *The History of Parliament: the House of Commons, 1754-1790.*, ed. L. Namier, J. Brooke, 1964, available from Boydell and Brewer.

McCall, Hugh. *The history of Georgia: containing brief sketches of the most remarkable events, up to the present day.* 2 vols. 1811-16. Atlanta: A.B. Caldwell, 1909.

McCandless, Peter. "Revolutionary Fever: Disease and War in the Lower South, 1776-1783." *Transactions of the American Clinical and Climatological Association*, vol. 118, 2007, pp. 225-249.

McCrady, Edward. *The History of South Carolina in the Revolution.* 1901. New York: Russell & Russell, 1969.

McGillivray, Robert. "A Tribute to Virtue." *Clan Chattan: The Journal of Clan Chattan* XII.5 (2011): 269-271.

---. "Colonel Anne of the '45." *Clan Chattan: The Journal of Clan Chattan* XI.2 (2002): 70-79.

McGuire, Thomas J. *Battle of Paoli.* Mechanicsburg, Pa.: Stackpole Books, 2000.

McIntosh, Lachlan, "Journal of the Siege of Charlestown, 1780." *University of Georgia Libraries Miscellanea Publications, No. 7: Lachlan McIntosh Papers in the University of Georgia Libraries*. Ed. Lilla Mills Hawes. Athens: University of Georgia Press, 1968. 96-122.

McLynn, Frank. *The Jacobites*. London: Routledge & Kegan Paul, 1985.

Meacham, Jon. *Thomas Jefferson: The Art of Power*. New York: Random House, 2012.

Meldrum, E. Alexander. "Loch Moy and its Islands." *Clan Chattan: The Journal of Clan Chattan* XII.5 (2011): 264-268.

"Message depicts S.C. in Revolutionary War: Columbia museum buys rare British letter describing Charleston in 1780." *The State* 30 Nov. 2008: B6. (Reprinted from *The Post and Courier* of Charleston, S.C.)

Migliazzo, Arlin C. *To make this land our own: Community, identity, and cultural adaptation in Purrysburg Township, South Carolina, 1732-1865*. Columbia: University of South Carolina Press, 2007.

"Military Establishment in St. Augustine 1763 – 1784" in the Miscellaneous Documents Collection, *University of Florida Digital Collections*, https://ufdc.ufl.edu/UF00047638/00001/pdf/0.

Mitchell, Frances Letcher. *Georgia Land and People*. 1900. Spartanburg, S.C.: The Reprint Company, 1974.

Moncreiffe of that Ilk, Sir Iain and David Hicks. *The Highland Clans: The dynastic origins, chiefs and background of the Clans and of some other families connected with Highland history*. 1967. New York: Bramhall House, 1977.

Moultrie, William. *Memoirs of the American Revolution.* 1802. New York: The New York Times & Arno Press, 1968.

Mowat, Charles Loch. *East Florida as a British Province 1763-1784.* 1943. Gainesville: University of Florida Press, 1964.

Myers, Theodorus Bailey. *Cowpens Papers: Being Correspondence of General Morgan and the Prominent Actors.* Charleston: News and Courier Book Press, 1881. Available online through HathiTrust.

"North Carolina." *Clan Chattan: The Journal of Clan Chattan* XII.5 (2011): 284.

O'Hara, Charles. "Letters of Charles O'Hara to the Duke of Grafton." Ed. George C. Rogers, Jr. *South Carolina Historical Magazine* 65:3 (July 1964). 158-180,

O'Kelley, Patrick. *Nothing But Blood and Slaughter.* 4 vols. Barbecue, N.C.: Patrick O'Kelly, 2004.

Rankin, Hugh F. *Francis Marion: The Swamp Fox.* New York: Thomas Y. Crowell Company, 1973.

Rhodehamel, John H., ed. *The American Revolution: Writings from the War of Independence.* New York: Library of America, 2001.

Ripley, Warren. *Battleground: South Carolina in the Revolution.* Charleston: Post-Courier, 1983.

Rogers, H.C.B. *The British Army of the Eighteenth Century.* New York: Hippocrene Books, 1977.

Rose, D. Murray. *Historical Notes or Essays on the '15 and '45.* Edinburgh: William Brown, 1896.

Rowland, Lawrence S., Alexander Moore and George C. Rogers Jr. *The History of Beaufort County, Volume I, 1514-1861.* Columbia: University of South Carolina Press, 1996.

Saberton, Ian. *The Cornwallis Papers.* 6 vols. Uckfield, England: Naval & Military Press, 2010.

Savas, Theodore P. and J. David Dameron. *A Guide to the Battles of the American Revolution.* New York: Savas Beatie, 2006.

Scarlett, James D. "Another Highland Road." *Clan Chattan: The Journal of Clan Chattan* XII.5 (2011): 290-297.

Schecter, Barnet, *The Battle for New York: The City at the Heart of the American Revolution.* New York: Penguin, 2003.

Scheer, George F. and Hugh F. Rankin. *Rebels and Redcoats.* New York: The World Publishing Company, 1957.

"Sir Aeneas Mackintosh and Allan McDonald." *Clan Chattan: The Journal of Clan Chattan* X.4 (1998): 242.

Smith, David. *New York 1776: The Continentals' First Battle.* Oxford, U.K.: Osprey, 2008.

Southern, Ed, ed. *Voices of the American Revolution in the Carolinas.* Winston-Salem, N.C.: John F. Blair, 2009.

Spring, Matthew H. *With Zeal and Bayonets Only: The British Army on Campaign in North America, 1775-1783.* Norman: University of Oklahoma Press, 2008.

Stedman, Charles. *History of the Origin, Progress and Termination of the American War.* 2 vols. 1794. New York: New York Times and Arno Press, 1969.

Stewart, David. *Sketches of the character, manners and present state of the Highlanders of Scotland; with details of the military service of the Highland Regiments.* 2 vols. 1822. Edinburgh: John Donald Publishers, 1977.

Stokes, Thomas L. *The Savannah.* 1951. Athens: University of Georgia Press, 1982.

Sullivan, Buddy. *Early Days on the Georgia Tidewater: The story of McIntosh County & Sapelo.* Darien: McIntosh County Board of Commissioners, 1990.

Thane, Elswyth. *The Fighting Quaker: Nathanael Greene.* New York: Hawthorne Books, 1972.

Toffey, John J. *A Woman Nobly Planned: Fact and Myth in the Legacy of Flora MacDonald.* Durham, N.C.: Carolina Academic Press, 1997.

Treacy, M.F. *Prelude to Yorktown: The Southern Campaigns of Nathanael Greene.* Chapel Hill: University of North Carolina Press, 1963.

Trevor-Roper, Hugh. "The Highland Tradition of Scotland." *The Invention of Tradition.* Eric Hobsbawm and Terence Ranger, eds. Cambridge: Cambridge University Press, 1992: 15-41.

Troiani, Don. *Don Troiani's Soldiers of the American Revolution.* Mechanicsburg, PA: Stackpole Books, 2007.

Uhlendorf, Bernard A., trans. and ed. *The Siege of Charleston with an account of the province of South Carolina: Diaries and letters of Hessian officers from the von Jungkenn Papers in the William L. Clements Library.* Ann Arbor: University of Michigan Press, 1938.

Vining, Elizabeth Gray. *Flora: A biography.* New York: J.B. Lippincott, 1966.

Ward, Christopher. *The War of the Revolution.* 2 vols. Ed. John Richard Alden. New York: Macmillan, 1952.

Wilson, John. *The Gazetteer of Scotland.* 1882. Lovettsville, Va.: Willow Bend Books, 1996.

Wright, Jr., J. Leitch. *Florida in the American Revolution.* Gainesville: University Presses of Florida, 1975.

Young, Thomas, "Memoir of Major Thomas Young," published in *Orion Magazine,* Oct. and Nov. 1843. Reprinted in several sources, including *Traditions and Reminiscences Chiefly of the American Revolution.* Ed. Joseph Johnson. 1851. Spartanburg, S.C.: Reprint Company, 1972. 446-54.

Index

www.ingramcontent.com/pod-product-compliance
Ingram Content Group UK Ltd.
Pitfield, Milton Keynes, MK11 3LW, UK
UKHW022028190726
13853UKWH00005B/2162

9 798218 056254